BIG LITTLE BOOK OF
PLAYBOY
PARTY JOKES

BIG LITTLE BOOK OF
PLAYBOY
PARTY JOKES

EDITORS OF PLAYBOY

Illustrations by LeRoy Neiman

Main Street
A division of Sterling Publishing Co., Inc.
New York

A Main Street Book

©2004 **PLAYBOY**

Published 2005 by Sterling Publishing Co., Inc.
387 Park Avenue South, New York, NY 10016
Distributed in Canada by Sterling Publishing
c/o Canadian Manda Group, 165 Dufferin Street
Toronto, Ontario M6K 3H6
Distributed in Great Britain by Chrysalis Books
64 Brewery Road, London N79NT, England
Distributed in Australia by Capricorn Link (Australia) Pty. Ltd.
P.O. Box 704, Windsor, NSW 2756, Australia

ISBN 0-7607-6476-X

Femlin illustrations by LeRoy Neiman
Designed by Jeffrey Rutzky

Printed in China

10 9 8 7 6 5 4 3

Contents

Preface

When people think of *Playboy*, the first thing that comes to mind, naturally, is beautiful women. Then they think of the top-notch articles. And the next association a reader makes with the word *Playboy* is hilarious jokes. Since the January 1954 issue, Hugh Hefner has been publishing *Playboy*'s Party Jokes in the pages of his magazine.

Hef is always cited as being at the vanguard of the sexual revolution. Of course that's true, but he also was one of the first to publish humor for adults, both in the form of essays by comedians and in the following jokes. The same year *Father Knows Best* premiered on CBS, Hef published his first joke:

The preacher's sermon was on the Ten Commandments. When he reached "Thou Shalt Not Steal," he noticed one of his parishioners, a little man sitting in the front row, became very agitated. When the preacher reached "Thou Shalt Not Commit Adultery," the man suddenly smiled and relaxed.

After the service, the preacher approached the man and asked him the reason for his peculiar behavior.

The man replied with an embarrassed smile, "When you talked about the Commandment, 'Thou Shalt Not Steal,' I suddenly discovered my umbrella was missing. But when you said 'Thou Shalt Not Commit Adultery,' I remembered where I'd left it."

I have edited *Playboy*'s Party Jokes for four years. Along with my colleagues, we weed through 5,000 jokes each month, 4,000 of which are submitted via email. Almost none of these are original humor. They are jokes that have traveled from inbox to inbox, or from a bartender to a customer. Some jokes we receive were around in the 1950s, and some are just hours old. Every month, I pick about twenty-five of the best jokes and fax them to Hef, who personally selects and edits the final dozen.

We pay the first person who submits a joke we publish $100. Every few months, I'll get an angry letter from a reader demanding money because he or she claims to be the person who mailed in the joke. These letters always amaze me because the writer is assuming he or she is the only person in the world who knows this particular joke. In reality, we get hundreds of the same jokes each month. But once a person commits a joke to memory, he assumes a certain ownership of it, almost as if he wrote it himself. That's the great power of humor.

On rare occasions, someone writes in to complain that a joke we published crossed the line into impropriety. I used to view these as rants from members of an uptight society. But now I realize that people get offended by jokes because at the heart of each gag is an issue that's not a laughing matter. We joke about terrorists because we're frightened by their actions. We joke about presidents because their decisions appall us. We joke about dumb blondes because we're in awe of their sexual power. We joke about Viagra because we fear getting old. Jokes help us face the issues that need facing up to. And when a joke offends a person, it's because he or she recognizes this. But I urge these people to consider what Bill Cosby once said, "You can turn painful situations around through laughter. If you can find humor in anything—even poverty—you can survive it."

But enough analyzing. A joke is simply supposed to make you laugh. I hope the following jokes from our archives will accomplish just that.

—Patricia Lamberti, Assistant Editor,
Playboy Magazine

The Younger Generation

LeRoy Neiman

The kindly old gentleman was visiting his daughter's home. He entered the room of his two grandsons and found them busy studying at their desks. The first boy was reading a book on aviation.

"What do you want to be when you grow up?" asked the grandfather.

"A pilot, sir," said the boy.

"And what do you want to be when you grow up?" the old gentleman asked the second lad.

The boy looked up from the latest issue of *Playboy*. "Nothing, sir," he said wistfully, "just growed up."

The farmer had borrowed a bull from a neighbor to service his two cows. He put the beast in the pasture and instructed his son to keep an eye on them. "As soon as the bull has finished, you come up to the house and tell me," he said.

When the farmer got back to the house, he found the Reverend there paying a social call. They were seated in the front room sipping tea when the boy burst in the door.

"Dad, Dad," he exclaimed, "the bull just fucked the brown cow!"

Greatly embarrassed, the farmer took his son outside. "Is that any way to talk in front of the Reverend?" he demanded. "Why couldn't you have said the bull 'surprised' the brown cow? I would've understood. Now go back down to the pasture and come tell me when the bull is finished."

A few minutes later the boy again burst into the room.

"Dad, Dad—" he exclaimed.

Fearing another breach of verbal etiquette, the father interrupted.

"I know, I know," he said. "The bull has *surprised* the white cow."

"He sure has," exclaimed the excited boy. "He fucked the brown cow again!"

A father was shopping in a department store with his small daughter, when the little girl suddenly pulled on his coat sleeve and said, "Daddy, I gotta go."

"In a few minutes, dear," the father replied.

"I gotta go *now*," the little girl insisted in a very loud voice.

To avoid a scene, a saleslady stepped forward and said, "That's alright, sir, I'll take her."

The saleslady and the little girl hurried off hand in hand. When they returned, the father asked his daughter, "Did you thank the nice lady for being so kind?"

"Why should I thank her?" retorted the little girl, as loud as before, "She had to go, too."

A little girl answered the knock on the door of the farmhouse. The caller, a rather troubled-looking, middle-aged man, asked to see her father.

"If you've come about the bull," she said, "he's fifty dollars. We have the papers and everything and he's guaranteed."

"Young lady," the man said, "I want to see your father."

"If that's too much," the little girl replied, "we got another bull for twenty-five dollars, and he's guaranteed, too, but he doesn't have any papers."

"Young lady," the man repeated, "I want to see your father!"

"If *that's* too much," said the little girl, "we got another bull for only ten dollars, but he's not guaranteed."

"I'm not here for a bull," said the man angrily. "I want to talk about your brother, Elmer. He's gotten my daughter in trouble!"

"Oh, I'm sorry," said the little girl. "You'll have to see Pa about that, 'cause I don't know what he charges for Elmer."

The little girl walked into the drugstore and asked the clerk, "Do you fit men for jockstraps here?" Bewildered but obliging, he replied, "Why, yes, we do."

"Well, wash your hands," said the little girl, "I want a chocolate soda."

The young mother skeptically examined a new educational toy. "Isn't it rather complicated for a small boy?" she asked the salesclerk.

"It's designed to adjust the tot to live in today's world, ma'am," the clerk replied. "Any way he tries to put it together is wrong."

The attractive nanny, with her small charge in tow, left the park to visit her boyfriend in his apartment. They had a hard time keeping their hands off each other, but they could only go so far with the child watching. Then the nanny hit on an idea.

"Bobby," she said, "go look out that window and I'll give you a dime for every red hat you see."

Delighted with the new game, Bobby ran to the window and stared intently at the passersby below.

Almost a minute passed before Bobby's voice popped up with, "I see a red hat!"

"That's nice," came the nanny's muffled reply.

"There's another one," said the boy a short time later.

"Keep counting," the woman managed to say.

"Oh, nanny!" Bobby exclaimed suddenly.

"What now?" she asked, breathing heavily.

"I just wanted to tell you that this is going to be the most expensive roll in the hay you've ever had, 'cause here comes a Shriners parade!"

"**W**hy don't you smile?" the teacher asked young Johnny.

"I didn't have any breakfast," Johnny replied.

"You poor dear," said the teacher. "But to return to our geography lesson, Johnny: Where is the Canadian border?"

"In bed with Mama—that's why I didn't have any breakfast!"

A middle-aged woman stood watching a little boy leaning against a building, smoking a Lucky Strike and drinking from a half-pint of Old Grand Dad. Finally, unable to bear it any longer, she stalked up to the lad and demanded, "Why aren't you in school at this time of day?"

"Hell, lady," said the boy, taking another swig of bourbon, "I'm only four years old."

One evening at dinner the small boy asked how he had been brought into the world. His father, a rather straightlaced type, tried to dismiss the question with a reference to the stork. Unsatisfied, the youngster asked where the father had come from.

"The stork brought me, too, son," the father replied.

The boy sat quietly for a few moments. Then: "What about Grandfather?" he asked.

"Yes, the stork brought your Grandfather, too," father snapped, about to lose patience with his son for posing questions that were obviously none of a small boy's business.

"Gee, dad," the child exclaimed, "do you mean this family has gone through three generations without having any sex at all?"

We went to see the latest James Bond flick not too long ago and during the obligatory love scene we heard a small voice near us in the darkened theater say, "Mommy, is this where he puts the pollen on her?"

A schoolteacher took her second-grade charges on a field trip to the county fair. There was a racetrack on the grounds and she asked them whether they would enjoy seeing the horses. The children enthusiastically exclaimed they would, but as soon as she got them inside the gate, they all asked to be taken to the bathroom. She accompanied the little girls, but sent the boys to the men's room alone. They trooped out almost immediately and announced that the urinals were too high for them to reach.

The situation was an awkward one, but after looking about to make sure she was unobserved, the teacher ushered the boys back in. She lined them up before the plumbing and moved methodically down the line. After lifting several, she came to one who was unusually heavy.

"Goodness," she exclaimed, "are you in the second?"

"Hell no, lady," came the startled reply. "I'm riding Blue Grass in the fourth."

Two little boys were engaging in the traditional verbal battle of little boys everywhere:

"My father is better than your father!"

"No, he's not!"

"My brother is better than your brother!"

"No, he's not!"

"My mother is better than your mother!"

A pause.

"Well, I guess you've got me there. My father says the same thing."

A middle-aged friend of ours read *Lolita* recently. "I can't understand what all the excitement is about," he told us. "I didn't find anything in it that could be considered even vaguely sensational—and neither did my twelve-year-old wife."

George was describing his new secretary enthusiastically to the family at dinner: "She's efficient, personable, clever, punctual, and darned attractive, to boot. In short, she's a real doll!"

"A doll?" said his wife, with a frown.

"A doll!" re-emphasized her oblivious husband.

At which point, their five-year-old daughter, who knew a little something about dolls, looked up from her broccoli to ask: "Does she close her eyes when you lay her down, Daddy?"

Wee Willie was walking with Wanda, his new girlfriend, carrying her books home from grammar school. Both were eight years old.

"Wanda," said Wee Willie with worshiping gaze, "you are the first girl I have ever loved."

"Dammit," said Wanda, "I've drawn another beginner!"

Bobby's mother had been away for a few weeks and was questioning her small son about events during her absence.

"Well," said the boy, "one night we had an awful thunderstorm. It was so bad that I got scared, and so Daddy and me slept together."

"Bobby," said Sandrine, the boy's pretty French au pair, "you mean 'Daddy and I.'"

"No, I don't," exclaimed Bobby. "That was last Thursday. The storm was on Monday night."

One day in school young Johnny wrote on the blackboard, "Johnny is a passionate devil." The teacher reprimanded him for this act, and made him stay after school for one hour. When he finally left the school that evening, all his friends crowded about, eager to hear what punishment he had received. "What did she do to you?" asked one little tyke.

"I'm not sayin'," Johnny replied. "But I will tell you it pays to advertise."

The grade-school principal dropped into the new third-grade teacher's room to see how she was adjusting to her first day of school. "There *is* one problem," she said. "That little boy in the first row belongs in second grade, but insists on remaining here, and he's so smart I hate to send him back."

"He can't be *that* smart," said the principal. "Ask him something."

The teacher called the boy forward and inquired, "What does a dog do on three legs that a man does on two legs and a lady does sitting down?"

"Shakes hands," said the boy.

"What has a cow got four of that I have only two of?" she went on.

"Legs," the boy replied.

"What is a four-letter word meaning intercourse?" she continued.

"Talk," he answered.

The teacher turned to the principal. "Well, what should I do?"

He drew her aside and whispered, "Better promote him to the *fourth* grade. *I* missed all three questions."

A stern father was taking his little son Johnny for a walk in the park when suddenly a honeybee settled on a rock in front of them. Just for spite, the boy smashed it with a rock, whereupon his father said, "That was cruel, and for being cruel you'll get no honey for a whole year."

Later, Johnny deliberately stepped on a butterfly. "And for that, young man," said the father, "you'll get no butter for a year."

When they returned home, Johnny's mother was busy fixing dinner. Just as they entered the kitchen, she spied a cockroach and immediately crushed it underfoot. The little boy looked at his father and said, "Shall I tell her, Dad, or will you?"

The pretty young schoolteacher was concerned about one of her eleven-year-old students. Taking him aside after class one day, she asked, "Victor, why has your schoolwork been so poor lately?"

"I can't concentrate," replied the lad. "I think I've fallen in love."

"Is that so?" said the teacher, holding back an urge to smile. "And with whom?"

"With you," he answered.

"But Victor," exclaimed the secretly pleased young lady, "don't you see how silly that is? It's true that I would like a husband of my own someday—but not a child!"

"Oh, don't worry," said Victor reassuringly. "I'll be careful."

"Tell me, Tommy," the elderly schoolmarm inquired of one of her fifth-grade students. "If you started with twenty dollars and gave seven of them to Nancy, five to Mary and eight to Judy, what would you then have?"

"A ball!" answered Tommy.

A newspaperman, in Atlantic City for the Miss America Pageant, was seated in a boardwalk bistro when an exceptionally cute young redhead sat down beside him. They began to chat and, after a number of drinks, he proposed that they buy a bottle and finish it in his room. She was agreeable—so much so, in fact, that before the bottle was half finished, she began to undress. Before she got into bed, the newspaperman casually asked her how old she was.

"Thirteen," she replied.

"Thirteen? Good Lord!" he exclaimed. "Put your clothes on and get out of here!"

"What's the matter?" asked the girl, pouting. "Superstitious?"

The young kindergarten teacher had just instructed her charges to come forward as their names were called and be prepared to draw something on the blackboard that had been the cause of excitement in their homes during the previous week. One by one the pupils came forward and sketched such items as report cards, television sets, mothers' new hats, and the like. When it came time for Johnny, the class cutup, to comply with the assignment, however, he walked to the board and simply made two white dots before returning to his seat. Suspecting that he was up to one of his usual pranks, the teacher advised Johnny that he had better be able to explain why those two dots were exciting if he didn't want to be kept after school.

"Well," said Johnny, "the other day you told us that those dots are also called periods—"

"That's correct," the teacher interrupted. "But what could possibly be exciting about two periods?"

"Beats me," replied Johnny. "But that's how many my older sister says she's missed, and it's causing an awful lot of excitement around our house!"

The Sunday-school teacher asked her class of youngsters if they could name any of the Ten Commandments and one kindergarten-aged boy stood up and announced proudly, "Thou shalt not omit adultery."

The expectant mother was in her seventh month when she decided to break the news to her small son.

"Darling," she said, "if you could have your choice, which would you like to have—a little brother or a little sister?"

"Well," said the child, "if it's not too much to ask, I'd really prefer a pony."

The precocious six-year-old, who had just completed his first day in the second grade at a progressive school, suddenly asked his parents, "What is sex?"

After an embarrassed pause, they finally managed to stammer out an explanation of the birds and the bees.

Puzzled, the tot pulled a school questionnaire from his pocket and asked, "How am I going to put all that information in this little space marked 'Sex'?"

A little girl stared with fascination at the pregnant woman walking alongside her in the park. "What's that?" she asked, pointing to the woman's blossoming stomach.

"That's my own sweet baby," said the mother-to-be.

"Do you love him?" asked the child.

"Of course I do," the woman said, "I love him very much."

Whereupon the little girl exclaimed accusingly, "Then how come you ate him!?"

The policeman was walking his beat when he saw two men fighting and a little boy standing alongside them crying, "Daddy, Daddy!"

The officer pulled the two men apart and, turning to the boy asked, "Which one is your father, lad?"

"I don't know," the boy said, rubbing the tears from his eyes. "That's what they're fighting about!"

Dressed as a pirate for Halloween, the small boy knocked on a door and was greeted by a matronly woman. "Aren't you a cute little pirate," she said. "But where are your buccaneers?"

To which the little boy replied, "Under my buccan hat!"

As the two little girls walked hand in hand to kindergarten, one confided, "I found a condom on the patio yesterday."

Asked her friend, "What's a patio?"

Mrs. Gregson was taking care of some correspondence when her precocious six-year-old daughter ran in and tugged at her sleeve. "Mommy, can I have a baby?"

"Of course not, dear," her mother replied, without missing a keystroke.

"Are you sure?" the little girl persisted.

"Very sure. Now run along, dear."

As she ran to rejoin her playmates in the yard, the child called out, "OK, fellas, same game!"

"I know how babies are made," boasted one small fry to another.

"That's nothing," the second small fry replied, "I know how they're not."

While lecturing the Sunday schoolers on the nature of sin and damnation, the rural minister asked one lad, "Do you know where little boys and girls go when they do bad things?"

"Yes, sir," replied the boy. "Back of Fogarty's barn."

Asked by his teacher to spell "straight," the third-grade boy did so without error. "Now," said the teacher, "what does it mean?"

"Without water."

"Gimme a double whiskey!" the little boy yelled to the barmaid as he entered the saloon.

"Do you want to get me in trouble?" she asked.

The lad replied, "Maybe later; right now, I just want a drink."

The little boy pointed to two dogs in the park and asked his father what they were doing. "They're making puppies, son," the father said. That night, the boy wandered into his parents' room while they were making love. Asked what they were doing, the father replied, "Making you a baby brother."

"Gee, Pop," the boy said, "turn her over—I'd rather have a puppy!"

"Would you boys like to play house with us?" asked the bravest of several little girls.

"Sure," replied one lad. "Which one of you is going to be the madam?"

On a picnic with his parents, Tommy got lost. He wandered aimlessly through the forest and then fell to his knees to pray. "Dear Lord," he implored, "please help me find my way out of here."

As he was praying, a bird flew overhead and dropped an answer squarely in the palm of his outstretched hand. "Please, Lord," the boy begged, "don't hand me that shit. I'm *really* lost."

The father was distressed by his thirteen-year-old son's preoccupation with breasts. The boy would repeatedly point to attractive girls and whisper, "Hey, Dad, look at the knockers on that one!"

The father finally took the boy to a psychiatrist, who assured him that just one day's intensive therapy could cure the boy. When the session was over, father and son got in the car and headed home. The boy remained silent as they passed a number of pretty girls. As they drove on, the father was inwardly complimenting the psychiatrist. Then his son piped up: "Hey, Dad, look at the ass on that mailman!"

Little Herbie was instructed by his mother to avoid any of the popular synonyms for urination and to substitute the verb "whisper."

That night, the boy approached his father, who had not yet been apprised of the new code. "Daddy," he said, "I want to whisper."

"All right, son," answered his father, "do it in my ear."

"All right, you bastards, fall in—on the double!" barked the sergeant as he strode into the barracks. Each soldier grabbed his hat and jumped to his feet, except one—a teenage private who lay in his bunk reading a book. "Well?" roared the sergeant.

"Well," observed the private, "there certainly were a lot of them, weren't there?"

After going through the line at a crowded mall cafeteria, three rambunctious teenage boys found they were forced to share a table with a kindly looking old lady. One of the lads decided to have a bit of fun at the woman's expense and, nudging one of his buddies under the table, suddenly remarked, "Did your folks ever get married?"

"Nope," replied his tablemate, picking up the put-on. "How about yours?"

"They never bothered," answered the first young man.

"That's nothing," interrupted the third, "my mother doesn't even know who my father is."

The elderly woman looked up from her coffee and said sweetly, "Excuse me, but would one of you little bastards please pass the sugar?"

Trying to sell his oracular A.I. database to the young marketing exec, the software developer invited his skeptical client to ask it a question—any question. The exec sat down and typed out his query: "Where is my father?"

The computer rapidly displayed the reply: "Your father is fishing in Michigan."

"This thing doesn't know what it's talking about," bellowed the prospective customer. "My father's been dead for twenty years."

Certain that his creation was infallible, the developer suggested, "Why don't you ask the same question in a different form?"

The exec thought for a moment and then typed: "Where is my mother's husband?"—to which he received the answer, "Your mother's husband has been dead for twenty years. Your father has just landed a three-pound trout."

The wealthy old gentleman and his wife were celebrating their forty-fifth wedding anniversary and their three grown sons joined them for dinner. The old man was rather irritated when he discovered that none of the boys had bothered to bring a gift, and after the meal, he drew them aside.

"You're all grown men," he said, "and old enough to hear this. Your mother and I have never been legally married."

"What?" gasped one of the sons. "Do you mean to say we're all bastards?"

"Yes," snapped the old man, "and cheap ones, too."

After watching a young maternity-ward patient determinedly thumb through a telephone directory for several minutes, a hospital orderly finally asked her if he could be of some help.

"No, thanks," said the young mother. "I'm just looking for a name for my baby."

"But the hospital supplies a special booklet that lists every first name and its meaning," said the orderly.

"That won't help," said the girl. "My baby already has a first name."

"Darling," said the young bride, "tell me what's bothering you. We promised to share all our joys and all our sorrows, remember?"

"But this is different," protested her husband.

"Together, darling," she insisted, "we will bear the burden. Now tell me what our problem is."

"Well," said the husband, "we've just become the father of a bastard child."

Little Johnny, with a grin,
Drank up all of pappy's gin.
Mother said, when he was plastered,
"Go to bed, you little love-child."

Two farmers were discussing their sons' progress in the big city university. Ezra said, "I don't rightly understand them *degrees* the boys are workin' fer. Do you, Cy?"

"Reckon so," replied Cy, modestly. "First one they get is called a B.S. And you know what that means."

Being a man of the world, Ezra knew.

Cy went on: "Well, sir, they work a little harder and they get this here M.S. That means More of the Same."

Ezra nodded.

"Then comes the hard part. They study night and day, put in years of readin', write all kinds of papers and then, if they're lucky, they get the highest one of 'em all. The Ph.D."

"And what does that stand fer?" asked Ezra.

"Piled Higher and Deeper."

The Dean of an all-women Christian college was lecturing her students on sexual morality.

"In moments of temptation," said the speaker to the class, "ask yourself just one question: Is an hour of pleasure worth a lifetime of shame?"

A somewhat less-than-virginal-looking student in the back of the room rose to ask a question of her own: "How do you make it last an hour?"

The farm had been mortgaged, and gladly, to give daughter a college education. Now, driving home from the station after meeting her at the train, farmer Johnson was greatly disturbed when his daughter whispered confidentially, "I have a confession to make, Pa—I ain't a virgin no more."

The old man shook his head sadly. "After all the sacrifices your Ma and I made to give you a good education, you still say 'ain't'!"

The curvy young junior in the cashmere sweater wiggled up to the professor after class and murmured in a honeyed voice, "I'm afraid I didn't do very well on that quiz today, professor. But I'll do anything to pass this course. Just *anything*."

The professor raised an eyebrow. "Anything?"

"Uh-huh," she cooed. "Anything you ask."

"Then study," he said dryly.

The Dean of Women at a large Baptist university recently began a speech to the student body with these memorable words: "The president of the university and I have decided to stop hooking up on campus."

The announcements of the professor's new book on astrophysics and his wife's new baby appeared almost simultaneously in the newspaper. Upon being congratulated on "this proud event in the family," the professor naturally thought of the achievement that had cost him the greater effort.

"Thank you," he replied modestly, "but I couldn't have done it without the help of two graduate students."

The two sorority sisters were chatting animatedly over a couple of Cosmopolitans. "How did you like the bridge party that the Sigs threw last night?" asked one.

"Fine," answered the other, "until the campus cops came and looked under the bridge."

"Oh, I had a wonderful time," said the young woman to her sorority sister. "Everybody said that Tommy and I were the hottest couple on the floor."

"I thought you said you weren't going to the Senior Dance," puzzled her friend.

"We didn't," she said. "Tommy took me to a pajama party."

An undergraduate acquaintance of ours discovered a way to cut classes at the correspondence school he's attending. He sends in empty envelopes.

Our Research Department has just come up with a stack of statistics proving that a considerable number of college students do *not* make love in parked cars. In fact, the report continues, the woods are full of them.

"Hey, Sally," said the undergrad to his girlfriend, "how come you're not wearing my fraternity pin?"

"It was such a nuisance, Bob!" Sally said playfully. "All the guys were complaining that it scratched their hands."

The current re-emphasis on standards and accountability in higher education is typified by one Midwestern university that has ruled that no athlete be awarded a letter unless he can tell at a glance which letter it is.

We know a progressive college professor who claims that you'll always have a student body where you find a faculty for making love.

An old fraternity brother told us about a gag an undergrad girlfriend of his pulled off during her last semester: She disguised herself as a boy, joined TKE, and the authorities never found out about it.

"Wait a minute," we objected. "If this girl joined a fraternity, she would have had to dress with the guys and shower with them!"

"Sure."

"Well then, someone must have discovered she was a girl!"

"Probably," said our friend, downing his drink. "But who'd tell?"

Once upon a time there were three coeds—a big coed, a medium-sized coed, and a little tiny coed. One night they came home from a dance, and the big coed said, "Someone's been sleeping in my bed!"

The medium-sized coed looked in her room and said, "Someone's been sleeping in my bed!"

And the little tiny coed said, "...Well, nighty-night, girls!"

Lecturing a class at the women's college on the anatomical intricacies of the male reproductive organ, the exasperated professor finally declared to an utterly stunned audience, "I don't know why you girls can't grasp this subject! You've had it pounded into you all semester."

Annoyed by the professor of anatomy who told racy stories during class, some members of a campus feminist group decided that the next time he started to tell one they would all rise and leave the room in protest. The professor, however, got wind of their scheme just before class the following day, so he bided his time; then, halfway through the lecture, he began, "They say there is quite a shortage of prostitutes in France—"

The girls looked at one another, arose, and started for the door. "Young ladies," said the professor, "Please sit down! The next plane doesn't leave until tomorrow afternoon."

Two young Atlanta engineers were reminiscing about their college days when one of them remarked, "I sure wish I could have gone to Georgia Tech."

Said his friend, "Oh, hell, you wouldn't have liked Tech too much. The only graduates they have are football players and whores."

"It just so happens that my wife graduated from Georgia Tech," the first snapped.

"Oh, really?" answered the friend, realizing his faux pas. "Er, what position did she play?"

Then there was the enterprising sophomore who aced her advanced biochemistry class by donating her body to science.

"**Y**our housemother tells me that you smoke pot, snort cocaine, and have had sex with almost every boy on campus," exclaimed the angry dean of women. "Don't you know what good clean fun is?"

"No," replied the coed. "What good is it?"

"**I** sent my boy to college to get an education," complained one father to another, "but all he seems to do is shack up with girls, smoke pot, and have a good time."

"Most college students do that today," replied his friend.

"That's the trouble," snapped the first chap. "I should have kept him home and gone to college myself."

The fifty-five-year-old woman went to her doctor and asked for a prescription for birth-control pills. "But you don't need them at your age," he said. She went on to explain that she had tried some recently and now found that she couldn't sleep without them. "But birth-control pills have no tranquilizing agent in them," the doctor informed her.

"Well, I don't know what they have or what they don't have in them, but I give them to my daughter before she goes out each night, and I'm telling you, doctor, I sleep much, much better."

Late Friday afternoon, a college senior dropped by the campus drugstore and purchased three dozen condoms. On Monday morning, he returned to the drugstore and in a loud voice complained, "Last Friday, I came in here and ordered three dozen prophylactics, and you only gave me twenty-four."

"I'm very sorry, sir," said the pharmacist. "I do hope we didn't spoil your weekend."

And, of course, you've heard about the bright young student who was awarded a full scholarship to the college of his choice—it paid for tuition, books, and bail money.

Her chest heaving with emotion, Susan confessed her tearful tidings to her mother.

"Mom," she said, "I'm pregnant."

"Oh, Susan!" lamented her mother. "Who is the father?"

She lifted her weeping face. "How should I know?" she wailed. "You never let me go steady!"

The young college physician was bewildered by the procession of unhappy young women regularly visiting his campus clinic for pregnancy tests. "There seems to be something in the air this time of year that causes young girls to get pregnant," he commented to an older colleague. "What is it, I wonder?"

"Their legs," replied his friend.

Mrs. Brown pulled Mrs. Green out of earshot of the porch, where Mrs. Green's lovely young daughter Carol sat.

"It's really none of my business," whispered Mrs. Brown, "but have you noticed what your daughter is doing?"

"Carol?" Mrs. Green responded apprehensively. "Why, no. What's she up to?"

Mrs. Brown leaned closer. "She's knitting tiny garments," she hissed.

Mrs. Green's troubled brow cleared. "Well, thank goodness," she said, smiling. "I'm glad to see she's taken an interest in something besides running around with boys."

During the history lesson about Vietnam, the professor illustrated what it was like when the draft was still in effect by telling the class a story. A young college student appeared at his draft board one morning wrapped in the Stars and Stripes. As he entered, he proclaimed at the top of his lungs, "No matter what happens, don't hold up my induction! Let me start now and you can complete my papers later! I don't need a physical! I don't need a uniform, basic training, guns, or anything! Just lemme at the enemy! I'll kill them with my bare hands! If they shoot me, I'll get up and keep on going! I'll rip their barbed wire with my teeth! I'll—"

The draft-board examiner looked at him in alarm and said, "You're crazy."

To which the student replied, "Write that down! Write that down!"

And this one: "Gee, Mom," the teenager complained, "none of the other guys are wearing lipstick!"

"Be quiet, stupid," his mother replied. "We're almost to the draft board."

"Young lady," the football coach asked, "what are you doing with that varsity letter on your sweater? Don't you know that it's against campus rules to wear a letter unless you've made the team?"

"Yes, sir," she said.

Calling on an attractive young student in his class, the theology professor asked, "Who was the first man?"

"If it's all the same to you, sir," replied the young woman, "I'd rather not tell."

Three young women were attending the same logic class given at one of the better universities. During a lecture the professor stated that he was going to test their ability at situation reasoning.

"Let us assume," said the professor, "that you are aboard a small craft alone in the Pacific, and you spot a vessel approaching you with several thousand sex-starved sailors on board. What would you do in this situation to avoid any problem?"

"I would attempt to turn my craft in the opposite direction," stated the first student.

"I would pass them, trusting my knife to keep me safe," responded the next.

"Frankly," murmured the last one, "I understand the situation, but I fail to see the problem."

Alarmed by rumors of immoral amusements among the student body, the young Dean of Students at a large Baptist university arranged to accompany a group of his students on their class trip, to be spent at a fishing lodge far from the temptations of civilization. The first night, the students held a lemonade dance in the lodge's great room. After the partying had been going for several hours without a single incident, the much-relieved prof said goodnight and went up to bed. He had hardly gotten beneath the covers when his door opened and a shapely young student in a flimsy nightgown entered. "Did you want me for something?" he asked in surprise.

"Not especially," the petite lass replied. "I just drew you, and when life hands you lemons, well, you know...."

And, of course, you've heard about the fellow who was hired to coach an all-girl softball team but spent the season in the batter's box.

One summer night, as the elderly couple sat on their front porch looking at the cemetery across the street, the woman remarked, "You know, dear, every time I think of our wonderful daughter lying over there, it makes me want to cry."

"I know," the man agreed, "it saddens me, too. Sometimes I even wish she were dead."

"What do you give a man who has everything?" the pretty teenager asked her mother.

"Encouragement, dear," she replied.

"I suppose," snarled the leathery sergeant to the private, "that when you're discharged from the army, you'll wait for me to die, just so you can spit on my grave."

"Not me," observed the private. "When I get out of the army, I never want to stand in line again."

"You should be ashamed of yourself," the mother reproached her daughter. "All your girlfriends are divorced already and you're not even married."

Two potheads were sitting on a small pier in the Florida Everglades, dangling their feet in the stagnant water. Suddenly an alligator swam up and snapped a leg off one of them.

"Hey, man," the unfortunate fellow said to his buddy, "like an alligator just totally bit off my leg!"

"Which one?" asked the cool friend.

"I dunno," said the first cat. "You see one alligator, you seen 'em all."

Three decrepit, gray-haired gentlemen were seated together in the park discussing their personal philosophies for achieving a ripe old age.

"I'm eighty-six," said the first, "and I wouldn't be here today if I hadn't scorned tobacco and alcohol in every form, avoided late hours, and the sinful enticements of the opposite sex."

"I owe my ninety-three years to a strict diet of blackstrap molasses, wheat germ bread, and mother's milk," said the second old man.

"When I was eighteen," the third man said, "my father told me that if I wanted to enjoy life as much as he had, I should smoke black cigars, drink nothing but hard liquor, and carouse with a different woman every night. And that's exactly that I've done."

"Incredible," said the first old man.

"Amazing," said the second, for their friend was obviously the grayest, most elderly appearing of the three. "Just how old are you?"

"Twenty-two."

Shed a tear for the beatnik who committed suicide, leaving this note: "Good-bye, cool world."

Sylvester was a sprightly ninety years of age when he married Elizabeth, who was a resoundingly ripe eighteen-year-old. As they prepared for bed on their wedding night, he asked her, "Tell me, sweet child, did your mother tell you the facts of life?"

She blushed furiously from her hairline to the tips of her toes. "No," she shyly murmured.

"That's a great pity," he said, "because I'm afraid I've forgotten them."

Two stoners won a transatlantic cruise in a joint-rolling contest. After they'd been on board for a couple of days they finally found their way to the deck. The first one said, "Man, look at all that water out there!"

"Yeah, man," the second replied. "And just think, like, that's only the top of it."

Then there was the little old lady who walked up to the Haight Street hippie and asked, "Cross-town buses run all night?"

Whereupon the young slacker snapped his fingers and replied, "Doo-dah, Doo-dah."

Two hipsters were sight-seeing in the Everglades when one suddenly stepped into quicksand and began sinking, while his fellow traveler calmly looked on.

"Hey, man," shouted the sinking swinger, "how about giving me a hand!"

"Sure thing, Dad," replied the other hipster, as he began clapping.

A youthful friend of ours in San Francisco describes hippiness as a warm poppy.

"Hey, man," one hippie said to another, "turn on the radio."

"OK," the second hippie answered, and then leaning over very close to the radio, he whispered, "I love you."

"**H**ey, lover," said the hipster to the beautiful chick he'd just met, "have you ever been picked up by the fuzz?"

"No," she answered, "but I bet it really hurts."

A scruffy young man was questioned by one of New York's finest for peddling dirty pictures.

"But you're mistaken," said the kid. "These pictures aren't dirty."

Selecting one, the policeman said, "Do you mean to tell me this isn't a dirty picture?"

The young man responded, "Don't be such a prude, officer! Haven't you ever seen five people in love?"

Dating

LeRoy Neiman

This is an oldie, but it has always been one of our favorites.

The young playboy took a blind date to an amusement park. They went for a ride on the Ferris wheel. The ride completed, she seemed rather bored.

"What would you like to do next?" he asked.

"I wanna get weighed," she said. So the young man took her over to the weight guesser. "One-twelve," said the man at the scale, and he was absolutely right.

Next they rode the roller coaster. After that, he bought her some popcorn and cotton candy, then he asked what else she would like to do.

"I wanna get weighed," she said.

I really latched onto a square one tonight, thought the young man, and using the excuse that he had developed a headache, he took the girl home.

The girl's mother was surprised to see her home so early, and asked, "What's wrong, dear, didn't you have a nice time tonight?"

"Nah, it was wousy," said the girl.

"I told my boyfriend I didn't want to see him any more," said the young woman to her friend, over lunch.

"What did he say?" the friend asked.

"Nothing. He just pulled the covers over his head."

The none too bright young fellow had been dating the same girl for more than a year and, one evening, the girl's father confronted him and wanted to know whether the lad's intentions towards his daughter were honorable or dishonorable.

"Gee," said the young man, swallowing hard, "I didn't know I had a choice!"

"Why did you and that boy spend so much time parked out front last night?" demanded the irate mother. "I could hear the giggling and squealing for a good half-hour."

"But, Mom," answered her daughter, "if a guy takes you to the movies you ought to at *least* kiss him good night".

"I thought you went to the Stork Club!" countered the mother.

"We did."

We just heard about the unlucky fellow who phoned his girlfriend to see if she was doing anything that evening. She said she wasn't, so he took her out. And sure enough, she wasn't.

"We're going to have a wonderful time tonight, dearest," said the young man to his date as he greeted her in the living room of her parents' home. "I have three tickets to the theater."

"But why do we need *three* tickets?" asked the voluptuous young lady.

"Simple," said he. "They're for your mother, father, and brother."

"I understand you took out the new accounts director last night," said one ad exec to another. "How was she?"

"Pretty bad," was the reply.

"Yeah," said the first exec, "you always were lucky."

A staff researcher has come up with proof that most girls wouldn't stay out late if fellows didn't make them.

The lights in the apartment were low and so was the music. "You say you can read my mind?" the handsome young bachelor demanded.

"Yes," replied his date.

"OK," he challenged, "go ahead."

"No," she said. "*You* go ahead."

Carol had been dating one man steadily for almost a year, and her mother was growing concerned.

"Exactly what are his intentions?" she demanded.

"Well, Mom, I'm really not sure," Carol said. "He's been keeping me pretty much in the dark."

When Cleo's parents threatened to forbid her to see her boyfriend unless she told them why he'd been there so late the night before, she finally began to talk.

"Well," she said, "I took him into the loving room, and—"

"That's 'living,' dear," her mother interrupted.

Said the happy girl, "You're telling me!"

Mist circled sluggishly in the air of the steam room as George and Charlie attempted to sweat out the excesses of the night before.

"How was your date last night?" George asked.

"Awful," Charlie responded. "Beautiful, but awful. The minute we got to her apartment, the phone started ringing—every guy in town wanted a date with her. We didn't have a moment's peace. Man, was I fed up!"

"Come on, Charlie," George twitted his friend, "don't you expect a beautiful girl to have her number in the phone book?"

"Yeah," growled Charlie, "but not in the Yellow Pages!"

One thing that can be said in favor of going steady is that it gets the youngsters home and in bed at an early hour.

The girl who will go to a man's apartment to see his etchings may not know anything about art, but she knows what she likes.

Anxious to be on time for his date, Carl nevertheless dropped into a drugstore to buy a pack of condoms. The pharmacist gave him a knowing smile, so Carl gave him a run-down on the expectations he had for the evening. "I met this girl at a party last week," he explained. "She is so fine! Anyway, her folks are going to the opera tonight and it will be just the two of us with the whole apartment to ourselves."

Carl was greeted with a warm hug at the door by Nancy, his date. They settled on the couch and turned on the TV. Her folks would be leaving in a few minutes, she explained. Her father wasn't home from work yet and as soon as he arrived, the parents would be departing for dinner and the opera.

Nancy's father arrived soon after and she introduced both parents to Carl.

"Say, why don't Nancy and I join you this evening?" Carl suggested.

"Oh, you children don't want to be spending your evening with us old folks," said Nancy's mother.

"Sure we do," said Carl, before the flabbergasted Nancy could say a word.

"I didn't know you liked opera," whispered the bewildered Nancy to her date as he helped her on with her coat.

"I don't," said Carl, "and I didn't know your father was a pharmacist, either."

A really promiscuous girl is one you can have a good time with even if you play your cards *wrong*.

A girl can be poor on history but great on dates.

Sipping her second iced tea, the green-eyed church secretary demanded of her equally attractive girlfriend, the minister's daughter, "You and Ben have been dating since you were kids, and the relationship doesn't seem to be going anywhere. Hasn't he got any ambitions?"

"Oh, yes," smiled her companion, "ever since he's been knee-high."

The dazzlingly curvy blonde appeared at her door in a strapless evening gown that defied gravity. "You look terrific!" said her admiring escort. "I can't see what holds that dress up!"

"Play your cards right and you will," she murmured.

Lily just couldn't imagine why she was so popular. "Is it my lovely hair?" she asked a friend.

"No."

"Is it my cute figure?"

"No."

"My personality?"

"No."

"Then I give up."

"That's it!"

All he had asked for was a little good-night kiss, but she haughtily rebuffed him with, "I don't do that sort of thing on my first date."

"Well," he replied, "how about on your last?"

The sweetest words any young man can hear from his girlfriend are, "There's really nothing to worry about—I kid you not."

The Jag zoomed along, with the native Californian sitting behind the wheel describing to his visiting chum the blind date they were on their way to meet. "She's young, she's rich, and her face is a picture," said the driver.

Before the evening had grown very old, the visitor found that the young lady was indeed young, had very glowing financial prospects, but she was on the plain side. The next morning, he challenged his friend: "I thought you said my date's face was a picture!"

His host yawned and replied, "Can I help it if you don't dig Picasso?"

The young woman came slamming into her apartment after a blind date and announced to her roommate, "Boy, what a character! I had to slap his face three times this evening!"

The roommate inquired eagerly, "What did he do?!"

"Nothing," muttered the girl. "I had to see if he was awake!"

"What," the girl quizzed her date, "is hot-blooded, passionate, and hums?"

The young man thought a bit, then said, "I don't know."

She smiled and replied, "Hmmmmm...."

"**I** nearly fainted when the guy I was out with last night wanted to make out," exclaimed the demure young woman to her date.

"Really?" said the man. "Then you're gonna die when you hear what I have in mind."

The pretty young woman was a trifle taken aback at her first visit to the Cheetah in New York City. After watching the wildly gyrating couples doing the grind and the new *discothêque* steps, she declined her escort's invitation to join them on the dance floor.

"Come on," implored the young man. "You can do it."

"I know I can," the girl replied, "but not standing up!"

One of the most expensive things in the world can be a woman who is free for the evening.

The disgruntled young woman was complaining bitterly to her roommate about the previous evening's blind date.

"Not only did that loser lie to me about the size of his yacht," she said, "but he made me do the rowing!"

As the young couple parked in a crowded lovers' lane, she sighed romantically, "It's lovely out here tonight—just listen to the crickets."

"Those aren't crickets," her date replied. "They're zippers."

"**N**ot that I believe in reincarnation," said the young man to his prudish date, "but what were you before you died?"

As their car stopped on the shoulder of a secluded road, the young man asked his date, "If I try to make love to you, will you yell for help?"

Said his date, "Only if you really need it."

The high school senior was parked in a secluded lovers' lane with his sexy date. "Wow!" he exclaimed. "It's so dark I can't see my hand in front of my face!"

"I happen to know," the girl said, "that neither of your hands is in front of your face."

"How about making the evening a Dutch treat?" cooed the delectable blonde to her handsome escort. "You pay for dinner and drinks—and the rest of the evening will be on me."

During a conversation with a kindly old minister, the young man asked, "Is it really such a sin to sleep with a girl?"

"Oh, no," answered the minister, "but you young boys—you don't sleep."

The couple was afloat in a canoe when a sudden thunder squall flashed across the lake. "Oh Lord," the young man prayed, "save us and I'll give up smoking and drinking… I'll give up betting on the ponies… I'll give up—"

Above the noise of the thunder came the girl's earnest plea: "Don't give up *everything*, George! Paddle!"

He drank with curvy Mabel,
The pace was fast and furious.
He slid beneath the table—
Not drunk, but merely curious.

Latest comment from the pundits regarding the population explosion: If the birth rate keeps increasing, there will soon be standing room only on the earth, at which time the birth rate should stop increasing pretty quickly.

Having repaired to what they thought was an isolated spot in the cemetery, the couple was proceeding to make love when a cop surprised them. "Didn't you see the sign at the entrance?" he railed. "NO ADMITTANCE AFTER DARK!"

"No," explained the young man, "we came in the other way, past the one that reads GET LOTS WHILE YOU'RE YOUNG."

The young woman was telling her mother about the great time she had at the mountain resort. "I met a man in the recreation hall and we played Ping-Pong all afternoon. It was so much fun!"

"Why, dear," remarked her mother, "I never knew you enjoyed Ping-Pong."

"I do now," the daughter said. "I'd hit the ball the wrong way and we'd both go after it under the table. Then he'd hit the ball the wrong way and we'd both go after it under the table. We played all afternoon. It was wonderful."

"But I don't understand," said the mother. "Where does the fun come in?"

"Under the table, of course!"

A medical journal reports that the most foolproof birth-control pill developed to date is an aspirin tablet—held firmly between the knees.

One of the members of the cabana club asked the lifeguard how he might teach a young woman of his acquaintance to swim.

"It takes considerable time and technique," the lifeguard said knowingly. "First you must take her into the water. Then place one arm about her waist, hold her tightly, then take her right arm and raise it slowly...."

"Thanks, this is really helpful," said the member. "I know my sister will appreciate it."

"Your sister?" said the lifeguard. "In that case, just push her off the end of the pier."

Martinis, my girl, are deceiving:
Take two at the very most.
Take three and you're under the table.
Take four and you're under the host.

"I went golfing with Scott yesterday," the girl told her sorority sister.

"Does he use the woods well?" asked her friend.

"I really don't know," sighed the first girl. "He insisted on playing golf all day."

The young woman relaxed on the bed, enjoying a cigarette; her boyfriend lay beside her, lost in thought.

"Darling," he said finally, "let's get married."

The young woman took a long drag on her cigarette and, without turning, said, "But dearest, who would have us?"

A twist on a well-known safety poster goes like this: DON'T DRINK AND PARK—ACCIDENTS CAUSE PEOPLE.

The Tennessee boy was trying to make time up North. "Honey," he purred to a luscious Yankee, "would it be all right if Ah kissed y'all?"

To which she replied, "Aren't my lips enough?"

"The trouble with Harold," commented Alfre to her roommate, "is that once he starts kissing you, he never knows where to stop."

"That's funny," said her friend. "The last time I went out with him, he found a great place to stop!"

The attractive middle-aged woman stormed into police headquarters and shouted at the desk sergeant that a man had grabbed and kissed her while she was walking through the park.

"What did he look like?" the desk sergeant asked.

"I really don't know," the woman replied.

"Lady, it's the middle of the afternoon on a clear, sunny day," the sergeant said in an exasperated voice. "How could a man grab and kiss you without you seeing what he looked like?"

"Well," she answered, "for one thing, I always close my eyes when I'm being kissed."

An older bachelor took a young woman of his acquaintance for a ride in his car, and after finding a suitable spot to park, kissed her several times lightly on the cheek and then murmured in her ear, "This is called *spooning*."

"If you say so," she said, "but I think I'd rather *shovel*."

A songwriter friend of ours has turned out another catchy one: *I Used to Kiss Her on the Lips, But It's All Over Now.*

A young woman's kisses usually leave something to be desired: the rest of her.

"Did you follow my advice and kiss your girlfriend when she least expects it?" the senior asked the new pledge to his frat.

"Oh, hell," said the kid with the black eye, "I thought you said *where*."

It's no fun to kiss a girl over the phone unless you happen to be in the same booth with her.

The beautiful Belinda knew that Mervin's romantic experience was minimal and she was surprised when he parked the car in a dark and romantic spot, then swept her into a passionate embrace. After several minutes filled with kisses, he drew back rather proudly, straightened his tie, and asked, "How was *that*?"

"You know, Mervin," she confided, "you're the first man I've met whose kisses make me sit up and open my eyes."

"Really?" he said, quite obviously pleased.

"Yes," she admitted. "Usually they have the opposite effect."

The party was a swinging scene, with all the lights turned low, when Clark espied a female form alone in a corner. He crept up behind her, and before she became aware of his presence, he'd clasped her in a passionate embrace and kissed her soundly.

"How dare you!" she shrieked indignantly, pulling away.

"Pardon me," Clark bluffed smoothly, "I thought you were my sister."

"You idiot," she responded tartly, "I *am* your sister!"

"Before we get married," said the young man to his fiancée, "I want to confess some affairs I've had in the past."

"But you told me all about those a couple of weeks ago," replied the girl.

"Yes, darling," he explained, "but that was a couple of weeks ago."

"Gee," mused the pretty young Mormon as she stared longingly at her older sister's new engagement ring. "It must be wonderful when you're married."

"As far as I'm concerned," her sister replied, "it's wonderful whether you're married or not."

The loving young couple wanted to marry immediately—but the girl's strong-willed and domineering mother adamantly opposed the union.

"I can't help it," said the distraught girl to her boyfriend. "Mother thinks you're effeminate."

Reflecting for a moment, he replied, "You know, compared with her, maybe I am."

"I'm going to have a little one,"
Said the girl, all gay and frisky.
And the boyfriend up and fainted
(Then she told him she meant whiskey).

Then there was the guy who was engaged to a beautiful contortionist—until she broke it off.

With their wedding date finally set, the Christian bride-to-be snuggled up to her fiancée and said, "Darling, I want to make love *before* we get married."

"But it's not long until July, dear," he replied.

"Oh," she exclaimed. "And how long will it be then?"

"Give me a kiss," the fellow ordered his lovely date.

"You'll have to make me," she teased.

"Not so fast," he protested. "All I want now is a kiss."

While attending an engagement party given by his friends, the reformed player cast an eye over the assembled guests. "You know," he declared to his best man, "I've slept with every girl here except my sister and my fiancée."

"That's interesting," his friend responded dryly. "Between the two of us, we've had them all."

She was a gorgeous girl.
And he a loving male.
He praised her shape in English,
French, Italian, and Braille.

The young man had invited his fiancée to meet his parents over cocktails at the Plaza. After his family had left, the girl wanted to know whether she had made the proper impression on them.

"I'm sorry to have to tell you this, dearest," the fellow said, "but while you were in the ladies' room, my mother told me that she considered you rather uncouth."

"Did you tell them that I attended Bennington *and* Mt. Holyoke?" she asked in surprise.

"Yes, dearest."

"Did you remind them that my family enjoys a particularly high standing in Bar Harbor?"

"Yes, I did."

"And I hope you told them of my considerable interest in the arts."

"Of course," said the young man.

"Then what's this 'uncouth' shit all about?" she asked.

Friends were surprised, indeed, when Frank and Jennifer broke their engagement, but Frank had a ready explanation.

"Would you marry someone who was habitually unfaithful, who lied at every turn, who was selfish and lazy and sarcastic?" he asked.

"Of course not," said a sympathetic friend.

"Well," retorted Frank, "neither would Jennifer."

Aware of his prospective father-in-law's flair for sarcasm, the young groom-to-be was nervous over the prospect of asking the man for his daughter's hand. Summoning the necessary courage, he approached the girl's father and, with the utmost politeness, asked, "May I have your daughter for my wife?"

"I don't know," came the reply. "Bring your wife around and I'll let you know."

Marriage

LeRoy Neiman

The sweet young bride-to-be was shopping for her wedding gown.

"Have you been married before?" asked the salesgirl.

"Why, no—why do you ask?"

"Well, when a girl has been previously married, it's customary to wear lavender rather than white."

"Oh. Well let's see what you have in white with lavender trim."

Nobody gave the bride away, but several young men at the wedding could have.

The reason no one ever gives the groom a shower is that everyone figures him to be all washed up anyway.

To the astonishment of his friends, Martin, as dedicated a player as ever cut a swath through the ranks of the fairer sex, announced his intentions to marry. Speculation ran high as to what his conduct would be after the nuptials, but Martin put an end to all doubt when he toasted the bridesmaids at the reception.

"Girls," he said warmly, his eyes flitting lightly across the room. "I want to wish you all the best of luck, and to extend the hope that each of you will, in the near future, take the place of the bride."

It was a beautiful reception, but the mother of the bride was worried that the newlyweds wouldn't have time to change and pack their clothes in time to catch their honeymoon flight to Rio. Seeing that the party was nowhere near breaking up, she finally approached the groom and whispered, "Don't you kids think it's time to go upstairs and get your things together?"

A young couple had been married in a large, expensive church ceremony, and they had finally reached the resort hotel where they were going to spend their honeymoon. The bride was extremely tired and nervous after the tension of the day, and she launched into an impromptu criticism of large weddings, emphasizing both the bother and the expense of such affairs. "It's ridiculous," she said finally. "Why, this wedding set my family back over twenty-five thousand dollars."

"Honey," interrupted the groom, "if you'll just shut up and come to bed, I'll try to give you your money's worth!"

We've heard about a preacher who officiated at so many shotgun weddings that he decided to rename his church Winchester Cathedral.

We recently attended a wedding where the bride was six months pregnant—the guests all threw puffed rice.

It was the night before the nuptials and the bride-to-be's uncle was unmercifully teasing his future in-law. "Are you going to be a man and do it tonight, or are you going to be a mouse and wait until tomorrow night?" he smirked.

Before he could stop himself, the nervous young man blurted out, "I guess I'm a rat—I did it *last* night!"

A young bride's mother was helping unpack after the honeymoon and was shocked to find her daughter's trousseau badly torn.

"Darling," she gasped, "didn't your husband like your trousseau?"

The Olympic swimming champ got married to a beautiful girl and, on their honeymoon, treated her to an exhibition of his swimming prowess. He leaped into the hotel pool, cleaved the water with expert strokes, and came up on the opposite side in a matter of seconds. His proud smile faded slightly when his lovely wife dived in and repeated his feat in half the time.

But, masking his bruised ego, he took her in his arms and exclaimed, "Darling, you're wonderful! Why didn't you tell me you were a swimming champion, too?"

"I'm not," she replied. "I was a streetwalker in Venice."

It was her wedding night and the young bride was in a romantic haze. "Oh, honey," she sighed, "we're married at last. It's all like a wonderful dream!" Her husband didn't answer.

A few moments passed, she sighed again, and said, "I'm afraid I'll wake up in a moment and find it isn't true." Still no response from her new spouse.

Another pause and another sensuous sigh, then, softly: "I just can't believe that I'm really your wife."

"Damn it," growled her mate. "As soon as I get this goddamn zipper unstuck you will!"

The newlyweds registered at their Miami Beach hotel. The concierge, a magnificent blonde, looked at them in surprise and said, "Why, *hello*, Teddy, how are you?"

A frosty silence prevailed until the couple reached their room, when the piqued bride demanded, *"Who* was that *woman?!"*

"Take it easy, honey," said the groom, "I'm going to have enough trouble explaining you to *her*."

Adjusting to marriage sometimes poses problems. We met a good friend of ours recently, the morning after his wedding, brooding over a drink in a local bar.

"What's the trouble?" we asked. "I should think you'd be the happiest man in the world today."

He shook his head sadly.

"What creatures of habit we are," he said. "This morning when I rose, half asleep, without thinking, I pulled a hundred dollar bill from my wallet and left it on the pillow."

We tried to console him—told him his wife wouldn't think anything of it.

"You don't understand," he said. "Half asleep, without thinking, she gave me fifty dollars change."

The young bride's mother had some old-fashioned ideas of marriage and passed them on to her daughter. "Never let your husband see you in the nude," she advised. "You should always wear something."

"Yes, Mother," replied the obedient girl.

Two weeks after the wedding, the girl and her brand-new husband were preparing to retire when the fellow asked, "Dear, has there ever been any insanity in your family?"

"Not that I know of," she answered. "Why?"

"Well," said her husband, "we've been married two weeks now and every night you've worn that silly hat to bed."

"Darling, I have a confession to make," said the shy young bride at their first breakfast together. "It isn't a big thing, but I feel I should have told you before. I suffer from asthma."

"Thank heavens!" said the groom, smiling. "Last night I thought you were hissing me."

The newlyweds were obviously suffering from exhaustion and after a routine examination, their doctor advised, "It's not unusual for a young couple to overdo things during the first weeks of marriage. What you both need is more rest. For the next month I want you to limit your sexual activity to those days of the week with an 'r' in them. That is, Thursday, Friday, and Saturday."

Since the end of the week was approaching, the newlyweds had no immediate difficulty following the doctor's orders. But on the first evening of scheduled rest the young bride found herself unusually passionate. Hubby fell asleep quickly, but she tossed and turned interminably and finally nudged her spouse into partial wakefulness.

Expecting daylight and confused because it was still dark, he asked, "What day is it?"

"Mondray," said his bride, cuddling against him.

After the lavish wedding reception, the newlyweds retired to their honeymoon suite. The groom turned down the lights and found something suitably romantic on the radio. Then he excused himself and returned in pajamas and robe. He opened a bottle of champagne and poured them each a drink, then took his bride by the hand and tenderly led her toward the bedroom.

"Damn," she muttered, "every time I go out with a guy it ends up the same way."

Mary and Bob, young newlyweds, were in bed in their cheap hotel room in Montego Bay, and she was so wonderstruck that she kept repeating over and over again, "Bobby, I just can't believe that we're really married."

Finally, a sleepy voice was heard through the thin plasterboard: "For chrissakes, Bobby, convince her—we wanna get some sleep!"

The newly wed young socialite was having her new house decorated and, while changing into something suitable for a lunch date with some old friends, she noticed what appeared to be her husband's handprint on the wall in the bedroom that had been freshly painted the day before. She went to the head of the stairs and called down to the painter who was now working in the living room.

"Pardon me, but would you like to come up here and see where my husband put his hand last night? It needs a little touching up," she said.

"I'd love to, lady," replied the painter, "but I've got to get done with this painting first."

Sheila and George were spending the first night of their honeymoon in a quaint medieval town in France. To add piquancy to the evening, Sheila suggested coyly that they make love every time the old night watchman rang his hourly bell. George smiled in delight at this prospect, but four rings later he pretended that he had to go out to get some cigarettes and staggered off to the watchman's tower.

"Listen, old man," he wheezed to that worthy, "do me a favor, will you? For the rest of the night, ring that bell of yours at two-hour intervals instead of hourly!"

"Ah," replied the ancient watchman, fingering his mustache, "I would be happy to oblige, *monsieur*, but I cannot do this."

"Why not?" George demanded. "I'll give you money, if that's what's troubling you!"

"Not at all," the old man responded. "You see, a beautiful young lady has already bribed me to ring the bell every half hour."

Never try to keep up with the Joneses; they might be newlyweds.

Sam and Arthur, expectant fathers both, nervously paced the floor in the waiting room of a maternity hospital.

"What tough luck," grumbled Sam. "This had to happen during my vacation."

"You think you've got troubles?" said Arthur. "I'm on my honeymoon."

The quiz show host was interviewing a pair of newlyweds, and his usual forced smile had grown so wide that the lower part of head seemed completely surrounded by teeth.

"So you've only been married six days?" he cried.

"That's right," the pretty bride replied hastily, "but it seems like six months!"

"How's that?" the host boomed jovially.

"Well," the girl answered thoughtfully, "I guess it's because we've done so much in such a short time."

The king had arranged a regal marriage for his daughter—a bond that would unite two great nations. Yet, because the young couple seemed so terribly formal around each other, the old monarch was worried that the union would not be a fruitful one. Posting a spy outside the royal bridal chamber, he demanded a full account of the wedding night's progress.

"It is hard to tell," said the king's spy the next morning. "When the prince entered the chamber, I heard the princess say, quite formally, 'I offer you my honor.' Then the prince said, with equal courtliness, 'Madame, I honor your offer.' And that is the way it went all night long—honor, offer, honor, offer."

Carter had been back from his honeymoon only a week when a friend asked him how he enjoyed married life.

"Why, it's wonderful!" was his enthusiastic reply. "It's almost like being in love."

The shy young man, wed three months, met his doctor on the street and very unhappily reported that—due to similar shyness on his bride's part—theirs was still a marriage in name only. "Your mistake," the doctor advised after hearing the gloomy details of repeated ineptitudes, "is in waiting until bedtime to make advances. The thought of the approaching moment creates tensions and impairs any chance of success. What you must do is take advantage of the very next time you both are in the mood." The young man thanked the doctor and hurried home to tell his bride of the heartening advice he'd received.

A week later, the doctor happened to meet the man again, and noticed that he was now smiling and quite self-possessed. "My advice worked, I take it?" he inquired.

The young man grinned. "Perfectly. The other night, we were having supper, and as I reached for the salt—so did she! Our hands touched…. It was as if an electric current ran through us. I leaped to my feet, swept the dishes from the table, threw her down upon it and there and then consummated our marriage!"

"That's wonderful. I'm pleased to hear things worked out so well," said the doctor, about to go on his way. The young man laid a hand upon his arm.

"There's just one hitch, though, doctor," he said, uncomfortably.

"What's that?" asked the medical man, puzzled by the other's sudden uneasiness.

"Well—" said the young man, "we can never go back to The Four Seasons again…."

On the first night of their honeymoon the bride slipped into a flimsy bit of silk and crawled into bed, only to find that her husband had settled down on the couch. When she asked why he was apparently not going to make love to her, he replied, "Because it's Lent."

"Why, that's the most ridiculous thing I've ever heard!" she exclaimed. "To whom, and for how long?"

"I must insist on knowing one thing," said the groom as he lay beside his bride in the darkness of their honeymoon suite. "Am I the first man to sleep with you?"

"You will be, darling," said his bride, "if you doze off."

When one of the two first-grade teachers at the posh suburb's new school left on her two-week honeymoon, the other volunteered to teach both classes in her absence. A few weeks later, at a housewarming party given by the newlyweds, the guests were somewhat taken aback as the groom introduced them to his wife's teaching colleague:

"And this, ladies and gentlemen," announced the grateful husband, "is the lovely lady who substituted for my wife during our honeymoon."

After spending his wedding night in a motel, the young man approached the desk clerk and asked for his bill.

"Our charge for a double room is eighty dollars apiece," advised the clerk. The newlywed grumbled something about the price being a bit steep, then dug out a roll of bills and peeled off four hundreds.

Have you heard about the newlywed who was so lazy that he took his wife to the bridal suite of a San Francisco hotel and waited for an earthquake?

Before leaving on her honeymoon ocean voyage, the lovely bride made a last-minute stop at a nearby drugstore to purchase some necessary pharmaceutical provisions. Rushing up to the man behind the prescription counter, the blushing newlywed exclaimed, "I've got to have a hundred seasick pills and a three-month supply of birth-control pills right away."

The pharmacist smiled knowingly, then with a note of genuine concern in his voice asked, "I know it's none of my business, young lady, but if it makes you sick, why do it?"

The honeymoon is over when a quickie before dinner refers to a short drink.

After a Sunday-morning wedding, the newlyweds boarded a plane for Bermuda and several hours later arrived in the bridal suite of a magnificent hotel. Overwhelmed with the sheer splendor of the resort, the bride nervously remarked, "I'm sorry to bother you, honey, but I don't have any idea of what to wear tonight."

"Darling," said her smiling mate, "you're putting me on."

"We're newlyweds and we'd like a suite," said the groom to the hotel clerk.

"Bridal?" inquired the clerk.

"Oh, no!" blurted out the bride. "I'll just hang onto his ears until I get used to it."

The groom awoke the morning after his wedding to find his innocent young bride in tears. "Why are you crying?" he asked.

"Look," she sobbed, pointing to his resting manhood. "We used it all up the very first night!"

Then there was the sleepy bride who couldn't stay awake for a second.

While inspecting their honeymoon motel room, the bride discovered a little box attached to the bed. "What's this for?" she asked her husband.

"If you put a quarter in," he answered, reaching into his pocket, "the bed starts vibrating."

"Save your change," she cooed. "A quarter in and I start vibrating, too."

Before retiring on his wedding night, the young minister turned to his bride and murmured, "Pardon me, darling, I'm going to pray for guidance."

"Sweetheart," his wife answered, patting him on the cheek. "I'll take care of the guidance. You pray for endurance."

A recently married friend of ours came home after a day at the office to find his hot young wife stretched languorously on the sofa, dressed in a revealing negligee. "Guess what I've got planned for dinner?" she cooed seductively. "And don't tell me you had it for lunch!"

The reception had ended and the newlyweds had just sneaked off to the honeymoon resort. After supper and champagne, the groom retired to the bedroom, but the bride pulled a chair up to the window and sat gazing out at the stars.

"Aren't you coming to bed?" called her impatient husband.

"No," she announced. "My mother told me this would be the most beautiful night of my life—and I don't want to miss a minute of it."

We know an octogenarian who married a woman in her late seventies—they spent their honeymoon trying to get out of the car.

On their wedding night, the honeymoon couple checked into an expensive Miami Beach hotel. Next morning, the groom telephoned room service and ordered a breakfast of bacon and eggs for himself and a plate of lettuce for his bride. "Are you sure she wouldn't care for anything else?" the puzzled clerk asked.

"Not right now," replied the chap. "I just want to see if she eats like a rabbit, too."

On their wedding night, the rather pious young man entered the bedroom and found his bride lying naked on top of the covers. "I expected to find you on your knees by the side of the bed," he said with a frown.

"Well, I will if you insist," she answered, "but it gives me hiccups."

As the young newlywed was telling a girlfriend how she had successfully taught her husband some badly needed manners, he suddenly dashed into the living room and said breathlessly, "Come on, honey, let's fuck."

The friend sat stunned as the husband scooped his bride into his arms and carried her into the bedroom. Some time later, the girl returned, smiling and adjusting her clothing. "See what I mean?" she beamed. "A week ago, he wouldn't have asked!"

Sounds drifting from the honeymoon suite kept the bellboy glued to the door. Between gasps, a male voice was saying, "Now will you let me?"

Throughout the night, the same exchange held the bellboy with his ear at the keyhole. As he was about to give up, he heard the man, in a plaintive voice, say, "Honey, it's almost dawn. *Now* will you let me?"

"Oh, all right," sighed a woman's voice. "Go ahead and take it out."

About to marry a girl in her early twenties, the spry octogenarian went to a marriage counselor and asked how he might keep his prospective bride happy. Shaking his head and laughing, the counselor said, "I think you should take in a youthful boarder."

Several months later, the old gent returned to the counselor and reported that his new wife was pregnant. "I see you took my advice about the boarder," said the counselor, chuckling.

"Yep," said the octogenarian. "And she's pregnant, too!"

One day, after a phone call from his wife, the blowhard office manager strutted into the lunchroom, chest puffed out with self-satisfaction, and proclaimed loudly, "Well, folks, my wife is pregnant!"

After a moment's silence, a small voice in the back of the room replied, "Who do you suspect?"

The beautiful eighteen-year-old girl, sobbing quietly at the funeral service for her seventy-five-year-old husband, was overheard confiding to a solicitous neighbor: "We had such a happy marriage for the six months it lasted. Every Sunday morning he would make love to me, and he'd keep time with the church bells that summoned you all to services." She sobbed a little, then said with rising animation, "And he'd still be alive today if it weren't for that damned fire engine that went clanging by!"

Eighty-five-year-old Will Jones hobbled down to the local bar to have a cold one and shoot the breeze with his friends. Mr. Jones was the talk of the town, as he had recently married a beautiful nineteen-year-old girl. Several of the boys bought the old man a drink in an effort to get him to tell of his wedding night, and sure enough, the old rascal fell right into the swing of it.

"My youngest son carried me upstairs and lifted me onto the bed with my young bride," the octogenarian recalled. "We spent the night together and the next morning my three other sons carried me off the bed." The small circle of men scratched their heads and asked the old boy why it took three of his sons to carry him off the matrimonial mattress when it took only his youngest boy to put him on.

He replied, "I was trying to fight them off!"

The two old maids lived their lonely lives together until, rather unexpectedly, a stranger arrived on the scene and whisked one of them away in matrimony. After the honeymoon, the new bride visited her unmarried friend and painted an ecstatic picture of married life.

"Our honeymoon," she said, "was like a cruise down the Mediterranean, a sail into a glorious sunset. It was *wonderful!*"

The second old maid was very much impressed and determined to get a man for herself. She showed her bankbook around town and eventually nailed a local gigolo. They were married at once and began their honeymoon.

They climbed into their wedding bed and in a short time the husband was flushed with excitement. The bride, however, was cool as a cucumber and decidedly unaffected by the proceedings.

"I simply don't understand it," she said rather indignantly as he worked away. "My friend told me that marriage was like a cruise down the Mediterranean—like a sail into a glorious sunset."

"Oh, she did, eh?" said the guy, now trembling with uncontrollable excitement. "Well, bon voyage, baby—I'm sailing without you!"

An optimist is a man who looks forward to marriage. A pessimist is a married optimist.

It was the first day for Joyce, the newly hired sales clerk in the maternity shop, and a hectic day it had been. The store had been crowded from the moment its doors opened, and the girl had sped from one customer to another without stopping. Now, just as she concluded a large sale and anticipated a breathing spell, the doors opened and a fresh flood of obviously expectant ladies poured in.

"Ye gods!" the exhausted salesgirl cried in anguish. "Doesn't *anyone* do it for fun any more?"

The understanding employer was only too glad to give his clerk the rest of the day off, after the young man explained that his wife was going to have a baby. When the clerk came to work the following morning, the boss called him into his office to offer his congratulations and inquired, "Was it a boy or a girl?"

"Oh, it's much too soon to tell," the clerk replied. "We have to wait months to find that out."

The unusually high birthrate in a suburb near our city was recently explained to us. Every morning at 6:15 the express comes roaring through town blowing its whistle.

It's too early to get out of bed, and too late to go back to sleep.

Our Research Department informs us that the bathroom is no longer the room where the most household accidents occur. That honor now belongs to the bedroom.

What's better than honor? Inner.

A priest engaged in social work attempted to explain the Church's views on birth control to a tough but friendly gang of teenagers that had gathered around him on the sidewalk in front of a favorite juke joint.

"When you're married, you have two choices," he said, "periodic abstinence and complete continence."

The teenagers thought about that for several moments, then the kid slouching against the wall announced, "I get it, man—rhythm and blues!"

Our Research Department reports that hearing aids may be instrumental in lowering the birth rate. They bolster this fantastic assertion by the following case history:

John and Susan X had produced a bouncing baby every single year of their married life until quite recently when Susan, who is hard of hearing, acquired the aforementioned apparatus. As Susan explains it: "Every night when we retire, John always turns to me and asks, 'Well, shall we go to sleep or what?' And before I got my hearing aid, I always answered, 'What?'"

It was while they were crushed together in passionate embrace that Harry decided the psychological moment was at hand to tell Marge.

"Honey," he whispered. "I want you to know that I think you're a wonderful person and that I've certainly appreciated your—uh—company these past three years, but as far as I'm concerned, cohabitation is just out of the question."

In reply, Marge uttered a small sigh of pleasure at the prospect of a quick marriage.

"No," Harry went on doggedly, "I mean, you're more like a sister to me."

At that, Marge's lovely eyes opened, and her lips parted in surprise.

"My God," she murmured, "what a home life you must've had!"

A none-too-likable, middle-aged tax lawyer of our acquaintance has announced that she much prefers the business world to marriage. "In my younger days," she boasts, "I could have married any man I pleased."

"Of course," observes a waggish friend of ours, "she never pleased anyone."

"**D**arling," she whispered, "will you still love me after we are married?"

He considered this for a moment and then replied, "I think so. I've always had a thing for married women."

Interviewing the sixty-five-year-old rodeo champion in Amarillo, Texas, the journalist remarked, "You're really an extraordinary man, to be a rodeo champion at your age."

"Heck," said the cowboy, "I'm not nearly the man my Pa is. He was just signed to play guard for a pro football team, and he's eighty-eight."

"Amazing!" gasped the journalist. "I'd like to meet your father."

"Can't right now. He's in Fort Worth standing up for Grandpa. Grandpa is getting married tomorrow. He's a hundred and fourteen."

"Your family is simply unbelievable," said the newspaperman. "Here you are, a rodeo champion at sixty-five. Your father's a football player at eighty-eight. And now your grandfather wants to get married at a hundred and fourteen."

"Hell, mister, it ain't quite like that," said the Texan. "Grandpa doesn't exactly *want* to get married. He *has* to."

Getting married is a good deal like going into a restaurant with friends. You order what you want, then when you see what the other guy has, you wish you had taken that.

We know a man who thinks marriage is a fifty-fifty proposition, which convinces us that he either doesn't understand women or percentages.

Sunday was to be the day of Joe's wedding, and he and his father were enjoying a late-night Rusty Nail together before they retired to gather strength for the next day's event.

Lifting his glass in a toast to his father, Joe asked, "Any advice before I take the big step, Dad?"

"Yes," the father said. "Two things. First: Insist on having one night out a week with the boys."

"Makes sense. And second?"

"Second: Don't waste it on the boys."

The gods gave man fire, and he invented fire engines. They gave him love, and he invented marriage.

George knew just what he wanted in a woman. "The girl I marry," he used to tell us, "will be an economist in the kitchen, an aristocrat in the living room, and a tiger in bed."

Now he's married and his wife has all the required traits—but not in the same order. She's an aristocrat in the kitchen, a tiger in the living room, and an economist in bed.

We've come across a refreshingly unique proposal of marriage: "Honey, how would you like to do this *every* night?"

Returning from his vacation, Roger asked for two weeks more in which to get married.

"But you just had two weeks off," protested his boss. "Why didn't you get married then?"

"What," exclaimed Roger, "and ruin my vacation?"

"I'll never marry a man who snores," said the pretty young Mormon.

"All right," replied her mother, "but be careful how you find out."

Marriage is like a long banquet with the dessert served first.

LeRoy Neiman

In her own eyes, Peggy was the most popular girl in the world. "You know," she said, with characteristic modesty, "a lot of men are going to be miserable when I marry."

"Really?" said her date, stifling a yawn. "How many are you going to marry?"

Marriage starts with billing and cooing but only the billing lasts.

The young man stood in the doorway unnoticed for several minutes before he had the courage to speak. Then, clearing his throat, he said, "Excuse me for interrupting you, sir, but I've come to ask for your daughter's hand in marriage."

"I see," replied the father, giving the youth a swift appraisal. "And tell me, young man, do you think you can make my little girl happy?"

"Oh, I can do that all right, sir," the boy exclaimed, obviously pleased to have been asked something to which he could respond with such a strong affirmative. "You should have seen her when I had her up in my room earlier this evening…"

We've heard of a persistent suitor who spent so much money on a young woman over a two-year period that he finally married her for *his* money.

We know a fun-loving young woman who insists she won't even consider marriage until she's gotten some experience under her belt.

The middle-aged suburban father was reading his newspaper when his daughter's boyfriend came to the house and asked to speak to him. "I realize this is only a formality," the young man declared, "but I want to ask for your daughter's hand."

"And where did you get the idea that this was just a formality?"

"From her obstetrician," replied the boy.

Sleeping the sleep of the just in her aisle seat, the attractive silver-haired woman in first class was awakened by a persistent tapping on her shoulder.

"Excuse me, are you awake?" asked the middle-aged man in the window seat.

"I am now," she said groggily.

"It's frightfully cold in here. I wonder if you would mind getting me a blanket."

"I've got a better idea, darling," she said. "Let's pretend we're married."

He chuckled softly. "Why, that sounds like a terrific idea," he said.

"Good," said she, rolling over. "Now get up and get your *own* damn blanket."

Florence and Emily, two sexy young brides who worked at the same law firm, had arranged to have lunch together, but as soon as they met, Emily could see that something serious was bothering her friend.

"Out with it, Florence," she commanded. "What's got you down?"

"I'm ashamed to admit it," Florence said. "But I caught my husband having sex!"

"Why let that bother you?" laughed Emily. "I got mine the same way."

The boss had listened in sympathetic silence as Sylvester went through the reasons why he needed, and felt he deserved, a raise. Then, with a benevolent smile, the CEO patted the younger man on the shoulder.

"Yes, Sylvester," he said kindly, "I know you can't get married on the salary I'm paying you—and some day you'll thank me for it."

Mrs. Farnsworthy felt bereaved but sympathetic when she got the news that Juliette, her jewel of a French maid, was leaving to get married.

"Ah, well," she said, seeing the glow of happiness on the girl's beautiful young face, "I am overjoyed for you, Juliette. You will have it much easier now that you're getting married."

"Yes, Madame," said the girl, "and more frequently as well."

A man is incomplete until he's married—then he's really finished.

Husband
& Wife

One guy we know is so suspicious that when his wife gave birth to twins, he flew into a rage because only one of them looked like him.

The fellows were kidding the one married man among them. "You've been married five years now, George," one of them said. "How come you have no children? Is your wife—" (he gave a stage wink) "—*unbearable?*"

"Or," interjected another, "is she inconceivable?"

"Maybe she's, uh, impregnable," joked a third.

The married man shook his head. "No, boys, got it all wrong. She's insurmountable and inscrutable."

"That wife of mine is a liar," said the angry husband to a sympathetic pal seated next to him in the bar.

"How do you know?" the friend asked.

"She didn't come home last night and when I asked her where she'd been, she said she had spent the night with her sister, Shirley."

"So?"

"It's a lie! *I* spent the night with Shirley."

The husband came strolling in the front door to discover his wife in the passionate embrace of his best friend.

"I love him, John," she said to her surprised spouse.

"See here," said the friend, "we're all too sophisticated to let a situation like this get out of hand. Tell you what let's do—we're both sporting men—I'll play you a game of gin rummy for her."

The husband thought about that for a moment.

"All right," he said, "but let's play for a penny-a-point on the side, just to keep it interesting."

The husband was disturbed by his wife's indifferent attitude towards him, and the marriage counselor suggested he try being more aggressive in his lovemaking.

"Act more like a romantic lover and less like a bored spouse," he was advised. "When you go home, make love to her as soon as you meet—even if it is right inside the front door."

At the next consultation, the adviser was pleased to hear that the husband had followed instructions. "And how did she react this time?" the consultant asked.

"Well, to tell the truth," the husband replied, "she was still sort of indifferent. But her book group went absolutely wild!"

The ship's captain returned from a two-year voyage to find his wife nursing a month-old baby. "Who did this?" he demanded. "Was it my friend Mike Fitzpatrick?"

"No," his wife said softly.

"Well then, was it my friend Bob Bigelow?"

His wife shook her head.

"Bill Connery!" he exclaimed. "Was it my friend Bill Connery?"

"*Your* friends, *your* friends," his wife said impatiently, "all the time, *your* friends! Don't you think I have any friends of my own?"

"A man is responsible for the good name of his family," said the lecturer grandly. "Is there a man among us who would let his wife be slandered and not rise to her defense?"

One meek little fellow in the back of the room stood up.

"What's this?" exclaimed the speaker. "You, sir—you would permit your wife to be slandered and not protest?!"

"Oh, sorry" apologized the little fellow, resuming his seat. "I thought you said 'slaughtered.'"

"You want to know why I've come home half loaded?" said the soused spouse. "Because I ran out of money, that's why."

Demonstrating once again the importance of punctuation, this telegram was once sent from an ailing wife to her husband: NOT GETTING ANY, BETTER COME HOME AT ONCE.

Over Gibsons, two gents were having a rousing battle about the charms of Jennifer Lopez.

"I say she's overrated," said one. "Take away her eyes, her hair, her lips, and her figure and what have you got?"

"My wife," said the other with a heavy sigh.

Walter arrived at his office late one morning and was greeted with laughter from the man in the office next door.

"What are you laughing at?" asked Walter.

"There's a big black smudge on your face," said his neighbor.

"Oh, that!" said Walter. "That's easy to explain. I saw my wife off on a month's vacation this morning. I took her to the station— she hates to fly—and kissed her good-bye."

"But what about the smudge?"

"As soon as she got on board, I ran up and kissed the locomotive."

"**Y**ou used to be the life of the party in the old days," reminisced one buddy to the other. "Does your wife still find you entertaining after six years of marriage?"

"No," answered the live one, "she hardly ever catches me."

Arthur sat brooding at his favorite bar. "Charley," he said to the bartender, "I'm a rat. I've got a lovely wife at home and instead of appreciating her, I've been out getting into trouble with another woman. But a guy can reform. I'm going home right now, Charley, and I'm going to tell her everything, beg her to forgive me, and start all over again as a model husband."

Thereupon, Arthur paid his tab, went home, told his wife everything, and begged her to forgive him so he could start over.

"I'll forgive you on one condition, Arthur," his wife said. "I want to know the name of the woman." But Arthur wouldn't tell.

"Was it Susan Lopez?" she asked. "I see how she's always looking at you."

"I can't tell you, dear," he said.

"I'll bet it was that Simpson bitch," the wife declared.

"My lips are sealed," said hubby.

"I know," exclaimed the wife, "it's that slut Paula Higgins!"

The next day Arthur was seated again at his favorite bar and as he sipped on a vodka Martini, the bartender asked how he'd made out with his good resolution of the night before.

"Well, it's a mixed bag," said Arthur. "My wife didn't quite forgive me, but she did give me three pretty good new leads."

We know a practical, if henpecked, husband who tells us that he really doesn't mind being in the doghouse as long as he can keep his tail outside.

"**F**or twenty-five long and wonderful years," mused the gentleman at the bar, "my wife and I were deliriously happy."

"Then what happened?" asked the bartender.

"We met."

She knew that these were to be her last few hours on this earth, so she called her husband to her side and in a halting voice told him her last request.

"I know," she said, "that you and Mother have never gotten along. But would you, as a special favor to me, ride to the cemetery in the same car with her?"

"All right," replied the unhappy husband, "but it will spoil my whole day."

"**W**hat are you nagging me about?" complained the husband. "I was in last night by a quarter of twelve."

"You were not, you liar!" cried the irate wife. "I heard you come in and the clock was striking three."

"And since when," said he, "isn't three a quarter of twelve?"

Henry was helping his son fly a kite in the back yard, but was having trouble getting it to stay up. His wife stood watching them from the porch. Henry had just run the entire length of the yard, trying to pull the kite into the air, only to have it thrash about uncertainly and plummet to the ground.

"Henry," called out his wife, "you need more tail!"

"I wish you'd make up your mind," said Henry, panting heavily. "Last night you told me to go fly a kite!"

Sam, the private eye, was giving his curvesome client a report.

"I trailed your husband into four bars and a bachelor's apartment," he said.

"Aha!" exclaimed the wife. "Go on, go on! What was he doing there?"

"Well, lady," Sam responded in an embarrassed tone, "near as I could make out, he was trailing *you*."

The suburban couple, middle-aged and married for nearly twenty-two years, were out for the Saturday-afternoon ritual with the grass, the bushes, and flowers. He was putting Vigor-Gro on the crab grass and she was pruning the rose bushes, but somehow their minds didn't seem to be on their work. The wife seemed especially discontent and was mumbling under her breath about something; then, quite unexpectedly, she stalked over to where the husband was standing, examining at close range a tree fungus on his favorite elm, and gave him a swift kick to the ankle.

"Ow-ouch!" exclaimed the husband, seizing the bruised appendage. "What the hell did you do that for?!"

"*That*," she said, stalking back to her rose bushes, "is for being such a lousy lover!"

The husband thought about this unexpected attack for a minute or two, then he turned and—just as resolutely as she had a few moments before—stalked over and gave his wife a swift and well-placed foot to the behind as she bent over, about to pluck an American Beauty.

"Ow!" she wailed. "You brute—why did you do *that*?"

"*THAT*," said he, returning to his elm, "is for knowing the difference!"

The two Madison Avenue types met on the suburban train platform.

"Hi, Charley," greeted the one, "how's your wife?"

"Compared to what?" responded the other.

A young politician, eager to gather votes, accepted the invitation of a local woman's club to speak on the subject of sex. However, fearing that his wife wouldn't understand, he told her that he planned to lecture on sailing.

A week after the speech, his wife ran into one of the ladies of the club, who mentioned how entertaining his talk had been.

"I just can't understand it," said the wife, "he knows so little about it."

"Come on, darling, don't be coy. His talk showed intimate acquaintance with the subject," said the matron.

"But he's only tried it twice," protested the wife. "The first time he lost his hat and the second he became seasick."

Although he kept bachelor's hours, Harry quite piously demanded absolute fidelity from his wife. Almost every night he would leave her at home with the children, bidding her farewell with a cheery, "Good-night, mother of three."

Then one night she called back just as cheerfully, "Good-night, father of one."

Now Harry stays home.

Some men are so interested in their wives' continued happiness that they hire detectives to find out the reason for it.

Some wives claim that if you give a man enough rope, he'll claim he's tied up at the office.

Then there was the man who wanted to get something for his wife, but no one would start the bidding.

A henpecked husband was heard to remark after his third Martini, "Give my wife an inch and she thinks she's a ruler!"

At a suburban dinner party, a curvaceous blonde was the center of attraction. She stood in the middle of the room surrounded by almost every man in the place. Finally, one woman turned to her husband and said, "I don't see what they see in her."

"I don't either," replied her husband as he started across the room. "I think I'll take a closer look."

A not-so-young housewife was bragging to her husband about her slim figure. "I can still get into the same skirts that I had before we were married," she said.

Without glancing up from his newspaper, her spouse replied, "I wish the hell *I* could."

"And my husband is very absent-minded," wailed the embarrassed bride to the marriage counselor. "Last night, while we were making love, the doorbell rang; and without saying a word, he jumped up and answered it."

"You mean he just got up and left you lying there?" the incredulous counselor asked.

"No," she sobbed, "he took me with him!"

A young wife whose ornery husband had grown neglectful decided to make a last-ditch effort to arouse his dormant interest by shocking him into jealousy.

"Darling," she purred one night, "the doctor I visited today said I had the most flawless face, full, well-rounded breasts, and the loveliest legs he'd ever seen."

"Did he say anything about your fat ass?" her husband asked her.

"Oh no, dear," she said without missing a beat. "Your name wasn't mentioned once."

"My sex life has improved immeasurably since my wife and I got twin beds," the executive confided to an associate.

"How can that be?" the associate asked.

"Well," replied the exec, "hers is in Connecticut and mine's in Manhattan."

"I've got an idea," said the attractive wife to her husband. "Let's go out tonight and have some real fun."

"Suits me," he answered. "If you get home first, leave the light on in the hallway."

At her wit's end, the young wife finally took pen in hand and wrote to an agony column:

"I'm afraid I married a sex maniac. My husband never leaves me alone—he makes love to me all night long, while I'm in the shower, while I'm cooking breakfast, while I'm making the beds, and even while I'm trying to clean the house. Can you tell me what to do?

Signed,

Worn-out

P.S. Please excuse the jerky handwriting."

A beautiful but obviously overwrought young Born-Again tearfully admitted to her doctor that after almost a year of marriage, her husband had not yet made love to her.

"No wonder you're nervous and upset," said the astonished physician. "Bring your husband to my office tomorrow afternoon and I'll have a talk with him."

The following day, she returned with her husband.

"I dislike prying into your personal life, my friend," the doctor said, "But you're not fulfilling your marital obligations."

"What do you mean, doctor?" the clueless husband replied. "I'm considerate, gentle, devoted, and a good provider, and they've just made me a deacon in our church."

"But what about your *sexual* obligations?" the doctor demanded.

"I don't understand," the husband replied.

The doctor tried to explain, but the good deacon just couldn't wrap his mind around it.

"All right," said the doctor at last, in exasperation, "then I'll *show* you."

He then asked the pretty wife to disrobe. After she had wriggled out of her clothes, the good medic proceeded to make passionate love to her. When he was finished, the doctor said "And *that's* what every married woman needs at least twice a week."

Seeing the happy glow on his wife's face, the husband could only agree. "Okay, doctor," he said, "we'll be back on Friday for another treatment."

Wishing to surprise her husband with a new wig she had just bought, the wife put it on and strolled unannounced into his office. "Do you think you could find a place in your life for a woman like me?" she asked sexily.

"Not a chance," he replied. "You remind me too much of my wife."

Worried about their lackluster sex life, the young wife finally persuaded her husband to undergo hypnotic treatment. After a few sessions, his sexual interest waxed anew; but during their lovemaking, he would occasionally dash out of the bedroom.

Overcome by curiosity, she followed him to the bathroom. Tiptoeing to the doorway, she saw him standing before the mirror, staring fixedly at himself and muttering, "She's not my wife… she's not my wife…. "

During a session with a marriage counselor, the wife snapped at her husband, "That's not true—I *do* enjoy sex!" Then, turning to the counselor, she added, "But this fiend expects it three or four times a year!"

"Your Honor," said the distraught woman, pointing to her husband, "he won't give me enough money to feed and clothe our four children."

"Young lady," the judge announced, "I'm going to see to it that you get at least eight hundred dollars a week."

At this, the husband jumped up and exclaimed, "That's mighty kind of you, your Honor! And I'll try to give her a couple of bucks myself."

"I think I've finally cured my husband of coming home in the wee hours of the morning," the wife proudly announced on New Year's Day. "Last night, when I heard him fumbling downstairs, I yelled, 'Is that you, Harold?'"

"How has that cured him?" questioned her friend.

"Well, his name is Charles."

"I always worry when you leave on a business trip," sobbed the salesman's lovely young wife.

"Don't worry about me, honey," he answered soothingly. "I'll be back before you know it."

"I know," she said. "That's what worries me."

Sitting in the doctor's office, the frustrated fellow unburdened himself of a tale of woe. His beautiful young wife, who had been delightfully passionate before they were married, had now lost all interest in sex.

"Try giving her these," said the doctor, handing him a bottle of pills. "One each evening with dinner."

The man complied, but the first night brought no reaction. On the second evening, he gave his wife two pills, but still no reaction. On the third night, he gave her half the bottle and, in disgust, swallowed the rest himself. Soon, his wife stretched out languorously on the couch. "Oh, darling," she said, "I want a man."

"That's funny," said her husband. "So do I."

"**M**y wife is the most suspicious woman in the world," complained the harried husband to a sympathetic friend. "If I come home early, she thinks I'm after something. And if I come home late, she thinks I've already had it."

When a funeral procession passed a golf course where four men were preparing to tee off for their regular Saturday-afternoon game, one of them turned toward the street, removed his cap, and held it over his heart. "Why did you do that?" asked his partner.

"Well," replied the fellow, "I thought it was the least I could do for my wife."

The attractive young housewife was a bit surprised when her husband's best friend dropped by one afternoon and offered five hundred dollars to make love to her. Thinking that the extra money would come in handy, she led him into the bedroom and fulfilled her part of the bargain. Later that afternoon, her husband returned from work. "Did David stop by today?" he asked casually.

"Yes, he did," she stammered. "Why do you ask?"

"Well," her spouse replied, "he was supposed to return the five hundred dollars I lent him last week."

We know a fellow who, upon being told by his shrewish wife that she would dance on his grave, promptly provided for a burial at sea.

When the woman learned her husband had taken a mistress, she demanded, "Does this mean that you've had enough of me?"

"No, my dear," he coolly replied. "It means that I *haven't* had enough of you."

The nonchurchgoer's wife persuaded him to attend a service on a hot summer Sunday. He was ignorant of the various rituals involved and his spouse seemed to constantly be whispering, "Stand up," "Sit down," "Kneel," "Stand up," "Sit."

Perspiring from all the activity, he took out a handkerchief to mop his brow and then laid it on his lap to dry. Seeing this, his wife leaned over and whispered, "Is your fly open?"

"No," he replied. "Should it be?"

We know a happily married philanderer who justifies his numerous affairs with the comment, "My wife doesn't care where I get my appetite, as long as I eat at home."

"I've just invented a cotton gin," Eli Whitney declared proudly as he emerged from his workshop.

"So what," his wife grumbled. "Who wants a fluffy Martini?"

The jaded husband called his voluptuous wife to tell her he'd discovered a new sexual position for them to try; his wife was excited by the prospect of something fresh in their usually uninspired intimacies—and she pressed for more information. "In this new position, we'll do it lying back to back," he said.

"Back to back?!" she said. "I don't understand how that's possible."

"It's quite simple," he replied. "I'm bringing home another couple."

"Morning, Howard," said the commuter, getting on the train. "How's the wife?"

"Just fine, George," came the response. "How's mine?"

It was the social event of the season: the identical twin sons of an oil tycoon married the twin daughters of a media mogul. Unfortunately, all four of the newlyweds got very drunk on their wedding night. Now, a year later, the newly arrived offspring are listed in *Who's Who*, but nobody is really sure who's whose.

A friend of ours was waiting in an airport security line recently and couldn't help overhearing the conversation the man behind him was having with the friend seeing him off.

"Thanks for putting me up while I was here, Sam," said the traveler.

"Glad to do it," said the other man.

"Thanks for the food and the drinks—everything was wonderful."

"It was a pleasure," said the man.

"And thank your wife, Sam—she was great," said the traveler, as our friend reached the metal detector. "I really enjoyed sleeping with her."

Our friend was rather taken aback by this exchange and, as they were retrieving their bags, he turned to his fellow traveler and said, "Pardon me, but I couldn't help overhearing your conversation. Did I understand you to say that you enjoyed sleeping with your friend's wife?"

"Well," said the man reflectively, "I didn't *really* enjoy it. But Sam is a hell of a nice guy."

"Your wife will probably hit the ceiling when you get home tonight," said the barfly to his drinking companion.

"Yeah," said the companion. "She's a lousy shot!"

The talkative woman was telling her husband about the bad manners of a recent visitor. "If that woman yawned once while I was talking," she said, "she yawned thirty times."

"Maybe she wasn't yawning, dear," said the husband, "She may have been trying to say something."

During a chance meeting of two old friends who had not seen each other in years, one of the men inquired about the other's wife.

"Oh, but of course, you couldn't know," said the second man sadly. "Doris has gone to heaven."

"I'm sorry to hear that," said the first man, who was a bachelor. Then, realizing that this might be misunderstood, he corrected himself, saying, "I mean, I'm glad!" Then, noticing the shocked look on his friend's face, he blurted, "That is, I'm awfully surprised!"

An undertaker called the next of kin to confirm the funeral arrangements desired for the dear departed. As luck would have it, the son-in-law—who was actually delighted to be rid of the old battle-ax—answered the phone.

"We're sorry to disturb you in this time of personal grief," the undertaker intoned solemnly, "but there appears to be some confusion as to whether the body of the loved one is to be buried or cremated."

"Let's not take any chances," came the prompt reply. "Do both."

We know a cynical husband who says it's better to have loved and lost than to have loved and won.

We know a young woman who had been married three times and was still a virgin: Her first husband, a psychiatrist, only talked about it; the second, a gynecologist, just looked at it; and the third was a gourmet.

It's been said that the trouble in the Garden of Eden wasn't caused by an apple—but by a green pair.

While visiting the livestock exhibit at a county fair with her husband, the overbearing wife asked one of the bull breeders how many times a week his animals performed their stud function.

"Oh, about four or five times," replied the owner.

Turning to her husband with a scornful look, she said, "You see, four or five times a week is not unusual among champions."

Realizing that he had contributed to the woman's abuse of her husband, the breeder quickly added, "Of course, we never use the same cow twice."

Harry, a golf enthusiast if ever there was one, arrived home from the club to an irate, ranting wife.

"I'm leaving you, Harry," his wife announced bitterly. "You promised me faithfully that you'd be back before noon and here it is almost nine P.M. It just can't take that long to play eighteen holes of golf."

"Now, wait," said Harry. "Let me explain. I know what I promised you, but I have a very good reason for being late. I got up at the crack of dawn, as you know, and picked up Fred at six A.M. But on the way to the course we had a flat tire and when I changed it I discovered that the spare was flat, too. So I had to walk three miles to a gas station to get the tire fixed and then roll it all the way back and put it on the car. After that, we got back into the car, drove a quarter of a mile and ran out of gas. I had to trudge all the way back to the gas station and back to the car again. Finally we got to the course and started to play. Everything was fine for the first two holes and then, on the third tee, Fred had a stroke. I ran back to the clubhouse but couldn't find a doctor. And, by the time I got back to Fred, he was dead. So, for the next sixteen holes, it was hit the ball and drag Fred, hit the ball and drag Fred...."

Jealously eying her next-door neighbor's new Versace coat, the young housewife asked how she had been able to afford such an expensive item.

"You probably won't believe it," her neighbor replied, "but I saved up the money by charging my husband twenty dollars every time we had sex."

That night, when her husband tried to fondle her, the young wife, determined to get a couture coat of her own, promptly stuck out her palm and demanded twenty dollars. Fumbling through his trousers, the husband complained that he had only sixteen dollars.

"For sixteen bucks," she said, "you can only sample my affection!"

After several minutes of extensive sampling, however, the aroused wife realized she wouldn't be able to resist her husband's advances much longer. In a final attempt to stick to her plan, she whispered in his ear, "Listen, if it's all the same to you, why don't I lend you four bucks until tomorrow?"

News item: Mrs. Bradley Fowler was granted a divorce after she told the judge her husband had spoken to her only three times since they were married. Mrs. Fowler was awarded the custody of their three children.

The rising exec married a co-worker's ex-wife, and his spiteful predecessor persisted in reminding him that he had received secondhand merchandise. "Hey, George," quipped the first husband one day at lunch, "how do you like handling worn goods?"

"It's great," George replied, "once you get beyond the used part."

The overweight, undersexed housewife was alone in the house watching her soaps when her husband burst through the front door, stalked into the bedroom without saying a word, and began packing his suitcase.

"Where are you going?" she demanded.

"I resigned from the firm today. I'm sick and tired of you and I'm going to Australia," was his reply. "I'm told that the young ladies there will gladly pay a hundred dollars a night for the services of a good man and I intend to live off the earnings from my lovemaking." He then continued to pack.

Suddenly, his wife pulled her suitcase from the closet and began packing her own clothing.

"And where do you think you're going?" he demanded to know.

"To Australia," she laughed. "I want to see how you're going to live on fifty dollars a month!"

Adam and Eve were walking in the Garden.

"Do you love me?" asked Eve.

Replied Adam, nonchalantly, "Who else?"

Returning from the funeral of his beautiful wife, the widower was disconsolate.

"I know how deeply grief-stricken you are," his best friend said, "but you're young and in time you will forget. You'll meet someone else with whom you will share real happiness."

"I know, I know," said the husband, "but what about *tonight?*"

"I have seven children and I've just found out my husband has never really loved me," said the distraught woman to her lawyer.

"There, there, my dear," said the attorney. "Just imagine the fix you'd be in today if he *had*."

A pair of suburban couples who had known each other for quite some time talked it over and decided to do a little conjugal swapping. The trade was made the following evening and the newly arranged couples retired to their respective houses. After about an hour of bedroom bliss, one of the wives propped herself up on an elbow, looked at her new partner, and said, "Well, I wonder how the boys are getting along."

Martin was known among his friends for the punctuality with which he sent his ex-wife her alimony payment each month. When asked the reason for his haste, he shivered and explained, "I'm afraid that if I ever should fall behind in my payments she might decide to repossess me."

Behind every successful man stands a surprised wife.

Many a wife thinks her husband is the world's greatest lover. But she can never manage to catch him at it.

The weeping bride poured out her heart to the eminent marriage counselor. "Isn't there some way—without turning into a nag—that I can keep my husband in line?"

The counselor scowled. "Young lady," he said, "your husband shouldn't have to wait in line!"

During a grouse hunt in Scotland two intrepid sportsmen were blasting away at a clump of trees near a stone wall. Suddenly a red-faced country squire popped his head over the wall and shouted, "You almost hit my wife, you daft bugger!"

"Did I?" cried the hunter, aghast. "Terribly sorry! Here, have a shot at mine—right over there."

The remarkably sexy wife of a busy husband recently won a divorce, charging her hubby with lack of attentiveness. "Can you believe that if anything ever happened to me," the woman demanded of the jury in her closing statement, "my husband wouldn't even be able to identify the body?"

Swinging
Spouses

leRoy Neiman

Pete was the playboy of the office. He kept the cubicle set bug-eyed with juicy tales of his conquests. One afternoon a bachelor in the office cornered him and asked, "Pete, how the hell do you do it? You're a married man, but you make Casanova look like a two-bit amateur. Come on, buddy, what's your secret?"

Pete was in a conversational mood. "I wouldn't do this for everybody, Eddie," he said, "but you're a friend, so I'll tell you my secret. Like all great plans, it's really very simple. It's all in the *approach!*

"Tonight, take the 5:21 out of Penn Station and get off at Great Neck. You'll find dozens of women there waiting for their husbands. Now there are always *some* husbands who have to work late. So all you have to do is be charming and let nature take its course."

The system was indeed simple, and also seemed foolproof. Eddie boarded the 5:21 that night with Pete's instructions fixed firmly in his mind. But he dozed en route and didn't waken till Plandome, two stops after Great Neck. He got off the train in a hurry and was about to catch a cab back to his destination when he noticed an unescorted female standing on the platform looking very available.

He sauntered over casually, lit her cigarette, and asked whether she'd like to have a nice quiet drink with him.

"I'd love to," she said, "but let's go to my place. It's near here and it's very, very quiet."

Everything went as planned. They had a small dinner at her place, some drinks, then they retired to the pleasures of the bedroom. They'd been enjoying themselves only a few minutes, however, when the door swung open and the woman's husband entered.

"Goddammit, Betty!" he cried. "What the hell's going on here? So this is what you do when my back is turned... And as for you, you bastard—I thought I told you to get off at Great Neck!"

"**I**'ve learned one thing about women," said the experienced one to his drinking companions. "You just can't trust a girl with brown eyes."

"It occurs to me," said one of his inebriated friends, "that I've been married nearly three years and I don't know what color eyes my wife has," whereupon he finished his drink, climbed from his stool, and hurried home to investigate. His wife was in bed, asleep. He crept up to her and carefully lifted an eyelid.

"By God! *Brown!*" he exclaimed.

"How the hell did you know I was here?" said Brown, crawling out from under the bed.

Two Englishmen struck up a conversation with an American in the club car of a train headed east out of Chicago.

"I say," queried the younger Englishman, "have you ever been to London?"

The American laughed. "I called it home for two years," he said. "Had some of the wildest times of my life in that old town."

The older Englishman, a little hard of hearing, asked, "What did he say, Reggie?"

"He said he's been to London, father," the younger Englishman replied.

After a lull in the conversation, the young man asked, "You didn't, by any chance, meet a Hazel Wimbleton in London, did you?"

The American almost fell off his chair. "Hot-Pants Hazel?!" he exclaimed. "My God, I shacked up with that one for three months, just before I came back to the States."

"What did he say, Reggie?" the older Englishman wanted to know.

"He says he knows mother," the younger Englishman responded.

Paul Revere's horse galloped down the country road. The life of the colonies depended on Revere's warning the people that the British were coming. He approached a farmhouse.

"Is your husband at home?" he called to the woman feeding chickens in the yard.

"He's back in the barn, Paul," she answered.

"Tell him to get his musket and go to the village square. The Redcoats are coming!"

The exchange of words had taken but an instant; Revere's horse had not broken its stride. The famous patriot thundered off toward the next farm.

"Is your husband at home?" Revere called to the woman in the doorway of the next farmhouse he approached.

"He's asleep in his room, Paul," she said.

"Tell him to get on his clothes," Revere cried. "The Minute Men are meeting at the village square. The British are coming!"

Horse and rider galloped on to still another home.

"Is your husband at home?" he called to the handsome woman who leaned out the window.

"He's gone to New Amsterdam and won't be back till Sunday," she said.

"Whoa-a-a!"

The husband finally wised up to the fact that his wife was something less than faithful. He put a private investigator on her tail, and within a week had the name and address of the "other man."

"No sonofabitch is going to break up my home," the husband snarled indignantly to himself. "My loving wife would be true to me today if this sneaky guy hadn't come on the scene!"

Still, the husband prided himself on his sophistication, and resolved to handle the situation in a businesslike way. He called in his secretary and dictated this letter:

"Sir:

It has been called to my attention that for some time now you have been carrying on an affair with my wife. So that we can settle this matter intelligently, please see me in my office at three P.M. sharp on Friday."

The "other man," amused by the husband's formal manner, called in his own secretary and dictated this reply:

"Dear Sir:

Received your circular letter this morning. Be advised that I will attend the scheduled conference on time."

A married man we know relaxed on a recent business trip by enjoying a lively weekend with a lively blonde who was *not* his wife. Not long after returning to the home office, however, a rather shifty individual paid him a visit and said, with the nasty innuendo of a professional blackmailer, "Remember that trip you took? Remember that blonde?" The answer to both questions was "Yes."

"Well, mister," said the unsavory one, "it just so happens that I have photographs of everything that you and her did."

"Everything?" asked our friend.

"*Everything!* See?" He spread a half-dozen highly detailed snapshots on the desk and after giving them a chance to make the proper impression, asked, "What are you gonna do about it, mister?"

"Well," drawled our friend coolly, "I'll take one of these, two of those, and five of this one over here. Can I have them tinted?"

A sharp rap on the door startled the two lovers.

"Quick, it's my husband," exclaimed the frightened woman. "Jump out the window!"

"But we're on the thirteenth floor!" the Casanova gasped.

"Jump," cried the woman. "This is no time to be superstitious."

Mrs. Culpepper was almost in tears. "Oh, Marie," she said to her maid, "I believe my husband is having an affair with his secretary."

"I don't believe it," snapped Marie. "You're just saying that to make me jealous."

"**D**octor," said the man on the phone, "my son has scarlet fever."

"Yes, I know," replied the doctor. "I came by your house and treated him yesterday. Just keep him away from the others in the house and...."

"But you don't understand," said the distraught parent. "He's kissed the maid!"

"Well, that's unfortunate. Now we'll probably have to quarantine her...."

"And, doctor, I'm afraid I've kissed the girl myself."

"This is getting complicated. That means you may have contracted the disease."

"Yes, and I've kissed my wife since then."

"Damn it," exclaimed the doctor, "now I'll catch it, too!"

Two longtime friends sipped Scotch in a local bar and talked about their troubles.

"And on top of everything else," said the first, "my wife has cut me down to just once a week."

"That's too bad," agreed his friend, "but it could be worse. I know two guys she's cut off altogether."

"**G**et this," the husband chuckled. "That ridiculous janitor of ours claims he's made love to every woman in the building except one."

"Hmmmm," said his wife, assuming a thoughtful, faraway expression, "must be that stuck-up Mrs. Frobisher on the fourth floor."

Jim Morgan had just returned from a month-long trip to New York when he met a good friend just outside his office.

"Jim," said the friend, "what's wrong? Your eyes are so red and bloodshot!"

"It happened on the trip," said Jim. "My very first evening in New York, I met this very attractive young woman in the hotel bar. We had a few drinks, then dinner in a nice restaurant down the street, and then back to the hotel bar for a nightcap. One thing led to another and she spent the night in my room.

"When I woke the next morning, she was sitting on the edge of the bed crying. I asked her what was troubling her and she told me she was married and that she was very ashamed of herself.

"Well, that got me to thinking about my wife and kids back here, so we both sat there on the edge of the bed and cried for about a half hour."

"But, Jim," said the puzzled friend, "that was almost four weeks ago. What does that have to do with your eyes being bloodshot today?"

"Well, look," Jim exclaimed, "you can't sit and cry your eyes out every morning for four weeks without making them a little red!"

Mrs. Applebottom grew angry with the French maid, and after a series of stinging remarks regarding the young girl's abilities as a cook and housekeeper, she dismissed her. But the girl's Gallic ancestry wouldn't allow such abuse to go unanswered. "Your husband considers me a better cook and housekeeper than you, Madame. He has told me so himself."

Mrs. Applebottom looked at the girl scornfully and made no comment.

"And furthermore," said the angry girl, "I am better than you in the bed!"

"And I suppose my husband told you that, too," snapped Mrs. Applebottom.

"No, Madame," said the maid, "the chauffeur told me *that!*"

One of our friends has a real problem. He received a note through the mail advising him, "If you don't stop making love to my wife, I'll kill you." The trouble is, the note wasn't signed.

Lord Duffingham returned from his grouse shooting somewhat earlier than usual and found Lady Duffingham in a rather compromising situation with his best friend, Sir Archibald Carpley. Lord Duffingham stood stiffly in the bedroom doorway and loudly berated his wife for her infidelity. With thunder in his voice, he reminded her that he had taken her from a miserable existence in the London slums, given her a fine home, and provided her with servants, expensive clothes, and jewels.

As Lady Duffingham was by this time crying inconsolably, his Lordship turned his wrath on his supposed friend: "And as for you, Carpley—you might at least stop while I'm talking!"

The king was waving to his loyal subjects from the steps of the palace when he spotted a beggar in the crowd who looked, beneath the dirt and rags, amazingly like his royal self. He had a guard bring the beggar to him and the crowd was likewise struck by the remarkable resemblance. The king was amused, for he knew that the king before him had had a well-deserved reputation as a ladies' man, as did he had himself.

"Tell me, my good fellow," said the king, smiling, "was your mother perhaps a servant in the royal palace?"

"No, Your Highness," said the beggar, "but my father was."

The jealous husband returned home from a business trip a day early and, discovering a strange coat in the front closet, stormed into the living room with the accusation that there was another man in the apartment.

"Where is he?" the husband demanded, as he stalked from room to room, searching.

"You're mistaken, dear," the wife insisted. "That coat must have been left by one of your friends the last time you threw a poker party. Since you've been gone, I haven't even *looked* at another man."

The husband searched through the entire apartment and, finding no one, decided his wife must be telling the truth. Apologizing for his unwarranted display of temper, he then went to the bathroom to wash up. He was running water in the basin when he noticed that the shower curtain was pulled closed. Rather peculiar, he thought. He ripped the curtain open and—sure enough—there was a strange man. But before the astounded husband could utter a word, the man jerked the curtain closed again, saying, "Please! I haven't finished voting yet."

The outraged husband discovered his wife in bed with another man.

"What is the meaning of this?" he demanded. "Who is this fellow?"

"That seems like a fair question," said the wife, rolling over. "What *is* your name?"

The very swank men's club had for years forbidden the presence of women in any of its stately rooms. One night a dignified member walked in and was shocked to discover a group of women chatting away in the very center of the study.

"What is the meaning of this?" he demanded of the club manager.

"We've decided to let members bring their wives in for dinner one evening a month," was the reply.

"But that's unfair," complained the disgruntled fellow. "I'm not married. Could I bring my girlfriend?"

The manager thought for a moment, and then replied slowly, "I think that might be all right... provided, of course, she's the wife of a member."

"Anything else, sir?" asked the attentive bellhop, trying his best to make the lady and gentleman comfortable in their penthouse suite in the posh hotel.

"No. No, thank you," replied the gentleman.

"Anything for your wife, sir?" the bellhop asked.

"Why, yes, young man," said the gentleman. "Would you bring me a postcard?"

"Do you cheat on your wife?" asked the psychiatrist.

"Who else?" answered the patient.

The hungover couple dawdled over a mid-afternoon breakfast, after a particularly wild all-night party held in their fashionable apartment.

"Honey, this is rather embarrassing," said the husband, "but was it you I hooked up with in the library last night?"

His wife looked at him reflectively, and then asked, "About what time?"

"You beast! You animal!" cried the young woman. "I'm going back to Mother."

"Don't bother," said the guy. "I'll go back to my wife."

"Your continual unfaithfulness proves you are an absolute shit," stormed the outraged wife, who had just caught her husband for the seventh time in a sportive romp with another woman.

"Quite the contrary," came the cool reply. "It merely proves that I'm too good to be true."

The young married couple had moved into an apartment next to a sexy model, and whenever the husband went over to borrow something it usually took him much longer than his wife thought it should. On one especially extended trip, his wife lost all patience and pounded several times on the wall between the two apartments. Receiving no answer, she called the neighbor on the phone.

"I would like to know," the wife said huffily, "why it takes my husband so long to get something over there!"

"Well," replied the woman coolly, "these interruptions certainly aren't helping any."

"**Y**es, you heard correctly," said Phillip rather pensively to the cute waitress. "My wife has run off with my very best friend."

"Oh, I'm terribly sorry, sir," said she. "I suppose he was a handsome scoundrel."

"I don't really know," said Phillip, brightly. "I've never met the guy."

The meek little bank clerk had his suspicions. One day he left work early and, sure enough, at home he found a strange hat and umbrella in the hallway and his wife was on the couch in the living room in the arms of another man. Wild for revenge, the husband picked up the man's umbrella and snapped it in two across his knee.

"*There!*" he exclaimed. "Now I hope it rains!"

With deep concern, if not alarm, Dick noted that his friend Conrad was drunker than he'd ever seen him before.

"What's the trouble, buddy?" he asked, sliding onto the stool next to his friend.

"It's a woman, Dick," Conrad replied.

"I guessed that much. Tell me about it."

"I can't," Conrad said. But after a few more drinks his tongue and resolution both seemed to weaken and, turning to his buddy, he said, "OK. It's your wife."

"My wife!"

"Yeah."

"What about her?"

Conrad pondered the question heavily, and draped his arm around his pal. "Well, buddy-boy," he said, "I'm afraid she's cheating on us."

Arriving home unexpectedly from a business trip, the husband found his wife in bed with his best friend, in what may be delicately described as a compromising position.

"See here," exclaimed the husband, "just what do you two think you're doing?"

"See!" said the wife to the man beside her. "Didn't I tell you he was an idiot?"

Joe had been out on the town with his latest mistress, a dazzling blonde, and as he returned home the rosy tints of dawn began to color the skies. Marshaling his inner resources, he managed an air of quiet sobriety before the suspicious eye and clapping tongue of his wife.

Suddenly, as he was undressing, she punctuated her harangue with a sharp, gasping intake of air.

"Joe," she asked through clenched teeth, "Where the hell is your underwear?"

Blearily, Joe perceived that his boxer shorts were, indeed, missing. Then inspiration struck.

"My God!" he cried, with aggrieved dignity. "I've been robbed!"

As they ran for their respective trains, Ralph called to his fellow-commuter Paul, "How about a game of golf tomorrow?"

"Sorry," Paul called back, "but it's the kids' day off, and I've got to take care of the maid."

Then there was the bandleader who spent all week working on a new arrangement only to discover that his wife wasn't going out of town after all.

Homer and his pretty wife were about to check out of the hotel, when Homer expostulated over the amount of the bill.

"But that, sir," explained the hotel manager, "is our normal rate for a double room with bath and TV."

"Yeah? Well, as it happens, we didn't use the TV."

"I'm sorry, sir," the manager replied firmly. "It was there for you to use if you'd wanted it."

"OK," Homer said, "but in that case, I'm going to charge you for making love to my beautiful wife."

"But, sir," spluttered the manager, "I did no such thing!"

"I'm sorry," Homer sneered, "but she was there for you to use if you'd wanted her."

At this reply, the manager became so flustered that he actually reduced Homer's bill. Homer was exultant at his *coup,* and for months afterward he told and retold the story at parties with great relish, while his wife rolled her lovely eyes heavenward to indicate her opinion of his boorishness. Finally, they took another trip. Homer was determined to pull the same stunt and, up to a point, he achieved the same success.

"Sir, that's our normal rate," said the young clerk.

"Very well, but we didn't use the TV."

"But, sir, it was there for you to use if you'd cared to."

Homer's eyes brightened in anticipation. "Well, in that case," he said smarmily, "I'll have to charge you for making love to my beautiful wife."

To Homer's chagrin, the clerk became very red in the face and began to stammer. Then he said, "OK, OK, I'll pay you. But keep your voice down, will you? I'm new at this hotel and you're apt to get me fired."

Carol was furious when she came home unexpectedly and caught her Harry in bed with a midget.

"You promised me two weeks ago that you would never cheat on me again," she stormed.

Harry shrugged his shoulders and murmured airily, "Well, as you can see, I'm tapering off."

Beauregard discovered his wife in the arms of her lover and, mad with rage, killed her with his .38 revolver. A jury of his Southern peers had brought in a verdict of justifiable homicide, and he was about to leave the courtroom a free man, when the judge stopped him.

"Just a point of personal curiosity, suh, if you're willing to clear it up?"

In reply, Beauregard bowed.

"Why did you shoot your wife, instead of her lover?"

Beauregard ran his finger lightly over his mustache.

"Suh," he replied, "I decided it was better to shoot a woman once than a different man each week."

"Say," said the recently married player in his usual confidential tone, "there are a lot of hot women at this party. If I find a chick who's ready, would you mind if I used your extra bedroom for a little quick in-out in-out?"

"Not at all," replied the gracious host, "but what about your wife?"

"Nothing to worry about," said the operator. "I'll only be gone a few minutes and she'll never miss me."

"No, I'm sure she won't miss you," agreed the host, "but fifteen minutes ago *she* borrowed the extra bedroom."

After two years in Kandahar, a Marine was shipped back to the States. Naturally, after a tearful shipside reunion, he and his beautiful wife went immediately to a hotel. Much later that night, a drunk, wandering the hall, banged on their door, shouting, "Let me in!"

"Good Lord," said the Marine, leaping from the bed only half awake. "I'll bet that's your husband!"

"Don't be silly," his wife said sleepily. "He's in Afghanistan."

Noah Webster's wife, returning from a long trip, discovered the lexicographer *flagrante delicto* with a pretty chambermaid.

"Mr. Webster!" she gasped. "I am surprised!"

"No, my dear," said Webster with a reproving smile. "You are shocked; *I* am surprised."

"I think you've made a mistake in my bill," said the patron, after three stiff, top-shelf Manhattans in a swank New York bar. "You've only charged me three bucks."

"No mistake," replied the bartender. "I only charge a dollar a drink."

"Fantastic," said the delighted patron. "But how, at a dollar a drink, can you afford to operate such a plush bar? Are you the owner?"

"No," confided the bartender. "The owner's upstairs with my wife. And what he's doing to her up there I'm doing to him down here!"

The defense attorney was bearing down hard. "You say," he sneered, "that my client came at you with a broken bottle in his hand. But didn't *you* have something in *your* hands?"

"Yes," said the battered plaintiff. "His wife. Charming, of course, but not much good in a fight."

In the Middle Ages, people who committed adultery were stoned; today, it's often the other way around.

It had promised to be a sensational divorce case, with the wife accused of incredible escapades, but thus far it had all proved rather disappointing, with nothing more than a few insinuations and vague generalities tossed back and forth. But this was the day when the wife was to take the witness stand for the first time, and the courtroom was filled to capacity. Testifying before her own lawyer, she projected an image of sweet innocence, as she told a tale of wifely fidelity and sacrifice. At long last the wife's direct testimony came to an end, and the husband's attorney was given the opportunity to cross-examine.

He first re-established her name, relationship to the plaintiff, and other details of identification. Then he picked up a paper from the table, studied it a moment, turned to her and asked, "Is it not true, Madam, that on the night of June twelfth, in a driving rain-storm, you had sexual intercourse with a certain circus midget on the handle bars of a careening motorcycle that passed through the center of Libertyville at speeds in excess of sixty miles per hour?"

The wife turned pale, but retained her remarkable self-control, and her voice was almost perfectly steady as she asked, "What was that date again?"

Harry constantly irritated his friends with his eternal optimism. No matter how bad the situation, he would always say, "It could have been worse."

To cure him of this annoying habit, his friends decided to invent a situation so completely black, so dreadful, that even Harry could find no hope in it. Approaching him at the club bar one day, one of them said, "Harry! Did you hear what happened to George? He came home last night, found his wife in bed with another man, shot them both, then turned the gun on himself!"

"Terrible," said Harry. "But it could have been worse."

"How in hell," asked his dumfounded friend, "could it *possibly* have been worse?"

"Well," said Harry, "if it had happened the night before, I'd be dead right now."

Originally scheduled for all-night duty at the station, Patrolman Michael Fenwick was relieved early, and thus arrived home four hours ahead of schedule. It was nearly two A.M., and hoping to get into bed without waking his wife, he decided to undress in the dark. But as he crossed the room to climb into bed, his wife sat up and sleepily asked, "Mike, dearest, would you go down to the all-night drugstore in the next block and get me a box of aspirin? My head is splitting."

"Certainly, sweetheart," he said, and feeling his way across the room, he crawled back into his clothes and stumbled out of the house and down the street to the drugstore. As he arrived, the pharmacist looked up in surprise.

"Say," he said, after taking Fenwick's order, "aren't you Officer Fenwick of the Ninth Precinct?"

"Yes, I am," said Fenwick.

"Well, then, what in the world are you doing in the fire chief's uniform?"

Having just returned from an extended business trip, the executive lay asleep beside his wife, who was dreaming she was in her lover's arms. Suddenly, in her dream, she imagined she heard a familiar step outside the bedroom door.

"Heavens!" she cried aloud in her sleep. "Get out, my husband's coming!" With that, her spouse leaped out of bed and bounded into the closet.

A wild-eyed young man rushed into Tony's crowded one-man barbershop at nine o'clock one morning and asked, "How many ahead of me?"

"Three" came the answer, and he ran out the door. At shortly after twelve he returned, asked the same question, the barber replied "Four," and again the young man sped off.

At three P.M. and five P.M. the previous scenes repeated themselves, but with only one difference: There was a noticeable decline in the young man's vigor as the day proceeded, and some of the spring had gone out of his step. The barber, concerned about a good and regular customer, instructed his sweeper to follow the lad and report back on what he was doing that was tiring him so.

Minutes later the sweeper rushed back into the shop and announced, "Better call your home right away, Tony, and tell your wife you're ready for that young man right now!"

The husband had arrived home unexpectedly, and now he stared suspiciously at a cigar smoldering in an ashtray. "Where did that cigar come from?" he thundered, as his wife cowered in their bed.

There was a pregnant pause, then from the closet a man's voice answered, "Cuba."

A young zoologist entered a cocktail lounge and ordered a triple Martini, explaining to the bartender that he was celebrating his first major achievement in the field of genetics. An alluring young woman at the other end of the bar asked if she might join him, since she was also there to commemorate an outstanding personal accomplishment.

"What a coincidence," said the zoologist. "I've just succeeded in breeding a very rare blue-eyed female pheasant for the first time in captivity. What did you do?"

"Nothing quite so significant," replied the girl. "It's just that, after ten long years of marriage, my doctor tells me I am finally pregnant. But how did you ever manage to breed your blue-eyed pheasant?"

"It was simple," he explained. "All I did was keep changing mates until I found the right biological combination."

"That's just what I did," said the girl, with a knowing smile. "What a coincidence!"

Two successful restaurateurs were discussing business when one suddenly dropped his head and solemnly announced, "Did you know that my married daughter is having an affair?"

"Is that so," said the other. "Who's catering it?"

Have you heard about the man who never worried about his marriage, until he moved from New York to California and discovered that he still had the same UPS man?

A pediatrician we know informs us that infants don't have nearly as much fun in infancy as adults have in adultery.

While riding home from work one evening, three commuters became friendly in the club car and after the third round, they began to brag about the relative merits of their respective marital relationships. The first proudly proclaimed, "My wife meets my train *every* evening, and we've been married for ten years."

"That's nothing!" scoffed the second. "My wife meets me every evening, too, and we've been married *seventeen* years!"

"Well, I've got you both beat, fellows," said the third commuter, who was obviously the youngest in the group.

"How do you figure that?" the first fellow wanted to know.

"I suppose you've got a wife who meets you every evening, too!" sneered the second.

"That's right," said the third commuter, "and I'm not even married!"

It was late afternoon in a small Nevada town and Joe, the owner of the local beer parlor, was lazily polishing glassware when his friend Mike, obviously agitated, came running in.

"Joe, baby," he shouted, "get over to your house quick. I just stopped off to see if you were home and I heard a stranger's voice in your bedroom. So I looked in the window and there—well, I hate to tell you, but your wife is in bed with another man."

"Is that so?" Joe replied calmly. "What does this guy look like?"

"Oh, I don't know—he's tall and completely bald."

"And did he have a thick red mustache?" asked Joe.

"Right, right!" Mike yelled.

"And did you notice if he had a gold front tooth?"

"Dammit, man, you're right!"

Pouring his friend a beer, Joe remarked philosophically, "Must be that jackass Cal Thompson—he'll screw *anything!*"

King Arthur, going on a two-year dragon-hunting expedition, ordered Merlin the Wise to make a chastity belt for Guinevere to wear while he was away. Merlin came up with a very unorthodox design—one that had a large gaping aperture in the area that would normally be most strongly fortified.

"That's absurd!" said Arthur. "It won't work."

"Sure it will," said Merlin. Picking up a spare magic wand, he passed it through the opening. Instantly, a guillotine-like blade came down and chopped the wand in two.

"Ingenious!" cried Arthur. After outfitting Guinevere with the belt, he rode off to slay dragons, his mind at peace.

Two years later, when Arthur came back, his first official act was to assemble all the Knights of the Round Table and send them to the court physician for a short-arm inspection. His frown grew severe as he learned that every member of the Round Table was nicked, cut or scratched. All but one: Sir Lancelot. Arthur called for him immediately and smiled at his best knight.

"Sir Lancelot," he declared, "you are the only one of my knights who did not assail the chastity of my lady Guinevere while I was off slaying yon dragons. You have upheld the honor of the Round Table, and I am proud of you. You shall be rewarded. You may have anything in the kingdom you desire. You have but to name it. State your wish!"

But Sir Lancelot was speechless.

After a round of golf, two men were changing their clothes in the country-club locker room. One of the men started putting on a pair of pantyhose and the other, quite astonished, said, "Since when did you start wearing *that*?"

Shaking his head resignedly, the first man replied, "Ever since my wife found it in the glove compartment of our car."

After twenty years of marriage, a couple mutually decided to get a divorce. To celebrate the granting of the decree, they dined out together. After the third glass of champagne, the husband confessed, "There's one thing I've always wanted to ask you, but I never had the nerve. Now that we're splitting up, your answer can't possibly hurt me, so please be honest. Why is it that five of our six children have black hair, but little Tommy is a blond? Whose child is Tommy, anyway?"

"I can't tell you," said the wife after a long pause. "It would hurt you too much."

"Oh, don't be ridiculous," the husband insisted. "I don't care who the father is. I'm just curious."

Finally, the wife acquiesced. "Well, if you really want to know, Tommy is *your* child."

Returning home for a forgotten briefcase, the husband found his pretty wife standing naked on the bathroom scales. Not bothering to enter the room, he reached in, patted her on the bottom and asked, "How much today, baby?"

"The same as always," she answered. "Two quarts of milk and a pound of butter."

"His family wasn't too pleased about our engagement," sighed the party girl to her roommate. "In fact, his wife was furious."

"Darling," cooed the wife sweetly over morning coffee, "do you remember those trout you spent two weeks fishing for back in April?"

"Sure," mumbled her husband through his newspaper.

"Well," she continued, "one of them called last night to say you're going to be a father."

"I don't really mind him being unfaithful," sighed the wife to the marriage counselor, "but I just *can't* sleep three in a bed."

After several years of marriage, the youthful stockbroker still couldn't keep away from other women; but he was fast running out of excuses to satisfy his jealous wife. One afternoon, he accompanied his attractive colleague from the floor of the stock exchange to her apartment and made love to her far into the night.

"My God!" he exclaimed, grabbing his watch from the nightstand. "It's three o'clock in the morning." Then, inspired, he dialed his wife. When she answered the phone, he whispered conspiratorially into the handset, "Don't pay the ransom, dear. I've just escaped."

Creeping around to the bedroom window, the private detectives saw their client's wife in bed with another man.

"Just as I suspected," said the first. "Let's go in after him."

"Great idea," the other replied. "How soon do you think he'll be finished?"

A middle-aged husband went to a doctor and explained that his wife was constantly nagging him about his vanishing potency. After giving him a bottle of pills, the doctor assured him that they would work wonders. A month later, the man returned, obviously satisfied with the results.

"The pills are terrific," he said. "I've been doing it three times a night."

"Wonderful," the doctor replied. "What does your wife say about your lovemaking now?"

"How should I know?" the fellow shrugged. "I haven't been home yet."

Noticing that her husband's relationship with the alluring young woman across the street was becoming more and more obvious, the suspicious wife awoke one morning to find herself alone in bed. Angered, she dialed her attractive neighbor and bellowed into the phone, "Tell my husband to get his ass across the street."

"Well, you know," the sleepy young woman's voice replied, "that's where he's been getting it for some time now."

Early one evening, the shrewish wife of a stock-market analyst returned home unexpectedly from a visit to her sister's house and discovered her husband in bed with a shapely blonde. "Harry, what the hell are you doing?" she bellowed.

"Didn't you hear?" the quick-thinking analyst asked. "I've gone public!"

We know a swinging suburban housewife who says there's as much difference between husbands and lovers as night and day.

In the midst of a passionate bout of lovemaking, the couple was interrupted by the phone ringing. The girl answered it, returning to bed a few seconds later. "Who was that?" her companion questioned.

"My husband," the sweaty but sultry young woman sighed, snuggling up against her bed partner. "He wanted to tell me he'll be out late because he's playing poker with you and some of the other fellows."

Have you heard about the wife who took a lover just to break the monogamy?

As the time drew near, the patient asked her obstetrician, "Will my husband be permitted to stay with me during the delivery?"

"Oh, yes," answered the physician. "I feel that the father of the child should be present at its birth."

"I don't think *that* would be a very good idea," the woman said. "He and my husband don't really get along all that well."

Fred and Elaine had been married for ten years when one evening at dinner Fred announced his intention of taking a mistress. His wife was shocked, but Fred pointed out that his two partners, Jim and Bob, both had mistresses and their wives had adjusted to the situation very nicely.

"All three girls dance in the chorus of the same nightclub," Fred explained, "and tomorrow night, I'm going to take you there to see them."

The next evening, Fred and Elaine went to the nightclub, and when the showgirls began their opening number, Fred said, "The blonde on the left is Jim's. The redhead next to her is Bob's. And the pretty brunette on the end is mine."

Elaine stared at the girls long and hard before answering, "You know something, darling? Of the three, I like ours best."

The Madison Avenue exec was dallying with both his secretary and the French maid, and on this particular evening he called home to make his excuses for a night out with the secretary. Babette, the French maid, answered the phone and the executive said in a very business-like manner, "Tell Madam she'd better go to bed and I'll be along as soon as I can."

"*Oui, monsieur,*" said Babette, "and who shall I say is calling?"

A retired four-star general ran into his former orderly, also retired, in a Manhattan bar and spent the rest of the evening persuading him to come to work for him as his valet.

"Your duties will be exactly the same as they were in the army," the general said. "Nothing to it—you'll catch on again fast."

Next morning promptly at eight o'clock, the ex-orderly entered the ex-general's bedroom, pulled open the drapes, gave the general a gentle shake, strode around to the other side of the bed, spanked his employer's wife on her bottom and said, "OK, sweetheart, it's back to the village for you."

The preacher's sermon was on the Ten Commandments. When he reached "Thou Shalt Not Steal," he noticed one of his parishioners, a little man sitting in the front row, became very agitated. When the preacher reached "Thou Shalt Not Commit Adultery," the man suddenly smiled and relaxed.

After the service, the preacher approached the man and asked him the reason for his peculiar behavior.

The man replied with an embarrassed smile, "When you talked about the Commandment, 'Thou Shalt Not Steal,' I suddenly discovered my umbrella was missing. But when you said 'Thou Shalt Not Commit Adultery,' I remembered where I'd left it."

In quest of his first mistress, the eager executive was plying a supple young lovely with food and drink. "I've rented a townhouse for you," he said, "and you'll have your own bank account and credit at all the *couturiers*. I'll visit you a couple of nights during the week and we'll spend all our weekends together. And if we find we've made a mistake, why, we can always separate."

After toying with the idea for a moment, the girl smiled and replied, "Sounds fine; but what'll we do with the mistake?"

Within a year after marrying one of a set of gorgeous identical twins, the exec found himself in court, asking for a divorce. When the judge demanded his reasons, the exec replied, "It's this way. My wife's sister visits us a lot and I sometimes come home and make love to her by mistake."

"But surely there's some difference between the two women," the bewildered judge said.

"You bet there is," responded the exec. "That's why I want a divorce."

Waxing eloquent on the sins of the flesh, the dynamic young preacher raised himself to full height, leaned over the pulpit, and boomed, "Brothers and sisters, if there are any among you who have committed adultery, may your tongue cleave to the woof of your mowf."

The surest sign that a man is in love is when he divorces his wife.

After the professional golfer made a five-footer on the practice green, his wife sued for divorce.

We know a religious fellow who loves his neighbor—but can't stand her husband.

"I had everything a man could want," moaned a sad-eyed friend of ours. "Money, a handsome home, the love of a beautiful and wealthy woman. Then, bang, one morning my wife walked in!"

Doctors, Lawyers, Indian Chiefs

A few friends had gathered in Bob's basement rec room for an evening of drinks and dancing. With the party in full swing, one of the women excused herself to go to the bathroom. This room, it seems, had been newly painted in a charming Provençal blue, with accents—window frames, door, even the toilet seat—in goldenrod. It was supposed to be a fast-drying enamel, but it hadn't dried fast enough, and the young lady found herself stuck. Her shrieks brought Joe's girlfriend, who, unable to do anything about the situation herself, summoned Joe. After several minutes of uncontrolled laughter, Joe managed to produce a screwdriver and detach the victim, permitting the girl to stand up. But they still couldn't get the paint off her butt, so they called a doctor.

"Did you ever see anything like this before, doctor?" the girl asked in embarrassment when the M.D. arrived.

"Well, yes," the doctor replied truthfully, "but I believe this is the first time I've ever seen one framed."

The doctor had just finished giving the young man a thorough physical examination.

"The best thing for you to do," the M.D. said, "is give up drinking and smoking, get to bed early, and stay away from women."

"Doc, I don't deserve the best," said the patient. "What's next best?"

"I just examined Nicole Kidman," said the bug-eyed doctor at the Hollywood film studio.

"And how is she?" his fellow physician wanted to know.

"My only wish is that the whole world should be in such good shape."

The young woman from Georgia went to the hospital for a checkup.

"Have you been X-rayed yet?" asked the doctor.

"Nope," she said, "but Ah *have* been ultra-violated."

"I don't know what's wrong with me, doctor," said the curvy call girl. "I feel tired, dragged out. Pooped. No pep. No get up and go. Is it vitamin deficiency, low blood count, or what?"

The medico gave her a top-to-toe examination and then his verdict. "Young lady, there's really nothing wrong with you. You're run-down, that's all. You've been working too hard. I suggest you try staying out of bed for a few days."

The attractive young woman was worried about her sailor boyfriend, away at sea, and complained to her doctor that she couldn't sleep at night. She requested some sleeping tablets, but the doctor suggested she try a psychological technique before resorting to drugs. "Since counting sheep and the other more usual methods have failed," he said, "try repeating this little ritual each night when you retire: 'Toes go to sleep, feet go to sleep, ankles go to sleep, legs go to sleep, thighs go to sleep' and so on, all the way to the top of your head. Concentrate on each separate part of your body as you direct it to sleep, and before you know it, you'll be in dreamland."

The young lady was dubious, but that very night, after turning out the light and getting into bed, she tried the doctor's suggestion.

"Toes go to sleep," she began. "Feet go to sleep, ankles go to sleep, legs go to sleep, thighs go to sleep…"

Suddenly the door to her apartment burst open and in walked her boyfriend, back from sea.

"Everybody up," she exclaimed. "*Everybody up!*"

The new patient was airing his woes to an understanding doctor. "After the first, I'm tired, Doc. After the second, my chest aches and I start getting pains in my legs. After the third, I feel like fainting and it takes half-an-hour for my heart and respiration to return to normal."

"Why don't you quit after the first?" inquired the doctor.

"How can I do that, Doc?" the patient asked. "I live on the third."

"Dear Dad," read the young soldier's first letter home. "I cannot tell you where I am, but yesterday I shot a polar bear...."

Several months later came another letter: "Dear Dad, I still can't tell you where I am, but yesterday I danced with a hula girl...."

Two weeks later came yet another note: "Dear Dad, I still cannot tell you where I am, but yesterday the doctor told me I should have danced with the polar bear and shot the hula girl...."

"Have you ever performed one of these delicate brain operations before?" asked the patient, as a nurse prepared to administer the anesthetic.

"Oh, yeah," said the man in white standing over him, "nothing to it."

"It's funny," said the patient, "but you look exactly like a bartender who works in a bowling alley where I bowl every Thursday night."

"I am," said the fellow with a smile, "but who says a guy can't better himself?"

With a bushel of apples, you can have a hell of a time with the doctor's wife.

A rather naive young man named Lester had recently reached manhood and had no idea why he was continuously nervous and tense. He went to see his doctor. The M.D. was not in, but his nurse was, a red-headed vixen who wore her uniform so tight that Lester's jitters noticeably increased. She asked him what was wrong and he told her. She eyed him appraisingly.

"That's easy to fix," she said. "Come with me." She led Lester into a small examination room, and there relieved his tensions.

As he was preparing to leave, she said, "That will be one hundred fifty dollars." And quite satisfied, Lester was pleased to pay.

Several weeks went by, and Lester found the same unrest growing in him again. He returned to the doctor's office and this time the doctor was in. He listened to Lester's symptoms, then wrote out a prescription on a piece of paper and handed it to him.

"This is for tranquilizers," the doctor said. "You can have it filled downstairs. That will be five dollars, please."

Lester looked at the small piece of paper for a few moments, then looked up at the doctor and said, "If it's all the same to you, doc, I'd just as soon have the hundred-and-fifty-dollar treatment."

The voluptuous young patient entered the dentist's office in an obvious state of agitation. She sat down in the chair and fidgeted nervously as the dentist prepared his utensils.

"Oh, doctor," she exclaimed, as he prepared to look into her mouth, "I'm so afraid of dentists. Why, I think I'd rather have a baby than have a tooth drilled."

"Well, miss," said the dentist impatiently, "better make up your mind before I adjust the chair."

The head doctor at the hospital was making his rounds and he paused before a group of newborn babies.

"What's the matter with this little fellow?" he asked. "He seems awfully puny and underweight."

"He's one of those artificial insemination babies," said the young nurse, "and he's been coming along rather slowly, I'm afraid."

"Confirms a pet theory of mine," said the doctor. "Spare the rod and spoil the child."

An exceedingly attractive young nurse walked calmly along the hospital corridor with a portion of her bosom exposed. A staff doctor, passing by, noticed the exposure and scolded her for this improper show of her charms. Blushing, the nurse murmured, "I'm sorry, sir, but it's these darn interns—they never put anything back when they're through with it."

A new shop opened in the heart of the little town, with no sign of any sort on its awning, door, or window, the nearest thing to identification being the large clock in the window. A gentleman whose watch had stopped happened to be passing by, and he went inside and asked if they would repair it.

"I'm sorry," said the clerk, "but this is not a watch-repair shop. This is a branch of the hospital on the next block. All we do here is perform hemorrhoid operations."

The man begged the clerk's pardon and started to leave, then turned with a puzzled frown. "Then what's the significance of the clock in the window?" he asked.

"Well," said the clerk, "what else *could* we put in the window?"

Completing her examination of the uncommonly attractive and well-equipped young patient, the doctor said solemnly, "You are a very sick young man. I don't want you returning to work this afternoon. Go home, get undressed, and get into bed. Drink about a third of this bottle of medicine I'm preparing for you…it will make you drowsy. I don't want you to answer your phone or let anybody into your apartment until you hear three short knocks.…"

A young man approached his family physician and said, "Doc, I'm afraid you'll have to remove my wife's tonsils one of these days."

"My good man," replied the doctor, "I removed them six years ago. Did you ever hear of a woman having two sets of tonsils?"

"No," the husband retorted, "but you've heard of a man having two wives, haven't you?"

A strapping young man entered a doctor's office on his lunch hour and addressed an attractive young woman in a white coat. "I've had a pain in my shoulder for a week. Can you help me?"

"Lie down on this table," she said, "and I'll massage it for you." After a few minutes, the handsome patient said, "Not that I mind, Doctor, but that isn't my shoulder."

The young woman smiled at the aroused patient and replied, "True, but I'm not a doctor, either."

A recent survey showed that nine out of ten doctors who preferred Camels have switched back to women.

"**D**octor," said the young woman, "I'd prefer being vaccinated where it won't show."

"All right," replied the physician, "but you'll have to pay in advance."

"Why do I have to pay in advance?" the girl protested.

"Because the last time a patient as pretty as you made that request," he explained, "I got so wrapped up in what I was doing I forgot to charge her."

The intern on duty at the hospital emergency room received a phone call late one night from a distressed mother who exclaimed, "Doctor, what shall I do—my husband just discovered that our two-year-old has eaten a whole tube of contraceptive jelly."

"Well," the intern drawled, "if it's really an emergency, why don't you have one of those all-night drugstores deliver?"

A lovely young woman decided to confide in her roommate. "The strangest thing has been happening to me," she said. "Every time I sneeze, I have an orgasm."

"I've never heard of such a strange illness," her friend answered. "What do you take for it?"

Came the smiling reply, "Black pepper!"

The doctor had just completed his examination of the teenage girl, when he addressed the girl's mother.

"Ma'am," he said, "I'm afraid your daughter has syphilis."

"Oh, dear," exclaimed the embarrassed mother. "Tell me, Doctor, could she have possibly caught it in a public lavatory?"

"It's possible," replied the physician after a moment's reflection, "but it would certainly be uncomfortable."

Every newspaper in New York sent a reporter and a staff photographer to the office of a local ophthalmologist when it was learned that he had recently performed a successful sight-saving operation on the wife of the country's most celebrated young artist, who, in addition to paying the doctor's usual fee, had gratefully insisted on painting one of his contemporary masterpieces across an entire wall of the doctor's waiting room. The mural turned out be an immense multicolored picture of a human eye, in the center of which stood a perfect miniature likeness of the good doctor himself. While cameras clicked and most of the newsmen crowded around the famous artist for his comments, one cub reporter drew the eye specialist aside and asked, "Tell me, if you don't mind, Doctor—what was your first reaction on seeing this fantastic artistic achievement covering an entire wall of your office?"

"Well," replied the physician, "my first thought was, 'Thank goodness I'm not a gynecologist!'"

The harried stockbroker was suffering from insomnia, never got to sleep before dawn, then slept right through the alarm and so never made it to the office on time. Upon being reprimanded by his boss, he decided to consult a doctor. The doctor gave him some sleeping pills, and that night he fell asleep immediately and experienced a pleasant rest. In the morning, he awoke before the alarm rang and jumped out of bed with new verve and vigor. When he arrived at his office promptly, he told his boss, "Those pills I got from my doctor really work. I had no trouble at all waking up this morning."

"That's nice," the boss replied. "But where were you yesterday?"

A young man sat next to a beautiful blonde in a bar and offered to buy her a drink. After some casual conversation, he asked her if she would care to go to his apartment for a nightcap and she agreed. Up in his apartment, she resisted his advances for over an hour until, in desperation, he exclaimed, "If you don't want to have sex with me, why did you agree to come with me in the first place?"

"I don't enjoy sex in the usual way," she explained. "But I'll let you make love to me if you promise to do it *my* way."

He was too aroused to argue.

"Then remove your shoe and stocking," she said passionately, "and take me with your big toe."

A few days later, his toe began to throb and he decided to have it examined by a doctor. The doctor looked at the toe and shook his head.

"I'm sorry to have to tell you this," the doctor said, "but you have gonorrhea of the big toe."

"I've never heard of such a thing," the young man said.

"It's a medical rarity," the doctor agreed, "but no rarer than the case I had this morning."

"Oh," said his patient, "what was that?"

"I treated a young woman with a case of athlete's vagina."

"No need for me to come out to the house," the doctor told the worried caller. "I've checked my files and your uncle isn't really ill at all—he just thinks he's sick."

A week later, the doctor telephoned to make sure his diagnosis had been correct. "How's your uncle today?" he asked.

"Worse," came the reply. "Now he thinks he's dead."

Then there was the Eskimo who rubbed noses so indiscriminately that he contracted snyphilis.

After a heart-transplant operation, the patient was receiving instructions from his doctor. He was placed on a strict diet, denied tobacco, and advised to get at least eight hours' sleep a night. Finally, the patient asked, "What about my sex life, Doc? Will it be all right for me to have intercourse?"

"Just with your wife," responded the doctor. "We don't want you to get too excited."

The voluptuous young patient was perched on the examination table when the doctor placed his hand on her bare breast. "You know what I'm doing, of course," he said, reassuringly.

"Yes," the patient murmured. "You're checking for breast cancer."

Encouraged, the doctor proceeded to caress her stomach. "Of course," he continued, "you know what I'm doing now, too, right?"

"Yes," she smiled. "You're checking my appendix."

At this point, the doctor could no longer control himself. He stripped off his clothes and began to make passionate love to her. "You know what I'm doing now, don't you?" he gasped.

"Yes," his patient answered. "You're checking for V.D.—and that's what I came here for."

"I just can't find a cause for your illness," the internist said. "Frankly, I think it's due to drinking."

"In that case," replied his patient, "I'll come back when you're sober."

During her annual checkup, the young woman was asked to disrobe and climb onto the examining table.

"Doctor," she said, "I just can't undress in front of you."

"All right," said the physician, "I'll flick off the lights. You undress and tell me when you're through."

In a few moments, her voice rang out in the darkness: "Doctor, I've undressed. What should I do with my clothes?"

"Your clothes?" answered the doctor. "Put them over here, on top of mine."

When the handsome gynecologist asked his new patient to disrobe, the beautiful young woman started to blush. "Haven't you ever been examined before?" he questioned.

"Oh, yes," she whispered, "but never by a *doctor*."

The tired doctor was awakened by a phone call in the middle of the night. "Please, you have to come right over," pleaded the panic-stricken mother. "My child has swallowed a condom."

The physician dressed quickly, but before he could get out the door, the phone rang again.

"You don't have to come over, after all," the woman bubbled. "My husband just found another one."

Upon finishing examining his new patient quite thoroughly, the obstetrician smiled and said, "I've got good news for you, Mrs. Smith—"

"Pardon me," interrupted the young lady, "but it's *Miss* Smith."

"Oh, I see," said the physician. "Well, Miss Smith, I've got bad news for you...."

The sixty-year-old patient explained his predicament to the doctor. He had recently married a gorgeous girl in her twenties, but unfortunately, every night at bedtime, when he and the lovely bride were ready and willing, he would fall asleep.

The doctor scribbled out a prescription and handed it to the patient. The old man's face lit up as he said, "You mean that now I'll be able to—"

"No," the doctor interrupted, "I'm afraid I can't do anything about *that*. But now at least she'll fall asleep, too."

Doctor Jones was called to examine his friend Frank, who at sixty-four had married a woman less than half his age. The doctor noticed that she was extremely attractive and quite voluptuous. After a thorough examination, he knew that the cause of his friend's illness was exhaustion. He wrote a prescription and was preparing to leave when the patient asked, "Well, Doc, what's wrong with me? Am I overweight?"

"No, Frank," answered the doctor with a sidelong glance at the young bride, "overmatched."

"Doctor," the worried exec told the psychiatrist, "I'm afraid I'm schizophrenic."

"Well," replied the doctor, "that makes four of us."

"**I**'ve got good news for you," said the psychiatrist. "You're a well man. It won't be necessary for you to continue the analysis any longer."

"How wonderful, doctor," said the patient. "I'm so very pleased, I wish there were something special I could do for you in return."

"Oh, that's not necessary. You've paid your bill and that's all that's expected."

"But really, doctor, I'm so elated I could kiss you!"

"No, don't do that. Actually, we shouldn't even be lying here on the couch together."

"**Y**ou're in remarkable shape for a man your age," said the doctor to the ninety-year-old man after the examination.

"I know it," said the old gentleman. "I've really got only one complaint—my sex drive is too high. Got anything you can do for that, Doc?"

The doctor's mouth dropped open. "Your what is too *what?*" he gasped.

"My sex drive," said the old man. "It's too high, and I'd like to have you lower it if you can."

"*Lower* it?!" exclaimed the doctor, still unable to believe what the ninety-year-old gentleman was saying. "Just what do you consider 'high'?"

"These days it seems like it's all in my head, Doc," said the old man, "and I'd like to have you lower it if you can."

We know an ingenious doctor who prescribed sex for insomnia. His patients didn't get any more sleep, but they had more fun staying awake.

A scientific friend informs us that celibacy isn't an inherited trait.

After returning home from an examination, the young woman phoned her gynecologist and asked, "Doctor, would you see if by chance I left my panties in your office?"

He looked in the examining room, returned to the phone, and told her, "I'm afraid they're not here."

"Sorry to trouble you, doctor," she replied. "I'll try the dentist."

Which reminds us of the dental joke about the Texas oilman who went in to see his dentist and, when asked which tooth was bothering him, replied, "Oh, just drill anywhere, doc. I feel lucky today!"

A man was complaining to a friend about an uncle who was staying with him: "I didn't mind when he wore my suits, I didn't object when he smoked my best cigars, drank my bourbon, and borrowed my car every night. But when he sat down at the dinner table and laughed at me through my own false teeth—that was too much!"

After the attractive blonde had seated herself, the young psychiatrist asked, "What seems to be the trouble?"

"Well," the shapely patient answered, blushing, "I think I may be a nymphomaniac."

"I can probably help you," said the doctor, "but I must tell you that my fee is one hundred fifty dollars an hour."

"That's reasonable," the girl quickly replied. "How much for all night?"

An inmate at the insane asylum was being examined for possible release. The first question the examining doctor asked was, "What are you going to do when you leave this institution?"

"I'm gonna get me a sling shot," said the patient, "and I'm gonna come back here and break every goddam window in the place!"

After six more months of treatment, the patient was again brought before the examining doctor for possible dismissal, and the same question was put to him.

"Well, I'm going to get a job," the patient replied.

"Fine," said the doctor. "Then what?"

"I'm going to rent an apartment."

"Very good."

"Then I'm going to meet a beautiful girl."

"Excellent."

"I'm going to take the beautiful girl up to my apartment and I'm going to pull up her skirt."

"Normal, perfectly normal."

"Then I'm gonna steal her garter, make a sling shot out of it, and come back here and break every goddam window in the place!"

The mother took her young daughter to a psychiatrist and explained to the good doctor that the girl thought she was a chicken. The doctor soothed her, observing that an overactive imagination is not uncommon in children, and asking how long the girl had suffered from the delusion.

"Almost two years," said the mother.

"Your daughter has imagined she is a chicken for nearly two years?!" the psychiatrist exclaimed. "Why have you waited so long before bringing her in?"

The woman looked embarrassed, then confessed, "We needed the eggs, doctor."

The new inmate at the mental hospital announced in a loud voice that he was the famous British naval hero, Lord Nelson. This was particularly interesting, because the institution already had a "Lord Nelson." The head psychiatrist, after due consideration, decided to put the two men in the same room, feeling that the similarity of their delusions might prompt an adjustment in each that would help in curing them. It was a calculated risk, of course, for the men might react violently to one another, but they were introduced and then left alone and no disturbance was heard from the room that night.

The next morning, the doctor had a talk with his new patient and was more than pleasantly surprised when he was told, "Doctor, I've been suffering from a delusion. I know now that I am *not* Lord Nelson."

"That's wonderful," said the doctor.

"Yes," said the patient, smiling demurely, "I'm Lady Nelson."

During the last day of a psychiatrists' convention, one of the doctors present at the closing lecture noticed an attractive female Ph.D. being pawed by the man seated next to her.

"Is he bothering you?" the observer asked the woman.

"Why should I be bothered?" she replied. "It's *his* problem."

Beverly stretched out on the psychiatrist's couch, forlorn and lovely. With genuine emotion she cried, "I just can't help myself, doctor. No matter how hard I try to resist, I bring five or six men with me into my bedroom every night. Last night there were ten. I just feel so miserable, I don't know what to do."

In understanding tones, the doctor rumbled, "Yes, I know, I know, my dear."

"Oh!" the surprised girl exclaimed. "Were you there last night, too?"

"**D**octor," said the obviously disturbed young man to his psychiatrist, "my biggest problem is that I always dream about baseball. Nothing but baseball."

"Don't you ever dream about girls?" asked the shrink.

"I don't dare," said the young man. "I'm afraid I'll lose my turn at bat."

Have you heard about the psychiatrist who gave his son a set of mental blocks for Christmas?

"**P**sychoanalysis is a lot of bunk," one imbiber said to his bar companion.

"Why do you say that?"

"I've been undergoing analysis for six months and today my analyst tells me I'm in love with my umbrella! Have you ever heard anything so ridiculous?"

"That's pretty crazy," agreed the friend.

"I would say that we certainly hold each other in sincere regard. But *love*? Please!"

A cute young woman was consulting a psychiatrist. Among other questions, the doctor asked, "Are you troubled at all by indecent thoughts?"

"Why, no," she replied, with just the hint of a twinkle in her eye. "To tell you the truth, doctor, I rather enjoy them."

"Oh, Doctor, you mean I'm finally cured?" the woman sighed happily.

"Yes Miss Willoughby," said the psychoanalyst, "I believe we now have your kleptomania firmly under control and you can go out in the workaday world just like anybody else."

"Oh, Doctor, I'm so grateful," said the woman. "I don't know how I'll ever repay you for your help."

"My fee is all the payment I expect," said the kindly analyst. "However, if you should happen to have a relapse, you might pick up an MP3 player for me—they're handy to have at the gym."

The analyst was concerned about the results of a Rorschach Test he had just given, for the patient associated every ink blot with some kind of sexual activity.

"I want to study the results of your test over the weekend," he said, "then I'd like to see you again on Monday morning."

"OK, Doc," the man agreed. Then as he was slipping on his coat, he said, "I'm going to a bachelor party tomorrow night. Any chance I might be able to borrow those dirty pictures of yours?"

Natalie, a ravishing and distraught young woman, took her troubles to a psychiatrist.

"Doctor, you must help me," she pleaded. "It's gotten so that every time a man takes me out, I wind up in bed with him. And then afterwards I feel guilty and depressed all day long."

"I see," nodded the psychiatrist. "And you want me to strengthen your will power."

"Heavens, no!" exclaimed the patient. "I want you to fix it so I won't feel guilty and depressed afterward."

The psychiatrist leaned back and placed the tips of his fingers together while he soothed the deeply troubled man who stood before him.

"Calm yourself, my good fellow," he gently urged. "I have helped a great many others with fixations far more serious than yours. Now let me see if I understand the problem correctly. You indicate that in moments of great emotional stress, you believe that you are a dog. A fox terrier, is that not so?"

"Yes, sir," mumbled the patient. "A small fox terrier with black and brown spots. Oh, please tell me you can help me, doctor. If this keeps up much longer, I don't know what I'll do...."

The doctor gestured toward his couch. "Now, now," he soothed, "the first thing to do is lie down here and we'll see if we can't get to the root of your delusion."

"Oh, I couldn't do that, doctor," said the patient. "I'm not allowed up on the furniture."

The psychiatrist was not expecting the distraught stranger who staggered into his office and slumped into a chair. "You've got to help me. I'm losing my memory, Doctor," he sobbed. "I once had a successful business, a wife, home, and a family; I was a respected member of the community. But all that's gone now. Since my memory began failing, I've lost the business—I couldn't remember my clients' names. My wife and children have left me, too; and why shouldn't they? Some nights I wouldn't get home until four or five in the morning—I'd forget where I lived.... And it's getting worse. Doctor—it's getting *worse!*"

"This is not an unusual form of neurosis," the psychiatrist said soothingly. "Now tell me, just how long ago did you first become aware of this condition?"

"Condition?" The man sat up in his chair. "What condition?"

An analyst was listening to a young patient with a problem of some consequence. "It's liquor, doctor," she sobbed. "I'm really a very nice girl, but just as soon as I've had a drink or two, I become uncontrollably passionate and I want to make love to whomever I happen to be with."

"I see," the analyst said thoughtfully. "Well, suppose I just mix us up a couple of Old-Fashioneds here and then you and I can sit down, nice and relaxed, and discuss this debilitating compulsion of yours."

A wild-eyed man dressed in a Napoleonic costume and hiding his right hand inside his coat entered the psychiatrist's office and nervously exclaimed, "Doctor, I need your help right away."

"I can see that," retorted the doctor. "Lie down on that couch and tell me your problem."

"I don't have any problem," the man snapped. "In fact, as Emperor of France I have everything I could possibly want: money, women, power—everything! But I'm afraid my wife, Josephine, is in deep mental trouble."

"I see," said the psychiatrist, humoring his distraught patient. "And what seems to be *her* main problem?"

"For some strange reason," answered the unhappy man, "she thinks she's Mrs. Schwartz."

The woman was enthusiastic about psychoanalysis and confided to a friend that she had undergone therapy. "You never knew this," she said, "but for years I was under the delusion that I was a fox terrier."

"And now you're completely cured?" asked the friend.

"That's right," said the woman proudly. "Just feel my nose— cold and wet."

Obviously on the verge of hysteria, the distraught woman entered the psychiatrist's office and, between sobs, managed to explain that her husband was suffering under the delusion that he was a refrigerator. "You can see what this is doing to me," the poor woman cried. "It's been weeks since I had a good night's sleep."

"I understand, my dear," the doctor reassured her. "But if you don't stop staying awake nights worrying about your husband's condition, you'll make yourself sick as well."

"It's not his condition that keeps me up," she wailed. "It's that damn little light that goes on every time he sleeps with his mouth open!"

Sinking uneasily into the depths of the psychiatrist's couch, the patient sighed, "Doctor, I have a problem." He loosened his collar and continued, "I've got one son in Harvard and another at Yale. I've just given them matching Ferraris. I have a townhouse on Fifth Avenue and a summer home in East Hampton and a sprawling ranch in Venezuela."

"Well!" smiled the psychiatrist, obviously impressed. "Either I missed something or you really don't have a problem."

"Doc," the harried chap croaked, "I only make seventy-five dollars a week."

"Doctor," explained the frustrated junior exec, "every night I have the same strange dream. Beautiful girls sneak into my apartment and try to seduce me."

"Well, what do you do?" asked the doctor.

"I keep pushing them away."

"Hmm. And what do you want me to do?"

"Please, doc," pleaded the man, "break my arms."

"I'm in love with my horse," the nervous young man told his psychiatrist.

"Nothing to worry about," the psychiatrist consoled. "Many people are fond of animals. As a matter of fact, my wife and I have a dog we're very attached to."

"But, doctor," continued the troubled patient, "I feel *physically* attracted to my horse."

"Hmmm," observed the doctor. "Is it male or female?"

"Female, of course!" the man replied curtly. "What do you think I am, queer?"

"I'm always forgetting things," the distraught man grumbled to the psychiatrist. "What should I do?"

"The first thing to do," the doctor prescribed, "is pay me in advance."

On his first visit to the psychiatrist, the nervous young man explained that his family made him seek help because he preferred cotton socks to woolen ones. "That's no reason for you to see me," retorted the physician. "In fact, I myself prefer cotton socks."

"Really?" the happy patient exclaimed. "Do you like yours with oil and vinegar or just a squeeze of lemon?"

The worried bachelor consulted a psychiatrist about his nymphomaniac girlfriend. "Doctor," he exclaimed in a shaky voice, "she'll stop at nothing to satisfy her bizarre sexual desires and unholy cravings—"

"I've heard enough, interrupted the psychiatrist. "Does she have a friend?"

"**I**'m perpetually exhausted," Joe told the psychiatrist. "Every night, I dream I'm driving a truck from Galveston to Chicago and in the morning, I wake up dead tired."

"Beginning tonight," advised the analyst, "you stop at Tulsa and I'll take it on to Chicago."

Later, at a bar, the relieved patient listened to a friend's problem. "Each night," related his buddy, "I dream that I'm being forced to satisfy four beautiful women. It's killing me."

Joe recommended his psychiatrist; but the next time the acquaintance came around, he was in worse shape than ever.

"What happened?" Joe asked him. "Didn't my shrink do anything about your problem?"

"Oh, he took away the chicks, all right," moaned the guy, "but now every night I dream I've picked up a damn truck in Tulsa and I have to drive it all the way to Chicago."

We just got the word about the legal secretary who told her amorous boyfriend, "Stop and/or I'll slap your face."

A lawyer friend tells us that you can't take it with you—especially when crossing a state line.

The editor of a small weekly newspaper, in a rage over several congressional bills that had recently been passed, ran a scathing editorial under the headline: "HALF OF OUR LEGISLATORS ARE CROOKS." Many prominent local politicians were outraged, and tremendous pressure was exerted on him to retract the statement. He finally succumbed to the pressure and ran an apology with the headline: "HALF OF OUR LEGISLATORS ARE NOT CROOKS."

"Have faith and ye shall be healed!" intoned the evangelist at the revival meeting. A woman on crutches and a man came forward. The evangelist asked, "What is your name, my good woman?"

"I'm Mrs. Hostetters," she answered, "and I haven't been able to walk without crutches for twenty years."

"Well, Mrs. Hostetters," he said, "go behind that screen and pray."

Turning to the man, he asked, "Now, sir, what is your name?"

"My name ith Thamuelth," he answered, "and I have alwayth thpoken with a lithp."

"All right, Mr. Samuels," the evangelist said. "Go behind that screen with Mrs. Hostetters and pray." After several minutes had passed, the revivalist announced, "I think the time has come. Witness these miracles. Mrs. Hostetters, throw your left crutch over the screen." The audience gasped as it sailed over. "Mrs. Hostetters, throw your right crutch over the screen." The crowd cheered as the second crutch appeared.

Encouraged, the evangelist commanded, "Mr. Samuels, say something in a loud, clear voice, so we can all hear you."

Samuels yelled back, "Mithuth Hothtetterth jutht fell on her ath!"

We overheard two young women discussing their marriage plans on a northbound subway last week. "So your boyfriend graduates from law school this June. I suppose you'll be getting married then."

"Oh, no, not right away," replied the other. "I want him to practice for at least a year first."

Then there was the lady barrister in London who dropped her briefs and became a solicitor.

And, of course, you've heard about the female lawyer who moonlighted as a call girl. She was a prostituting attorney.

When a utility company started moving its heavy equipment into the quiet suburban neighborhood, the local residents formed a protest committee and invited the offending firm's attorney to attend the committee's first meeting. Before the meeting could be called to order, however, the attorney decided to take the initiative and question each homeowner separately. Turning to a pretty widow on the committee, the lawyer said, "Now, as I understand it, the utility company is running its equipment around the clock, and the noise is disturbing your rest."

"What rest?" she interrupted. " You try spending a night in my bedroom. I promise you won't get a wink of sleep."

"Really, madam!" exclaimed another homeowner reproachfully. "If you're going to make offers like that, you might at least give the fellows from your own neighborhood first right of refusal."

An attractive young attorney we know consistently breaks the speed limit but rarely gets a ticket. Every time a policeman stops her, she simply lays down the law.

A young major was apprehended, completely nude, while chasing a woman through the lobby of a large hotel. However, his lawyer soon had him freed on a technicality. The Army manual specifically states that an officer need not be in uniform, provided he is properly attired for the sport in which he is engaged.

In 1894, Chief Sitting Bear had electric lights installed in the tribal latrine, thus becoming the first American Indian ever to wire a head for a reservation.

Miss-
Demeanor

The judge looked down at the attractive plaintiff. "You claim that the defendant stole your money from your stocking?" he asked.

"That's right, Your Honor," she answered.

"Well, why didn't you resist?" the judge asked.

The girl blushed and lowered her eyes. "I didn't know he was after my money, Your Honor," she said.

A husband returning from a trip was informed by his wife that a burglar had entered their apartment while he was gone.

"Did he get anything?" the husband anxiously inquired.

"I'll say he did," replied the wife. "It was dark and I thought he was you."

A young woman met her aunt downtown for lunch one afternoon and during the meal, the older woman asked her niece to deposit a paycheck for her at the bank where the girl worked. On her way back from lunch, the girl was accosted by a purse snatcher.

"Help, help," she screamed at a passing cop. "That man has taken my aunt's pay—my aunt's pay!"

"OK, lady," said the cop. "Cut out the pig Latin and tell me exactly what happened."

A friend of ours reports that he was innocently nursing a beer at his local watering hole when the Elvis-haired type with the pinkie ring occupying the next stool leaned over to him. "Hey, buddy," the wiseguy said confidentially, "you wanna buy a hot?"

"A hot what?" our friend asked.

"You name it," said the man with a smile. "I'm having a very good season."

Moving along a dimly lighted street, a friend of ours was suddenly approached by a stranger who had slipped from the shadows nearby.

"Please, sir," asked the stranger, "would you be so kind as to help a poor unfortunate fellow who is hungry and out of work? All I have in the world is this gun."

"Police?" came the voice on the phone. "I want to report a burglar trapped in an old maid's bedroom!" After ascertaining the address, the police sergeant asked who was calling. "This," cried the frantic voice, "is the burglar!"

A psychiatrist we know says that one good thing about being a kleptomaniac is that you can always take something for it.

On a road ten miles from Palermo, an American motorist was stopped by a masked desperado who, brandishing a revolver, demanded in a thick Sicilian accent that he get out of the car.

The motorist obeyed, pleading, "Take my money, my car, but don't kill me!"

"I no kill you, *signore*" replied the brigand, "if you do what I say." Whereupon, he told the motorist to unzip and masturbate then and there. Though shocked, the motorist did what he was told.

"Good," said the masked stranger. "Now, again!" The motorist protested, but the gun was menacingly waved, so, with extreme difficulty, he repeated the act.

"Again," commanded the desperado, "or I kill you!" Summoning superhuman resources, the exhausted motorist read the minutes yet a third time.

The bandit gave an order and a beautiful young girl stepped from behind the rocks. "*Now*," said the highwayman, "give my sister a ride to town!"

Before his daring escape from prison, an infamous criminal had been photographed from four different angles. The FBI sent copies of the pictures to police chiefs all across the country, with orders to notify Washington the moment an arrest was made.

The next day, the Bureau received an email from the ambitious sheriff of a small Texas town: "GOT THE PICTURES. ALL FOUR SHOT DEAD WHILE RESISTING ARREST."

It was tea-time in the dorm, and the air hung heavy in thick blue folds as a bunch of 'heads relaxed after class. Suddenly, a loud voice in the hall demanded that they open the door in the name of the law. The panicked kids frantically gathered their still-smoking joints and stuffed them in the cuckoo clock. The campus police entered, searched diligently, found nothing, and left. The bunch breathed a sigh of relief and made for the cuckoo clock just as the clock's hands announced three A.M. The little door popped open, the bird poked his head out and said, "So dudes, like, what time is it?"

The advance proofs of a cookbook for hipsters recently came our way. Wildest recipe is for a salad: You cut up lettuce, tomatoes, cucumbers, and green peppers. Then you add a dash of sinsemilla, and the salad tosses itself.

We know a guy who thinks a potholder is a cigarette case.

The doting father came home one night and was shocked to find his daughter and her friends getting high. Pulling the reefer out of the girl's mouth, he exclaimed, "What's a joint like this doing in a nice girl like you?"

Tripping heavily, the two acidheads were happily relating the details of their hallucinations to each other. Said the first, "Right now, I've a mind to buy all the jewels in the world. In fact, I'm going to buy up all the world's gold, its oil, its yachts, and yes, all those lovely naked women who are now dancing in front of me."

Raising an eyebrow querulously, his friend replied, "And where, may I ask, did you get the idea that I'd be willing to sell?"

The two stoners were staggering along a railroad track when one tiredly complained to the other, "I sure wish we'd get to the bottom of this flight of stairs."

"The stairs aren't the worst of it," grumbled the second. "It's the low handrail that bugs me."

And, of course, you've also heard about the ingenious chemist who invented an aphrodisiac insecticide. It didn't kill any bugs, but you could always swat two at a time.

The rape of the Sabine women by the Romans is a famous historical incident, but our Research Department has uncovered a hitherto unrevealed story.

It seems that Trebonius, the tallest, strongest, handsomest soldier in the Roman legions broke into a house where he found two luscious, sloe-eyed sisters and their elderly nurse. Chuckling with glee, he roared, "Prepare thyselves for conquest, my pretties!"

The lovely girls fell to their knees and pleaded with him. "Ravish us if thou wilt, O Roman, but spare our faithful old nurse."

"Shut thy mouth," snapped the nurse. "War is war!"

A stranger in town found his way to the most luxurious bordello. He entered, selected a gorgeous redhead, and was escorted to a resplendent bedroom of Hollywood proportions. Half an hour later, a satisfied smile on his face, he sought out the madam and took his wallet from his pocket. But the madam would not accept payment. She opened the drawer of a solid-gold cash register, counted out a hundred dollars and handed the money to him. Stunned and speechless, he staggered out.

A week later, he returned, chose a succulent blonde and was presented with two hundred dollars by the madam. Still puzzled, he took the money and left, feeling himself a very lucky fellow indeed.

The next night, he decided to pay another visit. After enjoying the services of a beautiful brunette, he walked up to the madam, held out his hand and waited for the money. He was unpleasantly surprised when she said, "Twenty-five dollars, please."

"Now, look here," he rejoined. "The first time I came in here, *you* gave *me* a hundred dollars. The second time, you gave me two hundred. How come I don't get paid tonight?"

"Tonight," replied the madam, "we ran out of videotape."

Back in the good old days, a traveler stopped at the mining town's best sporting house for a few hours of pleasure. As he cuddled up with a cute young employee, he noticed some men across the street digging around the foundation of a church. "What's going on?" he asked.

"Oh, that," she replied. "Last week, the town council passed a law that no bawdyhouse could be located within three hundred feet of a place of worship. So they've got till the end of the month to move that church."

Then there was the ninety-year-old man who tried to seduce a fifteen-year-old girl and was charged with assault with a dead weapon.

I met a woman who was willin'—
Now I'm takin' penicillin.

The lanky Texas ranch hand was still a virgin at twenty-one, so, on his first trip to the big city, he decided to visit a brothel and find out what he'd been missing. Upon securing the address of a rather exclusive establishment, he soon found himself lying in bed with an attractive partner. Sensing the lad was somewhat inexperienced, the professional gently took his hand and placed it on the source of her income. "Is this what you're looking for?" she whispered seductively.

"Well, I don't rightly know, ma'am," the cowboy murmured shyly. "I'm a stranger to these parts."

It was the young Englishman's first visit to Las Vegas and, in his innocence, he sought lodging in the city's red-light district. His money, however, was as green as his outlook, and the madam gladly offered him a room for the night. When a friend questioned him about his accommodations over lunch the following day, the young Briton replied, "Well, the room was very pretentious, you know, but *gad*, what maid service!"

"Though there are two dozen houses of ill repute in our town," said the candidate for mayor to his attentive audience at the political rally. "I say they are a menace, and I have never gone to one of them!"

From the back of the crowd a heckler called out, "Which one?"

Shortly after a new police commissioner took office, the local house of pleasure was raided and the girls were lined up outside for questioning by the police. A little old lady chanced to walk by and, noticing the commotion, asked what was happening. As a joke, one of the chicks told her they were standing in line for free lollipops. A few minutes later, a cop approached the elderly woman and asked, "Aren't you a bit old for this?"

"Officer," she cackled, "as long as they keep making them, I'll keep sucking them."

Having put in over three hundred miles behind the wheel during the first day of a cross-country business trip, the weary salesman was prepared to stop at the first motel along the road when he spotted a sign advertising: GRANDMA'S WHOREHOUSE 30 MILES AHEAD. His spirits understandably buoyed, the salesman drove on to Grandma's place, where he was greeted by a sweet old lady who silently led him to a plushly decorated waiting room and motioned for him to sit down. Without uttering a single word, she then left the room and returned momentarily with a picture of a beautiful young girl and a note stating that if he liked what he saw in the photo, the salesman should pay her fifty dollars and use the door at the far end of the room. The excited traveler quickly handed her the prescribed amount and rushed through the designated doorway, only to find himself standing back outside in the cold night air. Turning abruptly, he discovered a message painted across the door: CONGRATULATIONS! YOU HAVE JUST BEEN SCREWED BY GRANDMA.

Obsessed with the idea of pleasing all manner of customers with girls of the very highest order, an enterprising madam set up a three-story house of sport. She had ex-secretaries, selected for their efficiency, on the first floor; ex-models, selected for their beauty, on the second; and ex-schoolteachers, selected for their intelligence, on the third. As time went on, the madam noticed that almost all the play went to floor number three. She asked why, and the answer to the puzzle finally came from one of the steady customers.

"Well," said the sporting gentleman, "you know how those schoolteachers are—they make you do it over and over, until you get it right."

Then there was the young man who saved for years to buy his mother a house, only to find that the police department wouldn't let her run it.

"Signore," the Italian guide announced to his American client, "we are now passing the most fabulous brothel in all of Rome."

"Why?" asked the tourist.

A saleswoman friend of ours spent a couple of days in Miami last fall. Her first night there, a well-built blond dancer approached her in a club and said, "I'm selling—you buying?"

Our friend bought and thought no more about it till, a week later, she discovered she had a "case."

She visited a doctor and had it taken care of, and two months later business again took her to Miami and again she visited the same club. Sure enough, the same blond was there, and once again he approached her with, "I'm selling—you buying?"

"Well, that depends," said our friend, sipping her drink thoughtfully. "What are you selling tonight—cancer?"

Then there was the gigolo who bought a bicycle and peddled it all over town.

A street-walking acquaintance of ours has a new slogan that's certain to revolutionize the trade: "It's a business to do pleasure with you."

A doctor and his wife were out walking when a beautiful woman in a tight-fitting halter top and skirt nodded hello from a nearby doorway.

"And who was that?" questioned the wife.

"Oh, just a young woman I know professionally," said the doctor, reddening slightly.

"I see," said the wife. "Your profession or hers?"

Bill's sister was one of the most popular girls in Manhattan. She had more boyfriends than she knew what to do with and she never wanted for a thing. Bill was an impecunious musician, always in debt and constantly asking his sister for spending money.

"I don't understand you, Bill," she said in obvious annoyance one afternoon when he had tried to put the bite on her for a loan. "I don't have any trouble saving money, so why should you?"

"Well," he said, "you've got money coming in all the time from the very thing that's keeping me broke."

"I'm through going to psychiatrists," asserted the call girl. "I just can't get used to a guy who tells me to lie down on a couch and then sends me the bill."

Business was brisk for the pretty call girl at the bar, with a number of would-be customers gathered about her. "Bill," she said, "you can come over about seven-ish, and you, George, around eight-ish. Frank, I'll have time for you around nine-thirty-ish."

Then, obviously pleased with the prospects of a busy, busy evening, she spun around on her bar stool, surveyed the crowded club, and caroled, "Ten-ish, anyone?"

One of the recent cases investigated by an IRS inspector of our acquaintance was that of a young woman who listed her apartment rent as "expenses incurred while entertaining clients."

Charlie was taking his out-of-town pal, George, for a stroll through the city. As were admiring the scenery, George observed, "Hey, look at that good-looking girl over there. She's smiling at us. Do you know her?"

"Oh, yes: Betty—a hundred dollars."

"And who's that brunette with her? Man, she's really stacked!"

"Yep: Dolores—two hundred dollars."

"Ah, but look at that one. That's what I call really first class!"

"That's Gloria—four hundred dollars."

"My God," cried George, "aren't there any nice, regular girls in this town?"

"Of course," Charlie answered. "But you couldn't afford their rates!"

A ravishing professional girl of our acquaintance gets a grand and glorious feeling whenever a man makes love to her—but the grand always comes first.

In Rio on a business trip, Al found himself hampered, after working hours, by the fact that he didn't know the language. He was at once delighted and dismayed, therefore, when a surpassingly beautiful young Brazilian woman with a plunging neckline sat down at his restaurant table.

"Do you speak English?" he ventured hopefully.

"*Si*," she said with a bright white smile, "bot jus' a leetle beet."

"Just a little bit, eh?" Al repeated joshingly. "How much?"

"Seventy-five dollars," was the prompt reply.

Said Flo, a lady of the evening, to Dolores (another pro): "Can you spot me fifty bucks until I get back on my back?"

Rustic Ron stared at the bellhop in disbelief. "A hundred twenty-five dollars for a girl? That's ridiculous! Why, in Tennessee I can get a girl to clean my house, wash my clothes, cook my meals, and sleep with me all night for four pork chops a day."

"Then what," said the bellhop, "are you doing in Chicago?"

"Buying pork chops in bulk."

George, after tying on a whopper the night before, woke up in the morning to find a very unattractive woman sleeping blissfully beside him. He leaped out of bed, dressed quickly, and furtively placed a hundred dollar bill on top of the bureau. He then proceeded to tiptoe out of the room. But as he passed the foot of the bed, he felt a tug at his trouser cuff. Glancing down, he saw another female almost as homely as the one he'd left in bed. She gazed up at him soulfully and asked, "Nothing for the bridesmaid?"

Then there was the Japanese call girl who went broke because no one had a yen for her.

After an evening at the theater and several nightcaps at an intimate little bistro, the young man whispered to his date, "How do you feel about making love to a man?"

"That's *my* business," she snapped.

"Ah," he said. "A professional!"

Seeing an attractive young woman sitting alone in the cocktail lounge, the young man approached her politely and offered to buy her a drink.

"A motel!" she shrieked.

"No, no," he said, embarrassed, "I said a drink...."

"*You expect me to go to a motel with you!*" she shrieked even louder.

Definitely daunted, the young man fled to a dim rear booth of the lounge, to avoid the stares of the other patrons. A few minutes later, the girl came back to where he was seated and said softly, "I'd like to apologize for making you so uncomfortable at the bar. You see, I'm studying psychology at the university, and I wanted a chance to study the reactions of the people here."

To which the young man replied, in a resounding roar, "*Seventy-five dollars!*"

"I was in a phone booth talking to my girl, Your Honor," said the defendant, "and this cop came up, opened the door, grabbed me by the coat, and dragged me out."

"What did you do?" the judge asked.

"I didn't do anything—not until he grabbed my girl and dragged her out, too."

The American diplomatic courier had just arrived in the tiny Latin American capital. He strode briskly out of the airport terminal, self-importantly snapping instructions at the porters carrying his luggage and looking about impatiently for the car that was supposed to be there to meet him. He certainly had no time for the dirty little street urchins who trailed after him trying to sell everything from a shoeshine to their sisters.

"Hey, American," called out one lad especially worldly-wise for his years. "I get what you like, if you pay—feelthy pictures, marijuana, girls… boys… ?"

"I can't be bothered with this vermin," the undiplomatic messenger disdainfully proclaimed, brushing his ragged pursuers aside. "My business here is with the American ambassador!"

"Can do, *señor*," responded the boy. "But for an ambassador, you weel have to pay extra."

The wages of sin are high unless you know someone who'll do it for nothing.

One evening, after conducting a real hell-fire-and-brimstone revival meeting, the visiting evangelist decided to take a walk, and happened to wander into a nearby red-light district. On a corner, he saw a streetwalker leaning against a lamppost. The evangelist stopped and, in a powerful voice, he intoned, "Woman, I prayed for you last night."

"Well, you could've had me if you'd just come around," she purred. "I was standing right here all night long."

Have you heard about the ingenious call girl who found a better-paying position?

Then there was the gigolo who was so dumb he wound up working in a warehouse.

The impecunious young couple finally hit on a way to save money. Each time they made love, the husband would deposit all his change in a huge porcelain piggy bank in their bedroom.

After about a year of this, they decided to break open the bank and spend the money. Counting up all the proceeds, the husband remarked, "This is really strange—there's all this paper currency here: fives, tens, even some twenties. I don't remember putting in any bills."

"No," responded his wife, "but not everyone is as cheap as you are."

When one of the prostitutes passed away, the girls moped disconsolately around the house. "Good old Gloria," lamented one. "She could handle twenty men a night, drink a fifth of whiskey, and still have the strength to roll five drunks."

Hearing this, one of the others burst into tears. "Why is it," she sobbed, "that a girl has to die before anyone says anything nice about her?"

The luxurious Las Vegas hotel was engulfed in flames as the firemen battled the blaze and attempted to rescue the trapped guests. Just then, a man clad only in a towel came running from the hotel. "Have you seen a blonde girl running around naked?" he asked breathlessly.

"No, I haven't," a fireman replied.

"Well, if you do, you can have her," the man said. "She's already paid for."

The dazzling blonde met a well-attired gentleman at a plush cocktail lounge and they soon struck up an amiable conversation about human nature. "Would you sleep with a complete stranger for a million dollars?" the gentleman hypothesized.

"Yes, I think I would," the girl declared.

"Would you sleep with me for twenty-five dollars?" he asked.

"What do you think I am?" she retorted indignantly.

"We've already established that," he responded. "Now we're just haggling over the price."

Then there was the Old Testament prostitute who was arrested for trying to make a prophet.

Then there was the flight attendant who turned to prostitution but couldn't break the habit of greeting her customers with "Welcome aboard."

On a southbound train a few months after the Civil War, a young belle suddenly moved from her seat next to a businessman and sat beside a Confederate veteran who was on his way home from the front lines. "That carpetbagger offered me ten dollars to spend the night with him," the offended girl indignantly told the soldier.

The Southerner immediately drew his gun and shot the man. "Let that be a lesson to any other damn Yankees," he proclaimed in a loud voice. "Don't come down here and try to double the price of everything."

We know a swinging call girl who's a pleasure to be with—but she doesn't come cheap.

In olden days, man's greatest fear was that a woman would take it to heart; today, his greatest fear is that a woman will take it to court.

There was a generous area of disagreement between the attractive young widow and a bachelor friend she said had sired the latest addition to her brood. So they took their problem to court.

"Did you sleep with this woman?" asked the judge.

To which the defendant replied, sincerely, "Not a wink, Your Honor. Not a wink."

The courtroom was pregnant with anxious silence as the judge solemnly considered his verdict in the paternity suit before him. Suddenly, he reached into the folds of his robes, drew out a cigar, and ceremoniously handed it to the defendant.

"Congratulations!" said the jurist. "You have just become a father!"

"You are charged," said the judge, "with the serious offense of assault and battery upon your husband. How do you plead?"

"Innocent," said the shapely defendant. "I hit him because he called me a vile name."

"And just what did he call you?" asked the jurist.

"It's really too terrible to repeat—he... he called me a 'two-bit whore'!"

"That *is* bad," said the judge. "What did you hit him with?"

"A bag of quarters, Your Honor."

Then there was the freaky WAC who was court-martialed for contributing to the delinquency of a major.

A weekend golfer, having four-putted the last hole, threw his clubs into the golf cart and drove toward the clubhouse. Arriving there, he saw a squad car parked by the entrance. As he walked toward the locker room, a policeman stopped him. "Did you drive from the fifteenth tee about half an hour ago?" the officer asked.

"Yes."

"Did you hook your ball over those trees and off the course?"

"Yes, as a matter of fact, I did," replied the puzzled golfer.

With anger in his voice, the policeman continued, "Your ball sailed out on the highway, cracked the windshield of a woman's car; she couldn't see where she was going and ran into a fire truck; the fire truck couldn't get to the fire and a house burned down! What are you going to do about it?"

The golfer pondered a moment, picked up his driver, and said, "Well, I think I'm going to open my stance a little and move my left thumb around farther toward my right side."

"Gentlemen of the jury," said the defense attorney, now beginning to warm to his summation, "the real question here before you is, shall this beautiful young woman be forced to languish away her loveliest years in a dark prison cell? Or shall she be set free to return to her cozy little apartment at 4134 Seaside Street—there to spend her lonely, loveless hours in her boudoir, lying beside her little Princess phone, 1-858-962-7873?"

It takes a brave man to admit his mistakes, especially in the middle of a paternity-suit hearing.

The prosecuting attorney's voice reached fever pitch as he cross-examined the young male defendant. "You mean to sit there and tell this jury that you had a completely assembled still on your premises, and were not engaged in the illegal production of alcoholic spirits?"

"That's the truth," answered the defendant. "I acquired it as a conversation piece, just like any other antique."

"You'll have to do better than that," sneered the prosecutor. "As far as this court is concerned, the very possession of such equipment is proof of your guilt."

"In that case, you'd better charge me with rape, too," the defendant said.

"Are you confessing to the crime of rape, young man?" interrupted the incredulous judge.

"No, Your Honor," answered the defendant, indignantly. "But I sure as hell have the equipment!"

The stunning young woman was arrested for prostitution and taken to court. "Have you anything to offer the gentlemen of the jury on your own behalf?" asked the judge.

"Oh, no, Your Honor," she answered. "I've learned my lesson."

When the father discovered that his teenage daughter had been knocking boots with her boyfriend at a wild party, he insisted on having the kid arrested for statutory rape and the case was promptly brought to trial. The first witness was another kid who had attended the festivities. "If you actually witnessed the act," the prosecutor demanded, "why didn't you try to stop the defendant?"

"Well," the testifier admitted, "at the time, it was kinda hard to tell which one of them was gonna be the defendant."

The attractive grief-stricken widow had been living in seclusion at the home of her deceased husband's younger brother for several weeks. One evening, when she could no longer control her emotions, she barged into her brother-in-law's study and pleaded, "James, I want you to take off my dress." The brother-in-law did as she requested. "Now," she continued, "take off my slip." He again complied. "And now," she said, with a slight blush, "remove my panties and bra." Once more James obeyed her command.

Then, regaining her composure, she stared directly at the embarrassed young man and boldly announced, "I have only one more thing to say, James. Don't ever let me catch you wearing my things again!"

Then there was the transvestite from Yale who wanted to spend his junior year abroad.

Then there was the transvestite sailor who went down to the sea in slips.

When the young career girl consulted a doctor about her diminishing sexuality, she was given a hormone shot and told to call in a week. "Doctor," she wailed over the phone the next week, "my voice has become terribly low."

"That's not too unusual," replied the doctor. "Have you had any other reactions?"

"Yes," she moaned. "I've sprouted hair on my chest."

"My goodness," the doctor gasped. "How far down does it go?"

"All the way to my balls."

LeRoy Neiman

The storm smashed the great ship to pieces. One small boat of survivors found its way to a nearby island and safety. Realizing that they had been blown off the usual shipping route and would probably be on the island for many months before being rescued, the survivors proceeded to set up satisfactory living arrangements. Since the survivors included six women and one man, these "arrangements" were a little unusual.

It was agreed that rather than fight over the lucky fellow, each girl would take her turn, having him entirely to herself one day each week; and that he would have the seventh day to himself.

Being a normal sort of a guy, he threw himself into the situation with a great deal of enthusiasm. The first few weeks, he didn't even bother with his day of rest. As time passed, however, he began looking forward to that one day at the end of each week. Eventually, in fact, it was that day that filled his every thought; he longed to be off the island, to hear a masculine voice again, and to sleep, for days and days and days.

One morning, a Saturday, with the week almost at an end, he spotted a small raft on the horizon, and on it a figure. He waved frantically as the raft approached the island, and when it was near enough and he realized that the new arrival was a man, he dashed down the hill to the beach. As the man pulled himself out of the water, our friend threw his arms around him and cried, "Man, you've no idea how glad I am to see you!"

"Well goodness, honeybuns," said the new arrival. "I'm glad ta see you, too!"

"My God," croaked the weary one, "there go my Sundays!"

Two knights, resplendent in shining armor and mounted on handsome steeds, rode through the forest followed by their meek little page, who was huddled uncomfortably on his burro. As they arrived at a strange castle surrounded by the usual moat, one knight shouted the traditional "Tally-ho!" to inform the castle's proprietors that the travelers desired lodging for the night. The drawbridge was soon lowered and out came a wispy fellow, dressed in flowing robes of many colors. "Well, what can I do for you fellowth?" he lisped.

The tired knights, anxious for lodging but taken aback by their gayer-than-thou host, looked at each other in dismay, then one whispered to the other, "Promise him anything, but give him our page."

Two Jewish mothers who had lived in the same block in Brooklyn when their children were growing up, but hadn't seen each other in years, happened to meet at a luncheon in a swank hotel in Manhattan. After a tearful embrace, they retired to a corner to chat.

"And how are your two boys, William and Bernard?" the one woman inquired of the other.

"William is an attorney, and a full partner in an important New York law firm," the second woman responded with pride. "And it's *Doctor* Bernard, if you please! He has so many patients that even his mother needs an appointment to see her own son in the afternoon! And your son, Herman, how is he?"

The first mother gave a funny little smile.

"Well, you know, Herman is a homosexual—" she began.

"That's wonderful!" interrupted her friend. "And where's his office?"

Have you heard about the closeted Aussie who left his wife and returned to Sydney?

Did you hear about the young man who moved to Greenwich Village and turned prematurely gay?

The beautiful young career girl had one unhappy trait: She would fall head over heels in love with a different man each week, always with the conviction that her latest beau was *the* man of her dreams, with whom she could live happily ever after. One particularly devastating experience finally convinced her that she had to put an end to this distressing habit. She vowed to spend the next few evenings alone and repaired to her favorite bar to console herself. But, as luck would have it, she encountered a handsome well-groomed stranger, whom she couldn't resist approaching.

"Let me buy you a drink," the young man said, after she sat down next to him. "But I really must tell you that nothing will come of it."

His reserve intrigued her and after several drinks, her attraction to him had grown considerably. In fact, the more the fellow put her off, the more fascinated she became. Here, she thought, was a truly fine young man—who didn't try to take advantage of her like all the rest. Before she knew it, she had invited him to her apartment. "I'm just not the type of person who does that sort of thing," her new friend replied. "But I'll come along for the conversation."

His hesitance increased her ardor for him all the more. By the time they had reached her apartment, she was irresistibly drawn to him. Once inside, she reclined languorously on the couch and beckoned to him.

"Please," he pleaded. "I told you this couldn't work out."

"But you don't understand," she said. "I want you for my husband."

"That's quite different!" he said enthusiastically. "Send him in!"

"**I**s it true that you send flowers anywhere?" the man asked the FTD clerk.

"Of course," she said.

"Wonderful!" he exclaimed. "Send me to New York. I'd like to visit my boyfriend."

"**C**ongratulate me, Pop," said the stylish young man. "I'm in love with a girl."

"Son," observed his dad, "I'm happy with your choice."

Then there were the two gay judges who tried each other.

Then there was the gay Manhattanite who moved to Long Island so he could be listed in the Queens directory.

A youthful archeologist was sent to a deserted outpost in the Middle East to assist with an excavation project. "You're going to like it here," a colleague assured him on his arrival. "Friday nights, we get a truckload of booze from the village and have a great time."

"I'm afraid I'm no drinker," the archeologist protested.

The colleague shrugged. "On Saturdays, we bring in a busload of wild girls from the village and have an orgy."

"Gee," the archeologist mused. "I don't think I'd enjoy that at all."

"I say," blurted his colleague. "You're not queer, are you?"

"Of course not!" the fellow snapped testily.

"That's too bad," the colleague said. "You won't like Sunday nights, either."

The stylishly dressed young man sashayed into the Army recruiting office and enlisted. After subjecting the chap to an extensive physical and psychological examination, one of the board members declared, "Well, fella, it looks to me like you're going to make a good little soldier."

"Fabulous," replied the young man. "When can I meet him?"

To cut down on expenses, the two young women just starting their careers decided to vacation together and to share a hotel room. On the first night, one turned to her friend and rested her hand on her shoulder. "There's something about myself I've never told you," she admitted. "I'll be frank—"

"No," her friend interrupted, "*I'll* be Frank."

Then there was the gay tattoo artist who had designs on several of the local sailors.

When the Hollywood star announced his plans to vacation in Tangier, his agent told him to be sure to visit a very exclusive brothel there that specialized in unusual sexual practices. On his return, the star called his agent and announced that he'd taken his advice. "It was really quite an experience," he declared. "First the girl told me to strip and lie down on the bed. Then she covered me from head to toe with strawberry jam, sprinkled marshmallows over that, smothered it all with whipped cream, and topped it with a handful of almonds and maraschino cherries."

"Fantastic," the agent gasped. "And then she licked it all off?"

"Hell no," the star exclaimed. "It looked so good I ate it myself."

The family doctor, consulted by the hysterical parents of a pregnant teenager, told them he positively would not perform an abortion. "But when her time comes, I'll deliver the baby at a private hospital. Then I'll show it to one of my other patients—let's say a woman who's married and who's in for a gall-bladder operation—and tell her there's been a mistake, it wasn't her gall-bladder, she was pregnant, and here's the child."

All went as planned, but at the crucial time, there was no available female patient on whom to foist the infant. There was only a male—a priest, in fact. The physician, undaunted, decided to brazen it out. When the man of the cloth awakened from the anesthesia, he was informed that, by a miracle, he had been delivered of an offspring, a boy. Far from being shocked, the good cleric was overjoyed at this evidence of divine intervention and raised the boy as his own.

Years later, as the priest lay dying, he concluded that he must unburden his soul to his son. "I have always told you I was your father, but that is untrue," he confessed, and he told the lad about the "miraculous" incident at the hospital. "So you see, my boy," the priest announced, "I'm not your father. I'm your mother. The bishop is your father."

Rodney, the eldest son of a respectable Boston family, announced to his shocked father that he intended to live openly with his flamboyant boyfriend on Beacon Hill.

"Damn it, Rodney!" the parent responded, "Our family came over with John Winthrop and we've never had a scandal such as this."

"I can't help it, Father, I love him."

"But, for God's sake, son—he's Catholic!"

Two elderly farmers were leisurely strolling through a pasture when one stopped and remarked, "Here's where I got my first piece of ass and right over there's where her mother stood."

"Her mother," said his surprised companion. "What did she say?"

"Ba-a-a-a," came the reply.

The attractive young college junior was filing a report with the campus police regarding her encounter with an exhibitionist.

"Those nuts always seem to bother the nicest, most innocent girls," one officer said sympathetically. "I'm terribly sorry you were exposed to this experience."

"Oh, that's all right," said the undergrad. "It was really no big thing."

Young Quigly and his brother decided to attend a masquerade ball at the country club dressed in a rented cow costume. However, after an hour, they grew tired of their tandem togetherness and he suggested that they slip outside for a breath of fresh air. Still in the costume, the twosome was trotting across a nearby field when Quigly spotted a huge Hereford bull that was preparing to charge. "What are we going to do?" quavered his frightened sibling from his posterior position.

"I'm going to eat some grass," the lad croaked as the thundering hooves came closer. "But, ah, you might want to brace yourself."

Have you heard about the S&M fetishist who had to break a date because he was going to be tied up all night?

A colonel in the Foreign Legion, assuming command of a desert outpost, spied a camel tied up behind the enlisted men's quarters and asked his first lieutenant to explain its presence there. The lieutenant replied that the men, being without female companionship for long periods, had natural urges that required satisfaction, and the camel was used for that purpose. The colonel, being an understanding man, agreed that the camel could remain.

Several weeks later, the colonel himself felt a passionate urge welling up inside him and ordered the camel brought to his room. When the camel arrived, the colonel immediately set upon her with vigor. Having achieved satisfaction, the colonel turned around and discovered, with some embarrassment, that the lieutenant was still standing in the doorway.

"Well," the colonel said, breaking the silence after a moment, "is that the way the men usually do it?"

"Not exactly, sir," the open-mouthed lieutenant replied. "The men ordinarily use her to take them into town."

Then there was the masochist who was starved for affliction.

Two call girls were discussing their experiences of the last few evenings over cocktails when one asked the other, "Say, how did you make out with that eccentric millionaire you met yesterday?"

"He gave me five hundred dollars, but it wasn't worth it," said the second. "He wanted to do it in a coffin."

"No kidding?!" exclaimed her friend. "I'll bet that shook you up pretty good."

"Yeah," she confessed, "but not as much as it did the six pallbearers."

And then there was the raven-haired sadist who stood up and announced that she could whip any man in the house.

"Darling," she sighed, "love me like you've never loved me before!"

"Not in this state," he replied. "I could get ten years."

After patiently listening to their mother's garbled and mythical version of the facts of life, the precocious first grader said to his younger sister, "Gee, I never thought Dad was the kind of guy who would do it with a stork."

Then there was the unfortunate voyeur who was apprehended at the peek of his career.

Have you heard about the girl who was so ugly that Peeping Toms would reach in and pull down her shades?

Then there was the shoe fetishist who succumbed to Freudian slippers.

Two youths, newly arrived in ancient Crete, were on their way to consult the Delphic oracle when one stopped to admire a rather aristocratic woman who was entering the royal palace. "Come on, Oedipus," his friend sneered. "She's old enough to be your mother."

The Martian landed his saucer in Manhattan, and immediately upon emerging was approached by a panhandler. "Mister," said the man, "can you spare a dime?"

The Martian asked, "What's a dime?"

The panhandler thought a moment, then said, "You're right! Can I have a dollar?"

"It must be terrible to be lame," the woman remarked, dropping a quarter into the beggar's hat.

"It sure is, lady," he agreed.

"But wouldn't it be worse to be blind?" she asked.

"Much worse," replied the beggar. "People kept giving me slugs when I was blind."

Money

LeRoy Neiman

"**G**ood heavens, Doctor! What a huge bill," the patient protested.

"My dear fellow," the doctor replied, "if you knew what an interesting case yours was, and how strongly I was tempted to let it proceed to a post-mortem, you wouldn't complain at a bill three times as big as this."

"**I**'m awfully sorry, miss," said the store clerk, "but this fifty dollar bill is counterfeit."

"Damn it," she exclaimed, "I've been seduced!"

"**I**'m sorry, Samantha," he said, "I can never learn to love you."

"Gee, that's too bad," said Samantha, "and after I'd saved nearly seventy-five grand, too."

"Well, maybe just one more lesson…."

Coming home unexpectedly, the husband found his wife in bed with a naked man. He produced a pistol from a dresser drawer and was about to shoot the interloper when his wife pleaded, "Don't, don't! Who do you think bought us the house in the country, the Lexus, my sable wrap?"

"Are *you* the man?" asked the husband. The unclothed one nodded. "Then get your clothes on!" roared the husband, "You wanna catch a cold?"

A profound philosophy of life is reflected in the reply of a no-longer-wealthy roué who, when asked what he had done with all his money, said, "Part of it went for liquor and fast automobiles, and part of it went for women. The rest I spent foolishly."

It was painfully evident to the indignant father that all was not well with his attractive daughter. To his pointed questions, she tearfully admitted that motherhood was approaching and that the rich young layabout who lived on the next block was responsible.

With fire in his eyes, the father charged down the street and rang the bachelor's bell. The young man answered the door, still in his dressing gown and holding what appeared to be a Mai Tai. He readily admitted his guilt.

"Just what do you intend doing about it?" demanded the parent. The bachelor thought for a moment. "Well," he said, "if it's a girl, I'll give your daughter fifty thousand dollars. And if it's a boy, I'll give her a hundred thousand."

"See here," said the father. "If it's a miscarriage, will you give her another chance?"

"All right, lady," said the bill collector, "how about the next installment on that couch?"

The lady shrugged. "Better than having to give you the money, I guess."

A vice-president at our bank made the sage observation that women without principle draw plenty of interest.

A friend of ours observes that money can't buy love, but it can put you in an excellent bargaining position.

Men with money to burn have started many a girl playing with fire.

After the wealthiest man in the world passed away at a ripe old age, he was mourned on the front pages of newspapers throughout the world. On a mid-Manhattan street corner a short, bespectacled fellow in a rather worn gray-flannel suit seemed particularly broken up by the news. He clutched the paper to his chest and cried unabashedly, "He's dead! He's dead!"

"There, there," said the news dealer, trying his best to console him. "You mustn't carry on like that, sir. We've all got to go sometime. He wasn't related to you, was he?"

"No," sobbed the man. "That's just it!"

We've just been informed that the Internal Revenue Service has streamlined its tax form this year. It goes like this:

(A) How much did you make last year?

(B) How much do you have left?

(C) Send B

"Something the matter?" asked the bartender of the young, well-dressed customer who sat staring sullenly into his drink.

"Two months ago my grandfather died and left me eighty-five thousand dollars," said the man.

"That doesn't sound like anything to be too upset about," said the bartender, polishing a glass. "It should happen to me."

"Yeah," said the sour young man, "but last month an uncle on my mother's side passed away. He left me one hundred fifty thousand dollars."

"So why are you sitting there looking so unhappy?" asked the bartender.

"This month—so far—not a cent."

Two well-dressed, elderly women entered the business office and approached an executive.

"Sir," said one, "we are soliciting funds for the welfare and rehabilitation of wayward women. Would you care to donate?"

"Sorry," replied the exec, "but I contribute directly."

A friend of ours recently made a sizable contribution to the Home for Unwed Mothers. But he says next time he intends to give money.

A girl we know has met the rising cost of living by simply selling an extra key to her apartment.

The restaurant's coat-check girl was obviously new, and Jack watched in mild amusement as, fumbling frantically to find his coat, she knocked garments off the racks and entangled herself in the hangers. His amusement had changed to fury, however, when five minutes later the room was a jumble of outerwear and she still hadn't found his coat.

"Forget it!" he finally cried in rage. "I'll send somebody for it tomorrow!" And, seething, he strode out into the bitter cold of a snowstorm, clutching the lapels of his suit jacket. The girl ran after him.

"Hey, you cheapskate," she called, "what about my tip?"

Man's greatest labor-saving device is the love of a rich woman.

Affirmation of an ancient proverb comes from a sporty acquaintance of ours who assures us that two heads are indeed better than one, especially when they happen to be on the same coin.

Sam and Al had been partners for many years and they shared and shared alike in almost everything, including the affection of the attractive and rather hot-blooded accounting VP at the company they had founded. One morning Sam came into Al's office extremely upset.

"Al," he moaned, "a complication has come up. Our accounting director is going to have a baby. We are going to be a father."

But Al, who was the calmer of the two, sat his partner down and pointed out that a great many worse things could have happened to them: business could have fallen off, for instance. They agreed that the only thing to do was share and share alike, as they always had. They would see that their accounting director got the very best in medical care, and after the child was born he would want for nothing. A room of his own, fine clothes, and the best in schooling, and they would set up a trust fund immediately after his birth to guarantee him a college education. And the lucky youngster would have two fathers whereas many other kids didn't even have one.

Before they knew it, the big day had arrived. The two of them paced back and forth in the hospital waiting room, until Sam could stand it no longer.

"I'm too nervous up here," he said. "I'm going to go down and sit in the car. As soon as something happens, you come down and tell me."

Al agreed, and in less than an hour he was down on the street wearing a grave expression. It was obvious to Sam, even before his partner spoke, that something was wrong.

"What's the matter?" Sam asked, starting to choke up. "Is it bad news?"

His partner nodded.

"We had twins," Al said, "and mine died."

"My wife is always asking for money," complained a friend of ours. "Last week she wanted five hundred dollars. The day before yesterday she asked me for a hundred and twenty-five dollars. This morning she wanted three hundred and fifty."

"That's crazy," we said. "What does she do with it all?"

"I don't know," said our friend. "I never give her any."

There are more important things than money, but they won't date you if you don't have any.

A man who says he'll go through anything for a woman usually has her bank account in mind.

Silas, a self-made, illiterate millionaire, decided to thwart his ne'er-do-well son by leaving all his money to a local Christian college. But the son, banking on Silas' strait-laced attitude toward sex, wasn't ready to be counted out.

"Father," he said to the old man one day, "I hope you are aware that at that college—the one you've willed your money to—the boys and girls *matriculate* together."

Silas' eyebrows shot up and the son pressed his advantage. "Not only that," he said, "but the boys and girls use the same *curriculum*."

With that the old codger's face darkened and his son leaned forward to whisper, "But worst of all, Father, before a girl can graduate she has to show her *thesis* to the dean."

"That settles it!" roared Silas. "That infernal school won't get a penny from me."

So he left all his money to Harvard.

Many a young man is looking for an older woman with a strong will—made out to him.

Grosse Pointe's swankiest watering place had rarely seen such excitement as that evening when the suavely dressed young man jumped up from his table and proclaimed, "There's five thousand dollars for any woman in this place who'll let me fuck her my way." Pandemonium reigned and the crowd stood aghast as the bartender, maître d', and manager forcibly ejected the young fellow. He sat morosely on the curb in front of the lounge, until a beautiful young woman slipped out of the door, walked over to him, and asked if his offer still held. He said it did, and they promptly took a cab to her apartment. There she quickly stripped and got into bed. As he lay down beside her, she asked, "Incidentally, just what *is* your way?"

"On credit," he replied.

His last will and testament completed, the old man in the oxygen tent fondly told his son that all his wealth, stocks, bonds, bank account, and real estate would be his after the end finally came.

"Dad, Dad," whispered the weeping son, his voice emotion-choked, "I can't tell you how grateful I am, how unworthy I am…. Is there—Is there anything I can do for *you*? Anything at all?"

"Well, son," came the feeble reply, "I'd appreciate it very much if you took your foot off the oxygen hose."

The bleary-eyed, unshaven panhandler approached a passerby and said, "Mister, could I have $101 for a cup of coffee?"

"But," the man protested, "coffee only costs a buck!"

"I know," said the panhandler, "but coffee always makes me horny."

The young executive had taken more than a hundred thousand dollars from his company's safe and had lost it playing the stock market; he was certain to be discovered. In addition, his beautiful wife had left him. Down to the river he went, and was just clambering over the bridge railing when a gnarled hand fell upon his arm. He turned and saw an ancient crone in a black cloak with wrinkled face and stringy gray hair. "Don't jump," she rasped. "I'm a witch, and I'll grant you three wishes for a slight consideration."

"I'm beyond help," he replied, and told her his troubles.

"Nothing to it," she said, cackling. "Alakazam! The money is back in the company vault. Alakazam! Your wife is home waiting for you with love in her heart. Alakazam! You now have a personal bank account of two hundred thousand dollars!"

The man, stunned to speechlessness, was finally able to ask, "What—what is the consideration I owe you?"

"You must spend the night making love to me," she smiled toothlessly.

The thought of making love to the old crone repulsed him, but it was certainly worth it, he thought. Together they retired to a nearby motel, and in the morning, the distasteful ordeal over, he was dressing to go home when the bat in the bed asked, "Say, sonny, how old are you?"

"I'm forty-two," he said. "Why?"

"Ain't you a little old to believe in witches?"

The newly appointed chairman of the local fund-raising committee decided to call personally at the home of the town's wealthiest citizen, a man well known for his tightness with a dollar. Remarking on the impressive economic resources of his host, the committee chairman pointed out how miserly it would seem if the town's richest man failed to give a substantial donation to the annual charity drive.

"Since you've gone to so much trouble checking on my assets," the millionaire retorted, "let me fill you in on some facts you may have overlooked. I have a ninety-one-year-old mother who has been hospitalized for the past five years, a widowed daughter with five young children and no means of support, and two brothers who owe the government a fortune in back taxes. Now, I think you'll agree, young man, that charity begins at home."

Ashamed for having misjudged his host, the fund-raiser apologized for his tactlessness and added, "I had no idea that you were saddled with so many family debts."

"I'm not," replied the millionaire, "but you must be crazy to think I'd give money to strangers when I won't even help my own relatives."

The room was small, misty, and dim with pungent incense as the wrinkled gypsy woman looked up from her crystal at the gentleman seated before her. "I will answer any two questions you ask me," said the gypsy, "for fifty dollars."

"Isn't that price rather high?" asked the man.

"Yes, it is," said the gypsy. "Now what is your second question?"

A fool and his money are soon popular.

"**M**oney doesn't grow on trees," the beautiful showgirl declared as she stooped to adjust her jeweled platinum ankle bracelet, "but some limbs have a way of attracting it!"

In the presence of a client he wished to impress, a high-powered executive flipped on his intercom switch and barked to his secretary: "Miss Jones, get my broker on the line!"

The visitor was duly impressed, until the secretary's voice floated back into the room, loud and clear: "Yes, sir, stock or pawn?"

"**E**xcuse me, sir," the young man said, nervously entering the living room, where his girlfriend's father was reading the evening paper, "but there's something kind of important that I'd like to ask you. I was wondering whether, uh, that is, if you'd be willing to, er—"

"Why, of course, my boy," the father exclaimed, jumping to his feet and shaking the lad's hand vigorously. "I'll give my permission gladly, because my little girl's happiness is all that matters to me!"

"Permission?" the young man gulped, obviously confused.

"You want to marry my daughter," the father said, "and you have my blessing."

"Oh, no, sir," said the boy, "it's nothing like that. It's my car, sir. A payment was due last Thursday, and unless I can come up with a thousand bucks right away, they're going to repossess it, so I was wondering if you could loan me—"

"Certainly not," the father snapped, returning to the sofa and his paper. "I hardly know you."

A guy with money to burn has a good chance of finding a match.

The spirited bidding at Sotheby's in London was halted temporarily when the auctioneer held up his hand and announced, "One of the gentlemen in the audience has lost his wallet containing fifteen thousand dollars. He has asked me to tell you that he is offering a reward of five hundred dollars for its immediate return—no questions asked."

There was a brief hush in the hall, then a voice from the back was heard: "Five twenty-five!"

A debt-plagued fellow, hopelessly poring over a pile of bills, suddenly shouted, "I'd give a thousand dollars to anyone who would do my worrying for me!"

"You're on," answered his wife. "Where's the thousand?"

"That's your first worry," he replied.

"Of course I wouldn't accept money from a perfect stranger," the gold-digger told his buddy. "But then, nobody's perfect."

Two old friends, both prosperous businessmen, hadn't seen each other in some time and happened to meet on the beach at Miami. "What brings you here, Jack?" asked one.

"Actually, Fred, a tragedy. My business was burned to the ground, and I'm taking a vacation on part of the $250,000 insurance money."

"What a coincidence," responded Fred. "My business was destroyed by a flood and I got almost a million in insurance."

After a moment of thoughtful silence, Jack leaned close to his friend and whispered, "Tell me, Fred—how do you start a flood?"

The wealthy financier was sitting in his study when his eldest son came to him. "Dad," the boy stammered, "I got a girl in trouble and she wants two thousand dollars to keep quiet about it."

The father reluctantly wrote a check for the amount; but just as he finished signing it, his second son burst in with the same bad news, only this time the amount requested was three thousand dollars. While he was writing the second check, his youngest daughter appeared at the door of the study, weeping.

"Daddy," she sobbed uncontrollably, "I think I'm pregnant."

"Aha," the financier exclaimed gratefully. "Now *we* collect!"

After stopping his car on a deserted section of country road, the young man turned to his date and made some rather predictable advances. "Just a minute," the girl declared, pushing him away. "I'm really a prostitute and I have to charge you fifty dollars."

After he reluctantly paid her, they made love. Later, the man sat silently at the wheel. "Aren't we leaving?" the girl asked.

"Not quite yet," the fellow said. "I'm really a cabdriver— and the fare back is fifty dollars."

Encountering a sad-looking man standing on a street corner, the sweet old lady sympathetically walked over to him, pressed a five dollar bill into his palm, and said, "Chin up!"

Next day, as she passed the same corner, the man walked over to her and gave her twenty dollars. "Thanks for the tip, lady," he said. "Chin Up paid twelve-to-one."

Thomas Gladstone, a stockbroker, received an urgent phone call one afternoon. "My name is Walters," the caller announced. "About two weeks ago, my wife got a crazy idea and started turning tricks, asking me to line up customers for her."

"Just a minute," Gladstone protested. "You want Dr. Gladstone the psychiatrist. His name is right below mine in the phone book. Many people dial me by mistake."

"No mistake," came the reply. "I want you to invest all the money we're making."

When the bookie asked the inveterate horse player the secret of his consistent success, the gambler provided a simple explanation. "I'm just lucky, I guess. I just turn to the racing page, close my eyes, and stick a pin in it," he said.

"Lucky!" the bookie exclaimed in disbelief. "How did you pick this four-horse combination?"

"Well," the gambler admitted, "I didn't have a pin, so I used a fork."

Relatives of the late Charles Worthington were gathered to hear the reading of the will, and seated in a far corner was the svelte and stylish woman who had served the last two years as Mr. Worthington's personal secretary. The lawyer had almost finished and there had been no mention of the accomplished Miss Simpson, who was now perched uneasily on the very edge of her chair, taking in every word.

"And finally," the lawyer read, "to Miss Simpson, my beautiful but unavailable secretary, whom I promised to remember here: Hello, there, Miss Simpson!"

Then there was the compulsive gambler who drove to Las Vegas, pulled up to a parking meter, put a quarter in—and lost his car!

Some girls marry old men for money and spend the rest of their lives looking for a little change.

Two sisters were arguing about the upcoming marriage of their widowed father—a venerable gentleman in his sixties whose wife of forty years had died just a year ago. The bride-to-be was considerably younger than either of the two daughters.

"I really can't understand these May-December marriages," said the first of the sisters. "I can certainly see what December is going to find in May—youth, beauty, freshness, an upbeat attitude toward life—but what on earth is May going to find in December?"

"Christmas," answered the second.

Two friends were using adjoining booths in the men's room at an exclusive nitery when one of them noticed an appalling absence of tissue. "Hey, George," he called, "hand me some paper, will you?"

A disturbed voice replied, "Damn, there isn't any in here!"

"Any newspaper lying around?"

"No, don't see any…."

"Do you have an old envelope in your pocket? A letter, maybe? A handbill?"

"Sorry."

"Well, then—have you got two fives for a ten?"

Pitiable is the word for Milton, the manufacturer. He accumulated millions making men's suits, and lost it all making one skirt.

Latest rags-to-riches story—Texas style—concerns a young man from Dallas who inherited five million dollars, and proceeded to run it into a small fortune.

The stranger walked up to a Las Vegas craps table and laid down a thousand-dollar bet. He shook the dice, but as he threw them a third cube fell unexpectedly from his sleeve. The house operator was unruffled. He handed back two of the dice and pocketed the third, saying, "OK, roll again. Your point is fifteen."

We've just learned a secret method for returning from Las Vegas with a small fortune: Go with a large fortune.

The compulsive racetrack bettor promised to attend church each Sunday with his wife if she would agree not to nag him about the nags the rest of the week. The wife accepted the offer, hoping that this contact with religion might cure her husband of his gambling. On the very next Sunday, the couple were seated side by side in the center of the congregation; the husband seemed to be moved by the service, and he joined in singing the final hymn with such enthusiasm that several parishioners in the nearby pews were visibly impressed. As the couple emerged from the church, the husband acknowledged the smiles with which they were greeted, remarking in a whispered aside to his wife, "I'll bet you didn't expect me to make such an impression! It wouldn't surprise me if they wanted my barroom baritone in the church choir."

"You did very well, dear," his wife remarked, "except for one small thing. It's *Hallelujah*, not Hialeah!"

The Martian landed in Las Vegas and walked into a nearby casino. He passed a slot machine that suddenly whirred noisily, then disgorged a jackpot of silver dollars. The Martian looked closely at the machine and then said, "You know, you're nuts not to stay home with a cold like that."

It was eight A.M. at a Las Vegas casino and two lone bettors were still standing by a dice table awaiting further competition when a sporty brunette, attired in a business suit, happened by. "Although it's pretty early in the day," she announced, "I feel lucky this morning. I'd like to roll the dice once for twenty thousand dollars. Would the you two care to take me up on the wager?"

"Sure," answered one of the men, "we'll take your action."

"I hope you gentlemen won't mind," she then said, "but the only way I can get lucky is to roll the dice without my panties on." So saying, the lissome woman proceeded to remove her slacks and panties. With a shout of "Momma needs a new pair of pants!" she rolled the dice, gave a squeal of delight and yelled, "I win!" She then picked up her money, her slacks, and her underwear and made a hasty exit from the room.

The two men exchanged double-takes and one of them blurted out, "Hey, what did she roll, anyway?"

"How the hell should I know?" snapped the other. "I thought *you* were watching the dice."

We know a Texan who is so rich that he has an unlisted phone company.

At the height of the tourist season, a huge Texan replete with diamond-studded cuff links strode up to the desk of one of Miami Beach's most expensive hotels. He was followed by a caravan of bellhops, all of whom were carrying skis, ice skates, and other winter-sports gear. The perplexed clerk looked over the entourage and then said to the new guest, "Sorry to have to tell you this, sir, but we never have snow here in Miami."

"That's OK, son," boomed the Texan. "It's comin' with the rest of my luggage!"

A hitchhiker was picked up by a rich Texas oilman driving a big, bright-colored, richly upholstered, high-powered convertible. As they drove along the open highway, doing well over eighty, the young hitchhiker noticed a pair of very thick glasses on the seat between them.

"Are those glasses yours?" the hitchhiker asked nervously, noting that the Texan was staring intently at the road before him and the speedometer was still climbing.

"Yep," came the reply. "Wouldn't go nowhere without 'em. Cain't hardly see my hand in front of my face when I ain't got 'em on." And to the hitchhiker's dismay, when the Texan turned to talk, he squinted in his passenger's general direction, unable to make him out clearly on the seat beside him. Then sensing the hitchhiker's uneasiness, he added: "Ain't got nothing to fret over, though, sonny. This here windshield is ground to my prescription."

When she found out that the handsome young millionaire was fond of hunting, Joyce told him she was game.

The trouble with being kept is that the rent is always due.

The management of a faltering corporation offered a one thousand dollar award to those employees who turned in the best suggestions as to how the company could save money. One of the first prizes went to a young executive who suggested that in the future the award be reduced to twenty-five dollars.

Card playing can be expensive—but so can any game where you begin by holding hands.

We know a rabid, if somewhat slow-witted, football fan who is such a compulsive gambler that he lost fifty dollars on the last game of the season: twenty-five dollars when the opposing team scored a touchdown from their own fifteen-yard line, and another twenty-five bucks on the instant replay.

Harry and Fred were playing golf for money, ten bucks a hole. After the first, Harry asked Fred how many strokes he had taken. Fred answered five.

"I was home in four," said Harry smiling, "so that's my hole."

When they finished the second, Harry asked the same question.

"Wait a minute," Fred objected. "It's my turn to ask first."

Despite warnings from his guide, an American skiing in Switzerland got separated from his group and fell—uninjured—into a deep crevasse. Several hours later, a rescue party found the yawning pit and, to reassure the stranded skier, shouted down to him, "We're from the Red Cross!"

"Sorry," the imperturbable American echoed back. "I already gave at the office!"

An ex-husband we know once remarked that paying alimony is like pumping gasoline into another man's car.

"Cheer up," the exec advised his recently divorced colleague, "there are plenty of other fish in the sea."

"Maybe so," replied his despondent friend, "but the last one took all my bait."

We've heard of a new low in community standing: a man whose credit rating is so bad his cash isn't accepted.

Having spent the entire evening with the beautiful young prostitute, the businessman was surprised by the small fee she requested.

"It's not my place to advise you in such matters, my dear," said the executive, "but you're not doing yourself justice and, frankly, I don't know how you manage to get by on payments as small as this."

"Oh, it balances out," the pretty pro said with a smile wiser than her years. "I do a little blackmailing on the side."

The pretty model looked quite despondent, so the photographer asked what was bothering her.

"It's my boyfriend," she explained. "He was wiped out in the stock market—lost all of his money."

"You must feel very sorry for him," remarked the photographer.

"Yes," she replied wistfully, "he'll miss me terribly."

Divorce on grounds of incompatibility usually means either that he has lost his income or she her patability.

Show
Business

His lion trainer had quit without notice and the circus manager needed someone to replace him for the next night's show. He put an ad in the local paper and the next morning two applicants showed up outside his office. One was a rather ordinary-looking young man and the other a ravishing, redheaded beauty. Neither one of them looked very much like a lion trainer, but the manager was desperate.

"All right," he said, "here's a whip and a chair and a gun. Let's see what you can do with Big Leo over there. We'll let you have the first try, miss, but be careful—he's a mean one."

The ravishing redhead strode past the whip, and the chair and the gun and, empty-handed, fearlessly entered the cage.

Big Leo rose, snarling, then came charging across the cage towards her with a ferocious roar. When the lion was almost upon her, the girl threw open her coat. Underneath, she was stark naked. Leo skidded to a stop and crawled the rest of the way on his belly; he nuzzled the girl's feet with his nose, purred, and licked her trim ankles.

The astonished circus manager grinned happily and turned to the pop-eyed young man. "Well, young fella," he asked, "think you can top *that*?"

"Yeah," said the man. "Just get that stupid lion out of there."

After a particularly tiring performance stretched, encore by encore, into the wee hours, a sexy New York cabaret singer returned to her apartment and found a half-dozen handsome admirers waiting there. "How sweet of you boys to surprise me like this," she said, "but, really, I've had an awfully tough show tonight and I'm simply exhausted. I'm afraid one or two of you will have to go home."

Muster some sympathy for the dilemma of the out-of-work stripper: all undressed and no place to show.

It was cocktail hour in a swank lounge. Henry, a lingerie manufacturer, recognized the man sitting next to him sipping a Cosmopolitan as Bud Smiley, well-known reality-show host. Sensing a business opportunity, he introduced himself and his company to the star.

"Listen," he said conspiratorially, "how would you like to plug my product on your show?"

Bud lifted an eyebrow. "That all depends on what's in it for me," he said.

"Tell you what," Henry replied. "I'll send you one of our finest and filmiest negligees. How's that?"

Bud smiled indolently. "Like I said," he repeated, "That all depends on what's in it for me."

We just heard about the human cannonball who wanted to retire from his circus job.

"But you can't quit the show after all these years," moaned the circus director. "Where else can I find a man of your caliber?"

We suppose you've heard about the man on the flying trapeze who caught his wife in the act.

We just learned that one of the dancers from the strip joint disappeared last week and hasn't been obscene since.

We enjoyed a luncheon date the other day with a lovely Broadway showgirl who confessed she was unsuccessful in show business until she had her "no's" fixed.

The distraught female patient exclaimed to her psychiatrist, "I have no talent! I can't act! I can't sing! I can't dance! I want to quit show business!"

"Then why don't you?" asked the shrink.

"I can't," she sobbed. "I'm a star!"

"It's certainly nice to have someone like you with us this evening," said the night-club comic to the annoying ringside heckler, "and may I be the first to shake you by the throat."

Two chorus girls were talking things over between shows. "I've been out with hundreds of men," said the first, "but I haven't let one make love to me."

"Oh," said her friend, "which one was that?"

We know a gay swinger who never votes in an election. He simply doesn't care who gets in.

"Sam," said the agent, "I want you should meet Bubbles La Verne, a sensational new stripper I have just discovered. She will be a knockout as the featured performer in your club."

Sam looked the shapely dancer up and down, removed the cigar from his mouth, and said, "Well, don't just stand there, sweetheart. Undo something."

We have it on good authority that one of New York's biggest nightclubs is going to introduce a new act: a midget stripper. She'll entertain the customers who are under the tables.

A recent independent survey indicates that it's still possible for a young woman with little or no experience to make her way into show business.

A director was interviewing a pretty young actress who had just arrived in Hollywood from the East. After the usual questions, he looked her up and down and asked, "Are you a virgin?"

She nodded, then realizing a job might hinge on her answer, she added, "But I'm not a fanatic about it!"

The two television actors feigned friendship, but secretly hated each other's guts, and took great pleasure in giving one another the needle on any and all occasions. This particular evening they met, quite by accident, at a popular bar just off Broadway. The conversation started innocently enough, then one, with sudden inspiration, ran his hand over the other's bald head, and exclaimed, "By God, Fred, that feels just like my wife's ass!"

The other ran his own hand over his head, and nonchalantly retorted, "Well I'll be damned, Jim, so it does, so it does!"

You've undoubtedly heard about the high-paid movie director who was always trying to make a little extra.

A distinguished Shakespearean actor and an eminent English drama critic were lunching together in a London club when the conversation, as usual, turned to the Bard.

"Tell me this," asked the critic of the actor, "do you think that Shakespeare intended us to believe Hamlet had a sexual relationship with Ophelia?"

"I don't know what Shakespeare intended," said the actor, "but I usually do."

The dazzling movie star was applying for her passport.

"Unmarried?" asked the clerk.

"Occasionally," answered she.

The Hollywood star announced to her press agent that she was about to enter wedlock again, for the fifth time.

"Oh," said the agent. "Against whom?"

A several-times remarried Hollywood actress was confronted by a handsome young man at the premiere of her latest picture.

"Don't you remember me?" the swain enthused. "Three years ago you asked me to marry you."

"Oh, really?" said the actress. "And did you?"

The inroads of reality television have trebled unemployment among TV actors. Take, for example, the producer who came home unexpectedly one night and found his wife in the arms of one-time cop-opera star Antonio McKenzie.

"Hey!" cried the upset producer. "What are you doing?"

Antonio's manly brow knotted in concern. "To tell you the truth," he said earnestly, "not much of anything these days."

Leon, an unemployed actor, came shuffling dejectedly home after a fruitless day of visiting booking offices. But instead of the quiet comfort he expected, he found his apartment in shambles and Martha, his beautiful young wife, lying on the bed in hysterics. It was obvious that her clothes had literally been torn from her bruised and ravished body.

"Good Lord!" Leon cried. "Martha! What happened?"

"Oh darling!" she sobbed. "I fought and fought, but he—"

"Who did this awful thing? Who? Who was it?"

"He came here looking for you. He said it was very important. Finding me alone and defenseless, he…. Oh!"

"Who?" Leon roared. "Who?"

She hung her head and in a husky voice replied, "Your agent."

"My agent!" Sunlight suddenly flooded Leon's face. "Did he say whether he'd found a part for me?"

Two well-known actors were exchanging boasts at Sardi's. "Well, I've been doing all right," said the first one. "During the third act last night, I had the audience glued to their seats."

"Marvelous!" replied the second actor. "Damned clever of you to think of that!"

The director was patiently explaining the scene to the famous Method actor. "You've been on this desert island for twelve years. One morning, you awaken, crawl out of your lean-to, and start strolling along the beach. Suddenly you see this beautiful blonde girl lying on the sand beside her discarded life jacket. You rush forward, grab her in your arms, and start kissing her."

The actor nodded thoughtfully, then asked, "And what's my motivation?"

While making the rounds of producers' and casting directors' offices, Sally made a successful contact and as a result was offered a speaking role in a feature-length Western.

The first day's script called for her to be thrown from the horse into a clump of cacti. The second day, she had to jump from a cliff, her clothes on fire, into a mountain stream, and swim to shore. On the third day, she was cuffed around by the villain, and the director—a stickler for realism—reshot the scene five times. The fourth day, her boot caught in a stirrup, and a runaway horse dragged her for two miles.

Wearily, she managed to limp to the producer's office.

"Listen," she said hoarsely, "who do I have to sleep with to get *out* of this picture?"

After viewing the rushes of a Hollywood hopeful's screen test, the producer was less than enthusiastic: "My dear, it will take an act of Congress to get you into the movies."

The buxom young actress sighed, "That's what I thought— your apartment or mine?"

As the Shakespearean actor slipped off his trousers and prepared to join her in bed, the woman he had picked up at the after-party gave an appreciative whistle at his generous endowment.

"My dear," he cautioned in response, "we have come to bury Caesar—not to praise him."

Hoping to break into films, the aspiring young actress slept with a famous director, who promised to put her name in lights. Sure enough, the very next week there appeared on Sunset Strip a fifty-foot neon sign that flashed, ROBERTA STURGESS IS A PUSHOVER.

"In my last four shows," complained the Broadway actor, "I've played nothing but heels and cads and egotistical swine."

"Yes, it's a shame," agreed his colleague. "This type-casting is ruining the American stage."

"Well," exclaimed the young woman as she and her date left the movie theater, "that certainly was exciting! I wonder if the film was any good...."

As the horror movie was about to reach its terrifying conclusion, the young woman began fidgeting in her seat. The man sitting behind her leaned forward and inquired quietly, "Feeling hysterical?"

"No," she whispered, pointing to her boyfriend. "He's feeling mine."

A glamorous actress, whose best days were behind her, began finding herself without male companionship several evenings a week. To help pass the time—and perhaps catch a live one—she decided to attend one of those Hollywood charity meetings. She dozed quietly throughout the opening address, but awoke suddenly to hear the speaker say, "Now let's get out there and work like beavers!"

The actress nudged the person sitting next to her and whispered, "How do beavers work?"

The answer from the confused lady on her left was, "I'm not too sure, but I think it's with their tails."

The actress jumped to her feet and shouted as loud as she could, "Put me down for three nights a week!"

The young man took his girl to an open-air theater on their first date. After the first act he found it necessary to excuse himself. He asked the usher where the men's room was located and was told, "Turn left by that big oak tree, go straight ahead about twenty yards, then right another five."

In a few minutes he returned to his seat.

"Has the second act started yet?" he asked his date.

"You ought to know," she said coolly. "You were in it!"

"It was terrible, mother," complained the curvy teenager. "I had to change my seat four times at the movies."

"Some man started bothering you?" asked mother.

"Yes," said the girl, rolling her eyes. "Finally!"

They hadn't seen their friend in nearly five years—not since he had received a movie contract and moved to Hollywood. Now he was back visiting the Midwestern town where he had lived as a boy.

His friends were pleased to see him and anxious to learn if all the wild stories they had heard about life in Hollywood were really true.

"Nonsense," he replied. "Hollywood is no different than any other American city. Life out there is normal and well ordered: A movie actress isn't all that different from a legal clerk in Minneapolis or Milwaukee; a movie director is no more eccentric than the office manager of one of the businesses right here.

"Take my own case: I'm up early every morning and at the studio by eight-fifteen. I work a full, hard day and I'm home every evening by six. After dinner, I read the evening paper, and I'm in bed before ten.

"Why just the other day, I was saying to my wife and girlfriend as I handcuffed them to the headrest of our bed...."

In Hollywood, when a movie star tells a child a bedtime story, it usually goes like this: "Once upon a time, there was a Mama Bear, a Papa Bear, and a Baby Bear by a previous marriage...."

When the tabloid reporters speak of anticipating a blessed event in Hollywood, it invariably means the arrival of divorce papers.

Two young starlets were discussing the remarriage of a well-known Hollywood couple. "Well," said the one to the other, "I guess it was just another one of those divorces that didn't pan out."

We know a handsome young man of undeniable talent who went to Hollywood because he wanted to make love under the stars.

Johnny, a fourth-grader from Hollywood, was very proud because he had the most parents at the P.T.A. meeting.

Hollywood marriages are evidently losing their reputation for brevity: We've just heard about a producer who liked one of his wives so well that he decided to hold her over for a second week.

Then there was the very attractive, but somewhat confused, young hopeful who told the movie producer that she wanted to be a Stollywood harlot.

There's a new jewelry store in Hollywood whose business has suddenly leaped ahead of all the competition: It rents wedding rings.

We know a Hollywood actress who is an expert housekeeper: Every time she gets divorced, she keeps the house.

Hollywood is the only place we know where you can live happily and get married forever after.

The successful young rock star ordered a very expensive custom-made suit, but was wholly dissatisfied with the finished garment. "I told you to make the pants snug," he angrily remarked to the tailor. "I want them tight enough to show my sex."

"But sir," the tailor protested, "but if they were any tighter, they'd show your religion."

When her friends got word that Sabrina, a beautiful young starlet, had married Horace, an elderly producer worth two hundred million dollars, they all sent her Get Will cards.

Some people are music lovers. Other can love without it.

A true music lover is a man who puts his *ear* to the keyhole when he hears a girl singing in the tub.

Lots of women can be had for a song: the wedding march.

Whether or not a woman can be had for a song frequently depends on a man's pitch.

A good golfer has to break eighty, but a stripper only has to bust thirty-six.

You won't read about it in *Time Out*, but we occasionally go to a club where the music is so bad that when a waiter drops a tray everybody gets up and starts dancing.

Two sexy young starlets were sipping Stingers at the Formosa, in Hollywood.

"You remember that backless, frontless, sideless evening gown I wore to the premiere last week?" asked the first.

"Sure," said her friend, "it was a sensation!"

"I just found out it's a belt."

Advice to the exhausted: When wine, women, and song become too much for you, give up the singing.

Monkey Business

The police were investigating the mysterious death of a prominent businessman who had jumped from a window of his eleventh-story office. His private secretary could offer no explanation for the action, but said that her boss had been acting peculiarly ever since she started working for him a month ago.

"After my very first week on the job," she said, "I received a five-hundred-dollar raise. At the end of the second week, he called me into his private office, gave me a lovely black cashmere turtleneck, and said, 'This is for a beautiful, efficient secretary.'

"At the end of third week, he gave me a gorgeous pair of Manolo Blahnik pumps in my size. Then, this afternoon he called me into his private office again, presented me with this huge diamond bracelet, and asked me if I would consider making love to him and what it would cost.

"I told him I would, and because he had been so nice to me, it would only cost him a hundred, even though I was charging all the other boys in the office two hundred. That's when he jumped out the window."

"Who," raged the angry stockbroker. "told you that just because I've kissed you a few times you could loaf around the office and neglect your work?"

"The company attorney," answered his personal assistant.

One of the airlines recently introduced a special half-fare rate for women accompanying their husbands on business trips. Anticipating some valuable testimonials, the publicity department of the airline sent out letters to all the women who used the special rates, asking how they enjoyed their trip.

Responses are still pouring in, asking "What trip?"

One by one, the vice presidents of a large corporation were called into the boss' office. Then the junior executives were individually summoned. Finally the summer intern was brought in.

"I want the truth, Charles," the boss bellowed. "Have *you* been messing around with our accountant?"

"N-no, sir," the young man stammered. "I-I'd never do anything like that, sir!"

"All right, good," said the boss, "then *you* fire her."

"You know," said the office gossip to the knot of listeners around the water cooler. "I'd *never* say anything about Margaret unless I could say something good. And, brothers and sisters, is this *good....*"

After completing their shopping, Kelli and Serena were about to drive back to their apartment when Kelli realized that she'd forgotten to stop at the drugstore for birth-control pills. Rushing into the nearest pharmacy, she handed the prescription to the pharmacist. "Can you fill this quickly?" she asked. "I've got someone waiting in the car."

Then there was the clumsy file clerk who dropped her birth-control pills into the Xerox machine. It wouldn't reproduce for a month.

A handsome young production assistant we know enjoys telling us how the famous director he works for takes great pleasure in grabbing him by the knee when they go out together. "But yesterday," he confided over Mojitos, "she reached a new high."

Learning that several of his employees were tanking up on no-trace vodka Martinis during lunch hours, the wise company president issued the following memo:

"To all employees:

If you must drink during lunch, please drink whiskey. It is much better for our customers to know you're drunk than to think you're stupid."

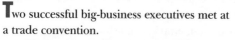

Two successful big-business executives met at a trade convention.

"So," said one, "how's business?"

"Well, you know how it is," replied the other. "Our line of work is like sex. When it's good, it's wonderful—and when it's bad, it's still pretty good!"

The young executive greeted his attractive boss warmly as he entered the office: "Good morning, Marge," he said, tossing his briefcase on his desk. "I had a dream about you last night."

Flattered but wishing to appear aloof, she casually inquired, "Oh, did you?"

"No," he replied. "I woke up too soon."

During the midmorning coffee break, the boss discovered a pair of very junior executives making love in the storeroom. "How can you explain this?" the boss steamed.

"Well," said Ms. Grayson, straightening her skirt, "neither of us drinks coffee."

Then there's the fast-rising executive who, on entering her newly decorated office, called her assistant onto the carpet because the young man forgot to order a couch.

It was a wild office party and—in the darkened mail room—two employees were making the most of it. "Oh, Jack," the curvy marketing VP sighed. "You never made love to me like this before. Is it because of the holiday spirit?"

"No," her partner replied, "it's because I'm Jonathan."

The morning after the office Christmas party, the husband woke up with an agonizing hangover. "I feel terrible," he complained.

"You should," said his wife. "You really made a fool of yourself last night."

"What did I do?"

"You got into a quarrel with your boss and he fired you."

"Well, he can go to hell."

"That's exactly what you told him."

"I did?" he said incredulously. "Good. Screw the old goat!"

"That's just what I did," his wife replied. "You go back to work on Monday."

When the handsome young personal assistant entered his boss' office one morning, she looked up from her mahogany desk and announced idly, "It's certainly going to be a beautiful day."

"I don't think so," replied the secretary. "The weather forecast is for snow."

"It's not going to snow!" contradicted the exec. "I'll lay you twelve to one."

"I'd rather not," the young man remarked. "That's my lunch hour!"

When the beautiful young intern failed to appear for the fourth straight day, her suspicious supervisor telephoned her apartment and demanded an explanation.

"I'm very sorry," she sighed breathlessly, "but I won't be in today."

"Well," he conjectured, "you must not be very happy in your present position."

"I'm very happy," she panted. "That's why I'm not coming to work."

Delighted by his good fortune, the handsome young man accepted a job as private secretary to a vice-president at a salary of $1,800 per week. But, arriving for work at nine o'clock the next morning, he was immediately summoned to the executive's office, where he learned that his responsibilities included making love to her. "I thought this might be part of the job," he sighed when they had finished. "But for $1,800 a week, I really can't object too much."

"Well, here's forty-five dollars for the past half hour," the executive said, reaching into her purse. "You're fired."

When Harry returned looking tanned and rested, his assistant asked him about his vacation.

"Well," he replied, "a friend of mine gave me the use of his hunting lodge—a quiet, secluded place. No night life, no parties, not another soul within a hundred miles."

"Did you enjoy yourself?" she asked.

"Who else?" he said.

Then there was the fellow who decided to start procrastinating but never got around to it.

The Fortune 500 CEO requested that the company's HR director screen the three attractive young women for the job of private secretary. Deciding to use a standard ploy, the personnel director asked each of the applicants the same question—"How much do two and two make?"

The first woman, a beautiful blonde, whispered "Four"; the second, a fetching brunette, responded with "Twenty-two"; while the third, a redhead with a twinkle in her eye, answered, "Four or twenty-two."

The following day, the consultant stopped by the CEO's office and reported his findings. "The first is solid and reliable," he opined. "The second has a vivid imagination but can't deal too well with reality. And the third is both clever and mature—she's the one I'd suggest we hire. What's your decision?"

"Well," the boss replied, after a moment of deep deliberation. "I think I want the one with the big tits."

Stunned by the incredible beauty of their new marketing director, the two senior partners resolved to make her adjustment to the firm their personal business. "It's up to us to teach her the difference between right and wrong," said the first.

"Agreed," said the second, adjusting his tie. "You teach her what's right."

"How did you spend the weekend?" the beautiful young executive asked her girlfriend.

"Fishing through the ice," her friend replied.

"Fishing through the ice? Whatever for?"

"Olives."

We're sure you've heard about the traveling salesman whose car broke down in a rain storm. He ran to the closest farmhouse and knocked on the door. A grizzled old farmer answered and the salesman pleaded for a place to stay the night.

"I can give ya a room," said the farmer, "but I ain't got no daughter fer ya to sleep with."

"Oh," said the salesman. "Well, how far is it to the next house?"

So then the ubiquitous traveling salesman said to the farmer, "Can you put me up for the night?"

Whereupon the farmer said, "Sure, but you'll have to sleep with my son."

"Good Lord," said the salesman, "I'm in the wrong joke!"

What must surely be the final version of the traveling salesman's gag has come our way. It concerns a hapless merchant on the move who ran out of gas on a lonely country road, trudged to the nearest farmhouse, and asked the young woman who came to the door if he could spend the night. Fearing becoming the punchline in a bad joke, the farmer stepped out from behind his daughter, promptly tied the man from head to toe, tossed him in the cellar, and called the police.

We know an insurance salesman who says his greatest successes are with young housewives who aren't adequately covered.

Shed a tear for the unfortunate shoe salesman with a lisp, who got slapped when he asked a miniskirted female customer to sit down while he "looked up her thize."

A traveling salesman we know writes passionate love letters to a beautiful farm girl in his territory. Her name is Sarah, but he always starts off his letters with: "Dear Hollyhock...."

We never understood this term of endearment till the other day, when we came across this in a gardening book: "HOLLYHOCK— *Does well in fence corners and behind barns, but not so well in beds.*"

"The Related Sale" was the subject of a pep talk given recently by the merchandizing manager of a drugstore chain. "For instance, if a customer wants razor blades," he told employees, "ask him how he's fixed for shaving cream and after-shave lotion. That way you can turn a small sale into a bigger one and earn a larger commission."

The youngest clerk was very impressed by the talk and decided to try the technique on his very next customer. This turned out to be a rather embarrassed gentleman who shyly requested a box of Kotex for his wife. Ten minutes later, the manager of the store was amazed to see the customer staggering out loaded down with assorted fishing equipment, tackle, nets, boots, and a one-man inflatable life raft. "What happened?!" the manager gasped, and the clerk modestly attributed his success to "The Related Sale."

"Related Sale!" exclaimed the manager. "But all he wanted was a box of—"

"I know. So I said, 'Look, mister, there isn't going to be much doing around your house this weekend. Why don't you take a fishing trip?'"

We spotted this ad in the personal column of a large metropolitan daily: "Gentleman who smokes, drinks, and carouses wishes to meet lady who smokes, drinks, and carouses. Object: smoking, drinking, and carousing."

The single-minded dedication required of those who apply themselves to the great advertising game is illustrated by the story of Harry and Joe, two Madison Avenue execs who met for lunch for the first time in months.

"Where," queried Harry, lifting his lunch and taking a sip, "has Charlie Harris been hanging out?"

"Haven't you heard? Charlie went to the Great Agency in the Sky."

"You're kidding!"

"Nope. He died last month."

"Good Lord! What did he have?"

"Nothing much," Joe said, reflectively. "A small toothpaste account, and a couple of department stores, but nothing worth going after."

A union official stomped over to an open lot where an excavator was being used. "A hundred men with shovels could be doing that job," he complained to the contractor.

"True," the builder retorted, "but why not a thousand men with teaspoons?"

A lively young advertising account exec wore tight knit dresses that showed off her figure, especially when she walked. Her hard-nosed boss motioned her into her office one afternoon and closed the door. Pointing to the young employee's tightly covered *derrière*, the older businesswoman asked, "Is that for sale?"

"Of course not!" the young woman snapped angrily, blushing in confusion.

Raising an eyebrow, the older woman replied quietly, "Then I suggest you quit advertising it."

On the first night of her fourth marriage, the bride turned to her husband and implored, "*Please*, darling, try to be patient with me in bed—I'm still a virgin."

"A *virgin*!" her mate exclaimed. "But you've been married three times before!"

"I know it's a little hard to believe, but it's the truth," she sighed sadly. "My first husband was a charming alcoholic, but he'd get loaded every night and by bedtime, he'd be dead to the world. My second husband was quite handsome, but on our wedding night, I discovered he was more attracted to my brother than to me. My third husband—the advertising executive—was a persuasive fellow, but he turned out to be a complete captive of his craft."

"What do you mean?" asked her astounded husband.

"Well," she said, "every night, all night long, he'd sit on the edge of the bed, telling me how great it was going to be...."

A *real-estate man's imperfections*
As a lover caused female rejections.
  "I'm deflated," he moaned.
  "They're erogenous-zoned,
But only for high-rise erections."

When Mr. Kreggemeier returned from Europe, his partner in a men's clothing store hung on his every word. "And I even was in a group that went to the Vatican," reminisced Kreggemeier, "where we were blessed by the Pope."

"The Pope!" exclaimed the other chap. "What does he look like?"

"A very pious man, reverent, spiritual, almost saintly," Kreggemeier answered, chin in hand and eyes to the ceiling. "I figure a size thirty-eight, short."

Then there was the guy who paid for a personal ad on an online matchmaking service for a wife and got two hundred replies, most of them from men, who wrote: "Please take mine."

Then there was the crooked crematory operator who sold the ashes to cannibals as "Instant People—Just Add Water!"

And of course you've heard about the pessimistic historian whose latest book has chapter headings that read "World War One," "World War Two," and "Watch This Space."

We know a waggish historian who says that George Washington was the only President who didn't blame the previous Administration for all of his troubles.

Playboys & Playmates

LeRoy Neiman

The prudish old maid found herself seated next to a sophisticated playboy at a formal affair. After a little, rather icy conversation, the lady attempted to dismiss the fellow with, "It's quite obvious that we do not agree on a single, solitary thing."

The playboy smiled. "Oh, I don't think that's quite true, madam," he said. "If you were to enter a bedroom in which there were two beds, and if, madam, there were a woman in one and a man in the other, in which bed would you sleep?"

"Well," the lady huffed indignantly, "with the woman, of course."

"You see, we agree," the playboy said, laughing. "So would I."

Then there was the playboy who suddenly decided to live a strictly moral life. First, he cut out smoking. Then he cut out liquor. Then he cut out swearing. Then he cut out women.

Now he's cutting out paper dolls.

We know of an overweight playboy who is unhappy about losing a hundred and five pounds last month. She was a beautiful blonde with a mind of her own.

A popular bachelor attached to the American Embassy in London had just returned from a weekend in the Midlands at a stately country home. When asked by a friend what sort of a time he had, he replied, "If the soup had been as warm as the wine, and the wine as old as the chicken, and the chicken as tender as the upstairs maid, and the upstairs maid as willing as the duchess, it would have been perfect."

She was, without question, the most beautiful woman he had ever seen in his life. He gulped down the last of his Martini and, without hesitation, walked to where she sat at the end of the bar.

"You must forgive my rudeness," he said, "but when I beheld you sitting here, the lights dancing in your hair like fireflies, I *had* to speak to you. I've never seen a woman as beautiful as you. I want to lay Manhattan at your feet, I want to pluck the stars from the sky for you—the very sight of you makes me feel capable of accomplishing these and a thousand other wondrous things. In fact, if you bid me welcome, we will fly this very night for Paris, then on to Venice, Rome, India, and finally Egypt for a trip down the Nile."

The young lady was utterly amazed by the handsome stranger who stood before her—bronzed face, hair prematurely graying at the temples, dark suit cut exactly so. She was quite literally speechless and could manage only to stammer, "Yes, well...."

"Then go prepare yourself, my Juliet, my Venus, my Helen of Troy. When you are ready, call me at the number on this card. My Rolls Royce will come for you and take you to my plane."

"Is this your private number?" she asked.

"Well," he said, "actually it's the delicatessen downstairs, but they'll call me."

We know an amorous millionaire who's terribly indiscreet, but so wealthy that he doesn't have to be. In fact, he begins each love letter to his girlfriends, "My Darling, and Ladies and Gentlemen of the Jury...."

A recent survey shows that the average young bachelor is more interested in high frequency than high fidelity.

A friend of ours claims to be the world's greatest lothario, and we're inclined to agree: He let us look at his carefully alphabetized little black book, and the forty-seventh entry was Annabelle Aarons.

Enervated by his life's hectic pace, the swinger determined to take a leisurely drive across the country. At first the pastoral sights pleased him, but by the time he got to Kansas, he was dying for some action. Pulling into the only gas station in a small town one Saturday evening, he asked the attendant, "Is there any nightlife in this town?"

"Not anymore," the station owner replied. "She moved to Chicago."

"Forgive me, Father," the embarrassed bachelor told his confessor. "I made love to a beautiful virgin last night."

"That's terrible," the cleric groaned. "Was it Cynthia Goodrich?"

"Please don't ask me that," the fellow pleaded.

"Was it the Carruthers girl?" the man of the cloth prodded him.

"I don't want to answer," he insisted.

"Well, was it Susan Fullerton?" the priest demanded.

"I simply refuse to tell you," the young chap declared firmly.

"All right, my son," the cleric sighed. "For admitting your guilt, you are forgiven, but you'd better see me again next week."

Leaving the church, the fellow met his best friend, who had waited for him outside. "How did your confession go?" the friend inquired.

"Not bad," the bachelor replied. "I got a week off and three new leads."

Sometimes when two's company, three's the result.

Most bachelors prefer girls who believe that children should be seen and not had.

The four men playing poker at the card table were being bothered by a fifth man, an irritating kibitzer. When the troublesome talker stepped into the next room to mix a drink, one of the players suggested, "This next hand let's make up a game nobody ever heard of—he won't know what the hell we're playing and maybe that will shut him up."

When the kibitzer returned, the dealer tore the top two cards in half and gave them to the man on his right. He tore the corners off the next three cards and placed them before the next player, face up. He tore the next five cards in quarters, gave fifteen pieces to the third man, four to himself, and put the last piece in the center of the table.

Looking intently at four small pieces of card in his hand, the dealer said, "I have a mingle, so I think I'll bet a dollar."

The second man stared at the pasteboards scattered before him. "I have a snazzle," he announced, "so I'll raise you a dollar."

The third man folded without betting and the fourth, after due deliberation, said, "I have a farfle, so I'll raise you two dollars."

The kibitzer shook his head slowly from side to side. "You're crazy," he said, "you're never going to beat a mingle and a snazzle with a lousy farfle."

A certain small New England town has had exactly the same population figure for the last half-century. This amazing condition is attributed to the fact that every time a baby is born, a man leaves town.

The man who is old enough to know better is always looking for a girl not quite that old.

Then there was the tidy fellow who never left his apartment in the morning without having his bed maid.

On impulse, the young man stopped at the flower shop and purchased a dozen roses for his girlfriend. When he presented them to her, she immediately tore off all her clothes and leaped onto the couch. "This is for the flowers," she announced, stretching languorously.

"Oh, come on," he replied, looking around. "Surely you have a vase somewhere in this apartment."

A friend of ours reports that he gave his girlfriend a diamond wristwatch, and the following night he gave her the works.

The best way to approach a woman with a past is with a present.

Breathes there a man with soul so dead,
Who's never to his playmate said:
"To hell with breakfast,
Come back to bed!"

As Mark fixed himself an Old-Fashioned while he waited for Peggy to get ready for their date, he could hear her singing in the shower.

"Sorry I'm so late," she finally called out to him, "but I was shopping and lost track of the time." Clutching a large towel about her, she edged into the room. "Would you like to see me in my new dress?" she asked.

Mark took appreciative note of her newly bathed charms straining at the confines of the barely adequate towel.

"I would like nothing better," he said with a smile.

A polite and rather timid young man, after buying his girlfriend a pair of Chanel felted wool and leather gloves as a birthday present, scrivened the following note to be sent along with them:

"Darling:

I hope you find these a welcome birthday gift, since you mentioned on our last date that you had lost your last pair. They are reversible, so if you get them soiled you can wear them inside out and thus wear them longer without having to wash them. I'm only sorry I cannot be there at your party to watch your smiling face as you try them on."

He left the note with the saleswoman, who promptly sent it off with the wrong gift: a pair of silk underwear.

It's a great life if you're weak enough to enjoy it thoroughly.

Men who are getting on in years should console themselves with the thought that when they get too old to set bad examples, they can always start giving advice.

While down South on a visit, the young Yankee made a date with a local woman he met at the pharmacy. When he called for her at her home, she was clad in a low-cut, tight-fitting gown. He remarked, "That's certainly a beautiful dress."

"Sho 'nough?" she asked, blushing.

"It sure does," he replied.

"Never put off until tomorrow what you can do today," a wise man once said, "because if you enjoy it today, you can do it again tomorrow."

---

*"**M**en seldom make passes*
At girls who wear glasses,"
So Dorothy Parker has said.
She said it quite rightly,
Specs are unsightly,
But no one wears glasses to bed.

A handsome PE instructor was having a seltzer with a twist at his neighborhood bar, when a dazzling woman approached him and began a flirtatious exchange. After a some time, she made a familiar proposition.

"No, thank you," he said politely. "This might sound strange to you, but I'm keeping myself pure until I meet the girl I love."

"That's certainly admirable, but it must be very difficult," the woman sympathized.

"Actually, it isn't as hard on me as you might think," he said. "But it has my wife pretty upset, that's for sure."

A man knows he's getting old when he runs out of gas after he runs out of gas.

A man knows he's old when his dreams about girls are reruns.

A man knows he's reached old age when he can't take "Yes" for an answer.

And, of course, you've heard about the Scotsman who wore a maxikilt. We're not sure if he was just trying to keep up with the styles or bragging.

You've undoubtedly heard about the number of magazines required to fill a baby carriage: a PLAYBOY, a *Mademoiselle,* and *Time.*

Many a young tomato has been cultivated by an old rake.

A friend of ours who rarely sleeps alone observes knowingly that one good turn usually gets most of the blanket.

A friend of ours says he's read so much about the terrible effects of smoking that he's decided to give up reading.

The golfer confidently eyed the next hole and remarked to his caddy, "This should be good for a long drive and a putt." His swing, however, hit the sod and pushed the ball only a few feet.

"Well," said the caddy, "looks like it's time for one hell of a putt."

"I'd like to buy some gloves for my girlfriend," the young man said to the attractive woman behind the counter, "but I don't know her size."

"Does this help?" she asked, placing her hand in his.

"Oh, yes," he answered. "Her hands are just slightly smaller than yours."

"Will there be anything else?" the clerk queried as she wrapped the gloves.

"Now that you mention it," he replied, "she also needs a bra and panties...."

"If I had my life to live over again," mused the old gentleman, "I'd make all the same mistakes—but I'd make them sooner."

And then there was the fifty-year-old bachelor who woke up one morning feeling like a twenty-year-old. Unfortunately for him, he couldn't find one who was willing.

"All I need in an apartment," says a bachelor we know, "is enough room to lay my head—and a few good friends."

The couple stepped up to the desk clerk of one of the city's nicer hotels. "I'd like a room with a bath for my wife and myself," said the young man.

"I'm terribly sorry, sir," said the clerk, "but the only room available doesn't have a bath—only a shower."

"Will that be all right with you, darling?" the man asked the young woman at his side.

"Sure, mister," she said.

"If I'm not in bed by ten o'clock," said one female barfly to the other, "I'm going home."

A flashy Mercedes-Benz roared up to the curb, where a beautiful young woman stood waiting for a taxi.

"Hi," said the gentleman at the wheel. "I'm going west."

"How wonderful," came the cool reply. "Bring me back an orange."

A most attractive redhead, window-shopping on Fifth Avenue, became aware of a well-dressed gentleman following her at a short distance. Somewhat flustered, she accidentally dropped her handbag and he immediately retrieved it for her.

"I dropped that bag accidentally," she said. "I want you to understand that I am not the type of girl you can pick up."

The gentleman smiled and said, "Madam, I am most assuredly not picking you up. I am picking you out."

Hgh and Ghg, a pair of newly arrived Martians, stood on a New York street corner leering at the traffic light across the way.

"Keep away from her or I'll knock your heads together," said Ghg to Hgh. "I saw her first."

"So what?" Hgh responded. "She winked at *me!*"

Just then the signal changed from GO to STOP. The Martians stalked off disgustedly.

"Some women can be such teases!" Hgh muttered.

"**D**id you pick up any Italian on your vacation?" the accountant asked her girlfriend from sales as they waited for the coffee to brew.

"I sure did," enthused the recently returned saleswoman.

"Let me hear you say some words."

"I didn't learn any words."

The other evening in a bar, a shy friend of ours spotted a really attractive young woman drinking alone a few stools away. He moved over and sat next to her, but was embarrassed about striking up a conversation with a total stranger. Instead, when she ordered her next drink, he ordered one of the same for himself and paid for both of them. She nodded her thanks, but still he could find no way to begin a conversation. This continued for nearly an hour, and the consumption of four more rounds by both of them.

Finally, emboldened by the liquor, and aware that the girl seemed to be getting a bit restless and might soon drift away and out of his life, he was horrified to hear himself blurt out, "Do you ever go to bed with men?"

"I never have before," she said, smiling, "but I believe you've talked me into it, you silver-tongued devil!"

A fellow we know is so jaded he has dropped all the subtle preliminaries usually expected by a girl in favor of the direct approach, which occasionally leads to trouble. For instance, we recently overheard the following conversation with a young woman he had just met at a cocktail party.

"I'm a man of few words. Will you or won't you?"

"Your apartment or mine?" the woman responded.

"Well," he said in an exasperated tone, "if there's going to be such a lot of discussion about it, let's forget the whole damn thing!"

A handsome young man who was cruising in his open convertible stopped beside an attractive young woman and invited her jump in. As she got in, she slyly informed him that she was a witch and could make him turn into anything she wished.

"Go ahead and try!" he answered with a smile; she leaned against him and whispered something in his ear. And sure enough, he turned into a motel.

Two industrial robots from the Toyota factory decided to leave the shop to investigate some of the human pleasures they had been hearing about. After several hours of individual exploration, one noticed the other standing on a corner in front of a mailbox and a fire-alarm box.

"Looks like we're going to get some action," said the new arrival, crossing the street.

"Forget it," answered the other under his breath. "The dumpy green one doesn't say a word, and as soon as you touch the red one, she screams her head off."

For five consecutive nights, the young man at the bar witnessed the same inexplicable phenomenon: Attractive women, whether alone or in groups of two or three, would wander in and soon be picked up by a dumpy little bald guy with a broken nose sitting in a corner booth. "I can't understand it," the man grumbled to the bartender after the sixth such incident. "I don't see how that guy does it."

"Me neither, Mac," said the sympathetic barkeep as he washed the mugs. "I've been watching him for weeks. He's not exactly handsome, he's a lousy dresser, and he hardly ever says a word. He just sits there, night after night, licking his eyebrows...."

As Patsy and Liz were strolling along the wharf one night in San Francisco, they noticed two strapping young sailors following them.

"Aren't those sailors out after hours?" Liz observed.

"I sure hope so," her friend replied.

We approve of this tactful variation on the age-old delicate question: One asks his date for the evening if she'd like to join him for breakfast. Receiving an affirmative reply, he then asks, "Shall I call you or just give you a little nudge?"

He'd shown her his etchings, and just about everything else of interest in his apartment and, as Jack poured the last of the Martinis into their glasses, he realized that the moment of truth with Louise had arrived. He decided to address the matter head-on.

"Tell me," he said, fingering a lock of her hair, "do you object to making love?"

She turned her lovely eyes up to his. "That's something I've never done," she said.

"Never made love?" cried Jack, appalled at the thought.

"No, silly," she said in rebuke. "Never objected."

We have nothing but admiration for the flair displayed by one beautiful woman in rejecting the advances of a playboy she had just met. She was attending a dinner party at a friend's apartment when her neighbor at the table propositioned her with, "Come on, Susan. Let's live for tonight."

She appraised him for a moment before responding, "Yes, but suppose we survive?"

"**H**ow about joining me for a cozy weekend in a four-star hotel?" he whispered in his date's ear.

"I'm afraid," she said, "that my newfound awareness of your self-avowed proclivities in the esoteric aspects of sexual congress precludes even the contemplation of such erotic confrontation."

"I don't get it," he said, looking confused.

"Exactly," she smiled.

"**I**f I refuse to go to bed with you," she said incredulously, "will you really commit suicide?"

"That," the oblivious playboy said grandly, "has been my usual procedure."

"**S**ay when," he said as he poured the Mojito for, and snuggled a little bit closer to, his date.

"Right after this drink," came the reply.

The farmer's daughter had gone to town to do some shopping and, on her way home after dark, encountered one of the neighboring farm boys returning from a day at the market. The two had walked together for a while when the girl said, "I'm almost afraid to be alone with you like this—you might try to take advantage of me."

"Take advantage of you?" the handsome lad gulped. "Here I am, carrying a pitchfork and a chicken in one hand, a washtub in the other and leading a goat. I could hardly take advantage of you."

"Well," she continued, "you could always stick the pitchfork in the ground, tie the goat to it and put the chicken under the washtub, couldn't you?"

"I've heard you're very shy," the young swain said to his date as they strolled through the moonlit park. "But you needn't worry about making conversation. I've devised a simple code that eliminates the need for talk: If you nod your head, it means you want me to hold your hand, and if you smile, it means you'd like me to kiss you. Isn't that easy? What do you think of my plan?"

She laughed in his face.

In the midst of one of the wildest parties he'd ever been to, the young man noticed a very prim and very beautiful girl sitting quietly apart from the rest of the revelers. Approaching her, he introduced himself and said, "I'm afraid you and I don't really fit in with this crowd. Why don't I take you home?"

"Fine," said the girl, smiling up at him. "Where do you live?"

The young couple had met early on New Year's Eve and began to really hit it off as the party progressed. "Listen," he finally said to her, "it's almost midnight—why don't we end the old year with a kiss?"

"Sounds good," replied his new friend. "Then we can go to your place and start the new one off with a bang!"

The evening had been going very well, but now, at the critical moment, the woman wouldn't let her date into her apartment. Worst of all, her excuse was thin: "My roommate's home."

Playfully, her date said, "In other words, I'm supposed to ignore this doormat that says *Welcome?*"

"Of course, silly!" she laughed. "There certainly isn't room enough for us on that little thing."

"**H**ow do you do so well with girls?" the frustrated sophomore asked his roommate.

"You've got to have a gimmick," the roommate responded. "For instance, I've painted a white circle on the dashboard of my car. My dates always ask about it. From there, I turn the conversation to white things in general, then to things symbolized by the color white, like virginity; and after that, it's easy to talk them into it."

"That sounds simple enough," the slightly clueless friend agreed. That evening, he painted a white circle on his dashboard before picking up his date.

"That's unique—to have a white circle painted on your dash," the girl said, soon after she got into the car.

"Yes, isn't it?" the young fellow replied. "Do you want to screw?"

The lonely executive had spent the whole evening at a dinner party complaining to her handsome neighbor at the dining room table about her husband's constant visits to his mother. "In fact, that's where he is tonight," said the woman. "What would you do if you were in my place?"

"Well," her neighbor smiled, "let's go over to your place and I'll show you."

The young man sat on the park bench with his date. He was certain his charming words and manner would win her over, just as they had so many others in the past.

"Some moon out tonight," he murmured.

"There certainly is," she agreed.

"Some really bright stars in the sky."

She nodded.

"Some dew on the grass."

"*Some* do," she said indignantly, "but not me!"

After repeatedly warding off her date's amorous advances during the evening, the young woman decided to put her foot down. "See here," she shouted indignantly. "This is positively the last time I'm going to tell you 'no'!"

"Good!" exclaimed her date. "Now we're getting somewhere."

Miss Bradshaw, a high school teacher who had been saving for several years, was finally off on her long-anticipated transatlantic cruise. Aboard ship, she wrote:

"Dear Diary:

"*Monday.* I felt singularly honored this evening. The Captain asked me to dine at his table.

"*Tuesday.* I spent the entire morning on the bridge with the Captain.

"*Wednesday.* The Captain made proposals to me unbecoming an officer and a gentleman.

"*Thursday.* Tonight the Captain threatened to sink the ship if I do not give in to his indecent proposals.

"*Friday.* This afternoon I saved sixteen hundred lives."

A lovely young Christian-school teacher of unsullied virtue was invited to go for a ride in the country with the gym instructor, whom she admired. Under a tree on the bank of a quiet lake, she struggled with her conscience and with the gym instructor and finally gave in to the latter. Sobbing uncontrollably, she asked her seducer, "How can I ever face my students again, knowing I have sinned twice?"

"Twice?" asked the young man, somewhat confused.

"Why, yes," said the sweet teacher, wiping a tear from her eye. "We're going to do it again, aren't we?"

An interloper at a meeting of the Society of Mayflower Descendants put the august group in a bit of a tizzy when he described his heritage by saying, "Actually, I'm descended from a long and successful line my mother fell for."

If Dorothy Parker will forgive us the paraphrase, it is our observation that men often make passes at girls who drain glasses.

A young American was wandering through the Montmartre section when he came upon a lovely young Parisienne who looked for all the world like Brigitte Bardot in her prime.

"Can I buy you a drink?" he asked, by way of striking up a conversation.

"No thank you," she said. "I don't drink."

"What about a little dinner with me in my hotel room?"

"No, I don't believe that would be proper," she said.

Having had no success with the indirect approach, the young man pressed directly to the point: "I am charmed by your beauty, *mademoiselle,* and will give you anything your heart desires if you will spend the night with me."

"Oh, no, no, *monsieur,* I could never do a thing like that!"

"Tell me," the young man said, laughing. "Don't you ever do anything the slightest bit improper?"

"*Oui,*" said the French girl with a smile. "I frequently tell lies."

A lovely southern belle we know is such a langorously slow talker that by the time she got through assuring a friend of ours that she wasn't that kind of girl, she was.

The inexperienced young man had heard that a good way to arouse sexual desire in a woman who proved impervious to the more usual forms of wooing was to forthrightly place her hand on his organ. Having parked with a date for more than an hour in the local lovers' lane, with nothing to show for it but some demure kisses, he decided to try this new technique. The response was instantaneous: The girl berated him with the longest stream of invectives he'd ever heard. Stunned, he tried to reply, but she refused to listen, insisting, instead, that he take her home at once.

As he pulled up in front of her house, she again started shouting imprecations. Finally, out of breath, she demanded, "Well, do you have anything to say for yourself?!"

"Yes, I do," was his pained reply. "Please let go."

Then there was the fellow who got badly scratched up fighting for his girlfriend's honor—turns out she wanted to keep it.

A man will often take a woman to his retreat in order to make advances.

The shy young man and his date were parked under a full moon. Placing his hand on her thigh, he whispered, "I love you."

With a deep sigh, the girl replied, "A little higher."

"I love you," came the falsetto reply.

We know a girl who hates losing her heart to a man, but who loves having him search for it.

A keyboardist friend of ours tells us the only thing better than roses on your piano is tulips on your organ.

Fred's convertible glided to a halt on the edge of the road.

"I suppose you're going to pull the old 'out of gas' routine," said his date.

"No," said Fred, "I'm going to pull the 'here after' routine."

"The 'here after' routine—what's that?" she asked.

"If you're not here after what I'm here after, then you're going to be here after I'm gone."

A friend of ours was at the bar one evening and overheard the following conversation.

"First, I'm going to buy you a few drinks and get you a little tight," said the guy.

"Oh no you won't," said the girl.

"Then I'm going to take you to dinner and ply you with a few more drinks."

"Oh no you won't."

"Then I'm going to take you to my apartment and keep serving you drinks."

"Oh no you won't."

"Then I'm going to make passionate love to you."

"Oh no, you won't!"

"And I'm not going to take any precautions either," said the guy.

"Oh yes you are!" said the girl.

On the Road

LeRoy Neiman

Overheard in a Corvette showroom: "This model has a top speed of a hundred and fifty-five miles per hour, and she'll stop on a dime."

"What happens then?"

"A small putty knife emerges and scrapes you gently off the windshield."

A friend informs us that the best way to cut off a cat's tail is to repossess his Jaguar.

The car sped off the highway, went through the guardrail, rolled down a cliff, bounced off a tree, and finally shuddered to a stop. A passing motorist, who had witnessed the entire accident, helped the miraculously unharmed driver out of the wreck.

"Holy shit!" he exclaimed. "Are you drunk?!"

"Of course," said the man, brushing the dirt from his suit-front. "What the hell you think I am—a stunt driver?"

If, as the scientists say, sex is such a driving force, why is so much of it nowadays found parked?

A friend of ours who is hooked on classic automobiles bought a vintage electric car the other day. It cost him ten thousand dollars—five for the car and five for the extension cord.

We know a superstitious sports-car enthusiast who, upon hearing that Saint Christopher—patron saint of automobile drivers and bachelors—had been decanonized, immediately switched to a Ralph Nader medal.

"I take the next turn, don't I?" asked the driver of the car.

The muffled reply from the backseat: "Like hell you do!"

The convertible glided silently to a stop on a lonely country road.

"Out of gas," he said, with a sly smile.

"Yes, I thought you might be," said his date, as she opened her purse and pulled out a hip flask.

"All right!" he said. "What do you have in there—Scotch? Bourbon?"

"Premium unleaded," she replied.

We've just heard about a new club called AAA-AA for people who are driven to drink.

In a whiskey it's age, in a cigarette it's taste, and in a sports car it's impossible.

The highway patrolman stopped a speeding car and, noticing the motorist's inebriated condition, arrested the man and delivered a stern lecture on the dangers of driving drunk. "Do you realize that you were going over seventy miles an hour?" the officer demanded.

"I know," the driver explained. "I wanted to get home before I had an accident."

A taxi driver was cruising for a fare when a pregnant woman, crossing against a red light, walked right in front of his cab. He slammed on the brakes and yelled indignantly out the window, "You better watch out, lady, or you'll get knocked *down*, too."

We know a modern Cinderella who, at the stroke of midnight, turns into a motel.

The angry woman's voice made the hotel manager wince. "I'm up here in room 1510," she ranted over the phone, "and I want you to know there is a man walking around in his room across the way with not one stitch of clothes on and his shades are up and... well, it's a shocking way to run a hotel!"

"I'll send the house detective up right away, madam," the manager assured her, and motioned for his minion of the law to scoot upstairs and see what the hassle was about.

The detective entered the woman's room, peered across the way, and said, "You're right, madam, he hasn't got any clothes on, but his window sill covers him from the waist down no matter where he is in his room."

"Oh yeah?" yelped the lady. "Stand on the bed!"

The house detective had been told to search the luggage belonging to the guest in room 1013 for any property belonging to the hotel.

"Did you find any towels in his suitcase?" asked the manager.

"Not a one," replied the detective, "but I did find a chambermaid in his grip."

A hotel reservations clerk we know recently got an email that read: "Do you have any accommodations where I can put up with my wife?"

Some of the best bedtime stories can be found in motel registers.

The proprietor of a combination dude ranch and resort hotel, the Westward Ho, found his business, which had been slow, suddenly booming after he hired a new bus driver to meet all incoming trains. Curious as to how the man managed to bring in so much new business, the owner questioned him about it.

"Ah really don't know," answered the Alabama native. "When that train comes chuggin' in, all ah do is hollah, 'Free bus to the Westward Ho House' and they all come pilin' in."

We just heard about the expensive new Miami Beach hotel that's so exclusive that Room Service has an unlisted number.

The young man-about-town enjoyed the lush life but couldn't always afford it, and so he huffily walked out of the Miami Beach hotel when he found out a room, meals, and golf privileges came to five hundred dollars a day. He registered across the street at an equally elegant hotel, where the same could be had for only a hundred dollars. The following morning he went down to the golf course and asked Scotty, the pro, to sell him a couple of golf balls. "Sure," said Scotty. "That'll be seventy-five dollars apiece."

"What?" exclaimed the bachelor. "In the hotel across the street they only charge a dollar a ball!"

"Naturally," replied the pro. "Over there they get you by the rooms."

Most major cities have a "dial-a-prayer" number for anyone requiring religious reassurance in the form of a brief, prerecorded sermon. Now there's talk of establishing a similar number for atheists. When you dial it, no one answers.

Two couples were enjoying their vacation together at a resort hotel. They were in the middle of a game of Scrabble in the lobby when a thunderstorm cut off the hotel's electricity, leaving little to do but retire to their rooms. Will was a rather devout chap, so before getting into bed with his companion, he said his prayers. As he got under the covers, the lights suddenly went on and he discovered he was in the wrong room. He instantly jumped up and dashed for the hallway. "You're too late!" called the girl from the bed. "My boyfriend doesn't pray."

The Texas oil millionaire, an old-time wildcatter who had been so busy making money all his life that he'd never had time to learn to read and write, took the pen from the hotel clerk and signed the register with an X. Then, after a thoughtful glance at the blonde he had picked up in a nearby cocktail lounge, he drew a circle around the X.

"I've had people sign their name with an X before," remarked the curious clerk, "but what's the circle for?"

"Shucks, sonny," whispered the oilman. "When a man checks into a strange hotel with a gal he's just met, y'all can't expect him to use his right name!"

Then there were the two honeymooners who wanted to fly United, but the flight attendant wouldn't let them.

A friend of ours who flies business class a good deal says that his pet peeve is when a hot flight attendant checks to make sure he's all buckled in and then asks, "Is there anything you'd like?"

Many a man who thinks he's going on a maiden voyage with a girl finds out later from her lawyer that it was a shakedown cruise.

After checking into the large motel complex, the self-styled evangelist read in his room for several hours, then sauntered over to the bar, where he struck up a conversation with the pretty bartender. After she had finished working, they shared a few drinks and then retired to his room. But when the evangelist began removing her blouse, she seemed to have second thoughts. "Are you sure this is all right?" she asked. "I mean, you're a holy man."

"My dear," he replied, "it is written in the Bible."

She took him at his word, and the two spent a very pleasant night together. The next morning, however, as the girl was preparing to leave, she said, "You know, I don't remember the part of the Bible you mentioned last night. Could you show it to me?"

In response, the evangelist took the Gideon Bible from the night stand, opened the cover, and pointed to the flyleaf, on which someone had inscribed, "The bartender puts out."

During her first visit to Las Vegas, the lovely, if somewhat inexperienced, young schoolteacher readily succumbed to the advances of the first man she met—a bellboy. Following their frenzied lovemaking, she breathed in his ear, "Wouldn't it be more discreet if you got me a room where the door would stay closed?"

"Yes, ma'am," he said. "But this isn't your room— it's the elevator."

The forgetful professor had left his umbrella in his hotel room when checking out; he noticed it on the way to the train station and, still having time to spare, he hurried back. He found the room and was about to ask a passing chambermaid to open it for him, when he became aware of voices within and realized that in the brief time since his departure, the room had been let to new occupants.

"Whose little baby are you?" asked a youthful male voice from behind the door, and the question was followed by the sound of kisses and a girlish giggle.

"Your little baby," said the youthful female voice.

"And whose little hands are these?" asked the boy.

"Your little hands," responded the girl, with more giggles and more kisses following.

"And whose little feet are these?" More kisses and giggles of delight. "And whose little knees... and whose little...."

"When you get to an umbrella," said the professor through the door, "it's mine!"

A wealthy gentleman was badly bitten by bugs while riding on a certain railway line. Arriving at his destination, he wrote the company an indignant letter and received a prompt reply. It was, said the letter, the first complaint the company had ever had of this nature. Inquiry had failed to reveal any explanation for this unprecedented occurrence. Nevertheless, a number of new precautions were being taken to make absolutely certain such an unfortunate incident never happened again. The letter was signed by the CEO of the railway.

The gentleman was well satisfied with this reply and was returning it to its envelope when a slip of paper fell out onto the floor. The hastily scribbled note on it read: "Send this guy the bug letter."

While visiting New York City, a lovely French girl found herself out of money just as her visa expired. Unable to buy an airplane ticket back to France, she was in despair until an enterprising sailor made her a sporting proposition. "My ship is sailing tonight," he said. "I'll smuggle you aboard, hide you down in the hold, and provide you with a mattress, blankets, and food. All it will cost you is a little love."

The girl consented and late that night the sailor snuck her on board his vessel. Twice each day, thereafter, the sailor smuggled a large tray of food below decks, took his pleasure with the French stowaway, and departed. The days turned into weeks and the weeks might have turned into months, if the captain hadn't noticed the sailor carrying food below one evening and followed him. After witnessing this unique bit of barter, he waited until the sailor had departed and then confronted the girl, demanding an explanation. She told him the whole story. "Hmm," mused the captain. "A clever arrangement, and I must say I admire that young seaman's ingenuity. However, miss, I feel it is only fair to tell you that this is the Staten Island Ferry."

When a smart girl travels by train, she gives the boys in the club car a wide berth.

On the old Concorde, you knew you were moving faster than sound when the flight attendant slapped your face before you could get a word out.

"Your fare, ma'am," requested the handsome train conductor. She smiled at him sweetly and replied, "You're not so bad yourself."

The prudish landlady suspected that her comely new boarder was breaking the no-men-upstairs rule of the dwelling. Finally, the busybody stormed up to the young woman's room, banged on the door, and called out, "Miss Reynolds, are you entertaining gentlemen in your room?"

"I must be," came the reply. "They all keep coming back for more!"

The pretty young woman approached the ship's steward. "Can you tell me where I might find the captain?" she asked.

"The captain is forward, miss," he replied.

"That's all right," she said. "This is a pleasure cruise, isn't it?"

During the frantic rush hour on a New York subway train, a lecherous old man pressed close to a pretty young commuter and whispered in her ear, "You know, you're rather a tasty morsel."

"And do you know," she replied angrily, kicking him in the balls, "that it's impolite to eat with your hands?"

The cheery voice of the stewardess came over the airplane's intercom: "Good afternoon, ladies and gentlemen, this is your stewardess, Agnes Hotchkiss. I have some bad news and some good news to report.

"First the bad news. Your pilot and copilot are both drunk. There's been a malfunction in the radio and we've lost contact with the field. We're three hundred miles off course and expect to run into some heavy turbulence over the Rocky Mountains. And it appears that we have an insufficient fuel supply to reach an alternate airport.

"And now for the good news. We're making very good time."

There's a wonderful new French airline that is almost completely automated. You push a button and out comes your seat belt. You push a button on the seat belt and out comes your pillow. You push a button on your pillow and out comes the hostess. You push a button on the hostess and out come your teeth.

While dancing with a dapper Englishman, the American girl's brooch became unfastened and slid down the back of her gown.

She told her escort about it and asked him to retrieve the lost article. Somewhat embarrassed, but determined to please, he reached cautiously down the back of her gown. After a moment, he said, "Awfully sorry, but I can't seem to locate it."

"Try further down," she advised. He did, beginning to blush. Still no brooch. "Down still further," she ordered.

Looking around and discovering that he was being watched by every couple on the dance floor, the Englishman blushed even more deeply and confided in an undertone, "I feel a perfect ass."

"Never mind that!" she snapped angrily. "Just get the brooch!"

The visiting American was quite upset by his sudden drop in popularity. During his first two weeks in England, he had been invited everywhere, feted and entertained. Now, quite suddenly, his phone no longer jingled and no invitations crowded his mailbox. Perplexed, he called his friend, Reginald.

"Reggie, you can speak frankly with me, what's happened? I'm being virtually ostracized."

"Well, old boy," Reggie replied, "you'll remember that fox hunt you went on last weekend? Here in England it's customary to cry *'Tally ho!'* when you sight the fox—not, I'm afraid, 'There goes the little son of a bitch!'"

Three Frenchmen were discussing the meaning of the word *savoir-faire*. The first explained, "If you come home and discover your wife in another man's arms and you say, 'Excuse me,' that's *savoir-faire*."

"No, no," said another who was slightly older and more experienced, "that's not quite right. If you come home and find your wife in another man's arms and you say, 'Excuse me, proceed,' that's *savoir-faire*!"

The third Frenchman was still older and wiser, and he said, with a smile, "I'm afraid neither of you really understands the full meaning of the word. If you come home and discover your wife in the arms of another man and you say, 'Excuse me, proceed,' and he proceeds, then *he* has *savoir-faire*."

Lord Cramsfedder was startled out of his sleep by his trusted valet, Gordon.

"Oh, M'lord, there's a bounder in congress with her Ladyship," announced the servant.

Lord Cramsfedder leaped out of his bed, hastily slipped into his robe, and grabbed his fowling piece from the mantle. Together they proceeded upstairs on tiptoe, and cautiously pushed open the door to Her Ladyship's boudoir. The situation was immediately obvious. The outraged husband lifted the weapon, aimed carefully, and blasted away with both barrels.

When the smoke had cleared, Gordon looked in. "Oh, sir," he cried out, his voice filled with admiration, "a sportsman ever! You got him on the rise."

At breakfast one morning Lady Cribblesfram suggested to His Lordship that since their son, Reginald, was fast approaching manhood, someone should be telling him "about the birds and bees."

Lord Cribblesfram did not welcome discussion on matters so delicate, but he recognized a father's duty and so, that evening after dinner, he summoned his son to his study.

"Er... ahem... Reginald," he began uneasily, "Lady Cribblesfram and I both feel it is time you and I had a man-to-man talk on the subject of... uh... the birds and bees."

"Yes, pater," said Reginald brightly.

"Son, do you remember our trip to Paris last summer?"

"Yes, sir."

"And do you remember our visit to the Folies Bergère?"

"I do, pater."

"You will then, perhaps, remember our drinking with the two lovely ladies from the Folies?"

"I do, indeed, pater."

"And afterward, you remember our taking them to our hotel and what we did there?"

"Yes, sir."

"Well, son," said Lord Cribblesfram, wiping the perspiration from his brow. "It's very much like that with the birds and bees, too."

The French executive was traveling home by rail from a business conference in Paris. As he pulled aside the curtains of his berth, he discovered two beautiful girls there. A glance at their tickets told him that the girls were in the wrong car. Distressed, the beauties flashed him warm smiles and asked if they might stay where they were.

"My dear ladies," explained the executive, "I am a married man, a pillar of my community, and scandal has never touched me. One of you," he concluded, "will have to leave."

Three French boys, ages eight, ten, and twelve, were walking together down a Paris street and, passing an open window where a young bride and groom were consummating their marriage, stopped to watch. "Observe!" said the eight year old. "That lady and gentleman are fighting!"

"You are mistaken," said the ten year old, both older and more sophisticated than his comrade. "They are making love."

"*Oui*," said the twelve year old. "And badly!"

There was a young lady from France,
Who decided to just "take a chance."
For an hour or so,
She just "let herself go."
And now all her sisters are aunts.

A pair of good friends, Frenchmen both, were strolling down the Champs-Élysées one balmy afternoon when they spied two women approaching.

"*Sacré bleu*, Pierre," cried out the one in dismay. "Here come my wife and my mistress walking toward us arm in arm!"

"*Mon Dieu*, Henri," cried out the second. "I was about to say the very same thing!"

The wealthy Frenchman's beautiful wife had died, and while the husband stoically controlled his grief throughout the funeral proceedings, the wife's lover sobbed loudly and made an open display of his loss. The husband observed this demonstration patiently and then, when the services were over, walked over to the younger man, put his arm around him and said sympathetically, "Don't be so upset, *mon ami*. I plan to marry again."

In Paris, everybody dates until the *oui* hours.

Two French *bons vivants* were relaxing over an after-dinner cognac, following an especially enjoyable meal, when one, knowing of his friend's true appreciation for the grape, asked his dining companion, "*Dites-moi*, Paul, I am sure you would have no difficulty in eliminating song from your life, but what would you forgo if you were forced to choose between women and wine?"

Paul paused to inhale the bouquet of his cognac, then replied, "That, *mon ami*, would depend on their respective vintages."

Two young French boys were talking about sex on their way home from the cinema when the younger boy suddenly exclaimed, "As far as I can tell, *mon ami*, sex is just a big pain in the *derrière*."

"*Mais non, Jean-Luc,*" sighed his older confrere. "You're doing it wrong."

Seeing the sights of New York City via the Fifth Avenue bus, a prim young woman was scandalized to hear an obviously newly immigrated man saying to his attentive companion: "Emma coma first, I coma next, two assa coma together, I coma again, two assa coma together again, I coma once-a-more, pee-pee twice, then I coma for the lasta time."

The young lady was crimson-faced when he finished, and then, noticing a policeman seated nearby, she whispered to him, "Can't you arrest that awful man?"

The policeman stared at her, genuinely bewildered, and said, "For spelling Mississippi?"

A New York police captain was vacationing in Paris and decided to stop by the local *sûreté* office and spend the day acquainting himself with the latest in French crime-fighting techniques. After indulging in the usual amount of shoptalk with one of the French detectives assigned to welcome visiting law-enforcement officials, the New York cop asked, "What would you say is the most successful technique used by your country's police department?"

"Well, *monsieur*," the Frenchman mused, "in France we 'ave ze saying '*Cherchez la femme*,' which in English means 'Find ze woman.'"

Not very impressed with this rather romantic bit of Gallic philosophizing, the New Yorker demanded, "Do you mean to sit there and tell me that you actually catch more crooks by merely chasing after women?"

"*Mais non, capitaine*," came the indignant reply. "But we 'ave ze happiest police force in all of Europe."

A noted French physician maintains that if a man consumes a glass of brandy after dinner each evening for twelve hundred months, he will live to be a hundred years old.

Then there was the Eskimo girl who spent the night with her boyfriend and next morning found she was six months pregnant.

In what was considered by the Pyongyang brass a bold stroke of propaganda, the North Korean government recently sent an order to an American rubber company for a thousand gross of contraceptives, eighteen inches long and eight inches in circumference. The company filled the order, but countering propaganda with propaganda, labeled each container MEDIUM.

During a recent expedition into the remotest uplands of Central Africa, a group of anthropologists came upon an isolated village without electricity or any apparent connection to the modern world. In an attempt to make friends, the leader of the party tried to tell the natives what it was like in the civilized, outside world.

"Out there," he said, "we love our fellow man."

To this, the natives gave a ringing cry of "*Huzzanga!*"

Encouraged by this, the explorer continued: "We treat others as we would want them to treat us!"

"*Huzzanga!*" exclaimed the natives, with much enthusiasm.

"We are peaceful!" said the explorer.

"*Huzzanga!*" cried the natives.

With a tear running down his cheek, the explorer ended his fine speech: "We come to you as friends, as brothers. So trust us. Open your arms to us, your houses, your hearts. What do you say?"

The air shook with one long, mighty "HUZZANGA!"

Greatly pleased by the reception, the leader of the explorers then began talking with the natives' chief.

"I see that you have cattle here," he said. "They are a species with which I'm unfamiliar. May I inspect them?"

"Certainly, come this way," said the chief. "But be careful not to step in the *huzzanga*."

The bearded Cuban was describing his country to a U.S. women's club.

"Our most popular sport is bullfighting," he declared.

One woman, obviously upset at the thought of so bloody a spectacle, exclaimed, "That's revolting!"

"No," said the Cuban, smiling, "that is our second most popular sport."

The newly arrived North Korean diplomat was being given a thorough tour of Washington nightlife by his State Department escort. After watching a group of young couples in a dance club, the escort said, "I don't imagine you've ever seen anything quite like this in your country. Do you know what they're doing?"

"Yes," said the diplomat. "But why are they standing up?"

The well-traveled executive returned from his trip to Italy and called a friend in New York to meet him for lunch. "Did you do anything exciting over there?" the friend asked.

"Oh, you know the old saying," the exec shrugged. "When in Rome, do as the Romans do."

"Well, exactly what did you *do*?" the friend persisted.

"What else?" the businessman replied. "I seduced an American tourist."

An Italian cabdriver was telling a passenger that only real men drive taxis in Rome. "We use our left hand for signals and our right to wave at women," he proclaimed.

His passenger finally asked, "But how do you steer?"

"I told you," the cabby said. "Only *real* men drive taxis in Rome."

Then there was the Polynesian nymphomaniac who was always longing for Samoa.

Historians at the Aztec pyramids in Mexico have finally deciphered the last words of the famous emperor Montezuma, found inscribed upon an ancient scroll: "Will someone tell those damned Marines to stop singing in the halls?"

"**C**ertainly, America has its problems," the politician roared to the UN assembly. "But we're still the only people in the world who are free to criticize our courts, our Congress, and our President."

"That's what you think," the foreign diplomat retorted. "People all over the world are criticizing your courts, your Congress, and your President."

After a certain South American republic succumbed to revolutionary forces, the new regime decided its troops needed special uniforms. A tailor was called in and shown the design—fuchsia trousers, crimson boots, snow-white caps, and orange jackets with gold epaulets.

"Is this to be the uniform for the president's palace guard?" inquired the incredulous tailor.

"No," replied the newly minted officer in charge. "It's for the secret police."

"**B**ut how can you tell a militiaman from a regular Iraqi citizen?" the nervous private asked the seasoned sergeant.

"Simple," the sergeant drawled. "You just holler, 'To hell with Saddam Hussein!' and see how he reacts."

A few days later, while visiting the company hospital, the sergeant saw the private lying in a bed, badly battered. "What happened to you?" the sergeant asked. "Didn't you remember to do what I told you?"

"Sure I did," the private answered weakly. "I saw this guy coming out of the reeds and I yelled, 'To hell with Saddam Hussein!'"

"And what happened?"

"He yelled back, 'To hell with George Bush!'—and while we were standing in the middle of the road shaking hands, a tank ran over us."

Wining
& Dining

LeRoy Neiman

"**H**ow many beers does it take to make you dizzy?" he asked.

"Four or five," she retorted. "And don't call me 'dizzy'!"

A drunk and his inebriated friend were sitting at a bar.

"Do you know what time it is?" asked the drunk.

"Sure," said the friend.

"Thanks," said the drunk.

The connoisseur sat down at the bar and ordered a Martini.

"Very dry," he insisted. "Twenty parts gin to one part vermouth."

"All right, sir," said the bartender. "Shall I twist a bit of lemon peel over it?"

"Look, when I want lemonade, I'll ask for it."

Maybe you heard about the drunk who was staggering through the park and saw a young athlete doing pushups. "Washamatter, Mac?" inquired the lush. "Lose your girl?"

It was a large, lavish dinner party and many important dignitaries and members of society were there.

"I suppose I mustn't offer you wine," said the hostess to the guest of honor seated on her right. "Aren't you the chairman of the Temperance League?"

"Oh, no," replied her guest with a smile, "I'm the head of the Anti-Vice League."

"Oh, of course," said the embarrassed hostess, "I knew there was *something* I shouldn't offer you."

One of our favorite bartenders told us about a very proper Englishman who came into his place a couple of weeks ago. The fellow sat down at the bar, but didn't order. The bartender, an unusually friendly guy, asked him if he couldn't fix him a drink, on the house.

The Englishman shook his head. "Tried liquor once," he said. "Didn't like it."

The bartender then offered the Englishman a cigarette.

"No, thank you," he said. "Tried tobacco once. Didn't like it."

Still trying to be friendly, the bartender asked the Englishman if he would like to join a couple of friends seated at the bar in a few hands of poker.

The Englishman shook his head. "Tried gambling once. Didn't like it. I wouldn't be sitting in this place at all, but I promised my son I would meet him here."

"I see," said the bartender. "Your only child?"

The switchboard operator in a swank New York hotel received a call at a little past two in the morning from a somewhat inebriated man who wanted to know what time the hotel bar opened.

"At nine A.M., sir," she replied.

At three-thirty A.M. the phone rang again and the same man, this time obviously feeling no pain, asked the same question.

"Not until nine A.M.," she said a second time.

At five-fifteen A.M. the switchboard operator received still another call from the same guy, now completely plastered. Once again he asked the same question.

More than a little irritated, she snapped, "I told you, sir, you'll have to wait until nine A.M. to get in the bar."

"*Get in*, hell," croaked the drunk. "I want to get *out* of the damn place!"

We know a freewheeling Comp-Lit major who says that two Martinis usually make her feel like a new man.

A table of improper measures we came upon the other day informs us that it takes two pints to make one cavort.

The two buddies had been out drinking for hours when their money finally ran out.

"I have an idea," mumbled Al. "Lesh go over to my housh and borrow shum money from my wife."

The two of them reeled into Al's living room, snapped on the light, and, lo and behold, there was Al's wife making love on the sofa to another man. This state of affairs considerably unnerved Al's friend but didn't seem to affect the husband. "Shay, dear, you have any money for your ever-lovin' hushban?" he asked.

"Yes, yes," she snapped. "take my purse from the mantel and, for Pete's sake, turn off those lights."

Outside, they examined the purse, and Al proudly announced, "There's enough here for a pint for you and a pint for me. Pretty good eh, old buddy?"

"But, Al," protested his friend somewhat sobered by the spectacle he'd just witnessed, "what about that fellow back there with your wife?"

"The hell with him," replied Al, "let him buy his own pint."

After gunning his Mercedes the wrong way down a one-way street, the rather inebriated young man was asked where he thought he was going by an inquisitive police officer.

"I'm not really sure," confessed the drunk, "but wherever it is, I must be late, because everybody seems to be coming back already."

The young man was determined to win his girlfriend's heart that evening.

"I have loved you more than you will ever know..." he began.

"So I was right," she exclaimed, slapping him across the face. "You *did* take advantage of me last Saturday night when I was drunk!"

The wife of a friend of ours purchased a large grandfather clock at an auction and then sent her unhappy husband to pay for it and carry the thing home. Making matters worse, the guy had been to a formal dinner earlier in the evening and was still wearing his tux. He was having some difficulty with the unwieldy contraption when he collided with the drunk staggering in the opposite direction. The husband fell backward to the sidewalk, the clock on top of him.

"Why in blazes don't you watch where you're going!" the man demanded.

The drunk shook his head dazedly, looked down at the man in tails and at the grandfather clock that lay across him.

"Why don't you wear a wrish watch like everybody elsh?" he inquired.

Two inebriated gentlemen stood at the bar near closing time.

"I've an idea," said one, "lesh have one more drink and then go find us shum girls."

"Naw," replied the other. "I've got more than I can handle at home."

"Great," replied the idea man. "Lesh have one more drink and go up to your place."

A friend has described a pink elephant as a beast of bourbon.

A rather inebriated fellow on a bus was tearing up a newspaper into tiny pieces and throwing them out the window.

"Excuse me," said the woman sitting next to him, "but would you mind explaining why you're tearing up that paper and throwing the pieces out the window?"

"It scares away the elephants," said the drunk.

"I don't see any elephants," said the woman, smiling.

"Effective, isn't it?" said the drunk.

The father, passing through his son's college town early one morning on a business trip, thought he would pay his boy a surprise visit. Arriving at the young man's fraternity house, dad rapped loudly on the door. After several minutes of knocking, a sleepy voice drifted down from a second floor window, "Can I help you?"

"Does Ramsey Duncan live here?" asked the father.

"Yeah," replied the weary voice. "Go ahead and dump him on the front porch."

The six fraternity men came weaving out of the off-campus gin mill and started to crowd themselves into the Volkswagen for the rollicking ride back home. One of them, obviously the house president, took charge of the situation. "Herbie," he said, "you drive. You're too drunk to sing."

A man we know who's no stranger to the bottom of a glass assures us that he has no trouble leaping out of bed as soon as the first ray of sunshine comes through his window. Of course, he adds, his window faces west.

We know a bartender who says that water is a fine drink if imbibed with the right spirit.

Quaffing at his favorite bar one afternoon, the regular was particularly struck by the odd behavior of a man three stools down. As fast as the bartender could serve the man, he was tossing off hookers of bourbon. Somewhat alarmed, the regular moved over to the prolific imbiber and asked, "What kind of a way is that to drink good bourbon?"

"It's the only way I can drink since my accident," the man replied, throwing down two more shots in fast order.

"What kind of an accident was that?"

The man guzzled another one, shuddered, and then answered in hushed tones, "I once knocked over a drink with my elbow."

We were quite sympathetic the other evening at the sight of an obviously sozzled gentleman feeling his way around and around a lamppost and muttering, "S'no use, I'm walled in."

As the cop helped the bruised and battered drunk up from the pavement in front of the bar, he asked, "Can you describe the man who hit you?"

"Oh, yes," said the man. "That's just what I was doing when he hit me."

"**A**re you sure this is your house?" the cop asked the thoroughly splificated gent in the rumpled suit.

"Shertainly," said the drunk, "and if you'll jush open the door f'me, I'll prove it to you.

"You shee that piano?" the drunk began. "Thash mine. You shee that television set? Thash mine, too. Follow me, follow me."

The police officer followed as he shakily negotiated the stairs to the second floor. The drunk pushed open the first door they came to.

"Thish ish my bedroom," he announced. "Shee that bed? Thash my bed. Shee that woman lying in the bed? Thash my wife. An' shee that guy lying next to her?"

"Yeah," said the cop suspiciously.

"Thash *me!*"

Upon leaving a hotel bar one evening, an executive friend of ours noticed a drunk sitting on the edge of a potted palm in the lobby, crying like a baby. Because our friend had had a couple himself that night and was feeling rather sorry for his fellow man, he asked the inebriated one what the trouble was.

"I did a terrible thing tonight," sniffled the drunk. "I sold my wife to a guy for a bottle of Scotch."

"That is terrible," said our friend, too much under the weather to muster any real indignation. "And now that she's gone, you wish you had her back."

"Thas right," said the drunk, still sniffling.

"You're sorry you sold her, because you realize too late that you love her," sympathized our friend.

"No, no," said the drunk. "I wish I had her back because I'm thirsty again."

"**W**hat's that drink you're mixing?" the stranger asked the bartender in the exotic Caribbean bar.

"I call this a rum dandy," said the bartender.

"What's in it?" asked the stranger.

"Sugar, milk, and rum," said the barkeep.

"Is it good?" asked the stranger.

"Sure," said the bartender. "The sugar gives you pep, the milk gives you energy."

"And the rum?" asked the stranger.

"Ideas about what to do with all that pep and energy."

A high-powered business executive began to drop in at Milton's Bar regularly, and his order was always the same: two Martinis. After several weeks of this, Milton asked him why he didn't order a double instead of always ordering two singles.

"It's a sentimental thing," the customer answered. "A dear friend of mine died a few weeks ago, and before his death he asked that when I drink, I have one for him, too."

A week later, the customer came in and ordered only one Martini.

"How about your dead buddy?" Milton asked. "Why only one Martini today?"

"This is my buddy's drink," the man said as he gulped the Martini down. "I'm on the wagon."

He offered her a Scotch and sofa, and she reclined.

These days the necessities of life cost you about three times what they used to, and half the time you find they aren't even fit to drink.

Staggering into his apartment, the lush deposited himself in his bed and fell asleep. A half hour later he was awakened by a knock on the door. Wearily he struggled out of bed and, stumbling over almost every piece of furniture in the room, made his way to the door and opened it. Standing there was his drinking companion of an hour before.

"Gee, I'm sorry I woke you up, Joe," said the companion.

"Oh, that's all right," said Joe blearily. "I had to answer the door anyway."

A gravedigger, thoroughly absorbed in his work, dug a pit so deep one afternoon that he couldn't climb out when he had finished. With nightfall and the attendant drop in temperature, his predicament became more uncomfortable. He shouted for help and at last attracted the attention of a drunk staggering by.

"Get me out of here," the digger pleaded. "*I'm cold!*"

The inebriated one peered into the open grave and finally spotted the shivering digger in the darkness.

"Well, no wonder you're cold, buddy," said the drunk, kicking some of the loose sod into the hole. "You haven't got any dirt on you."

Some people have no respect for age unless it's bottled.

Having wandered helplessly into a blinding snowstorm, Sam, a notorious drinker on vacation in Colorado, was greatly relieved to see a sturdy Saint Bernard dog bounding toward him with a small keg of brandy strapped to his collar.

"At last," cried Sam. "Man's best friend—and a great big dog, too!"

A castaway was washed ashore after many days on the open sea. The island on which he landed was populated by savage cannibals who tied him, dazed and exhausted, to a thick stake. They then proceeded to cut his arms with their spears and drink his blood.

This continued for several days until the castaway could stand no more. He yelled for the cannibal king and declared, "You can kill me if you want to, but this torture with the spears has got to stop. Dammit, I'm tired of being stuck for the drinks!"

Discovering too late that a watermelon spiked with vodka had accidentally been served to a luncheon meeting of local ministers, the restaurant's owner waited nervously for the clerics' reaction.

"Quick, man," he whispered to his waiter, "what did they say?"

"Nothing," said the waiter. "They were all too busy slipping the seeds into their pockets."

The voluptuous blonde was chatting with her handsome escort in a posh restaurant when their waiter, stumbling as he brought their drinks, dumped a Martini on the rocks down the back of the woman's dress. She sprang to her feet with a shriek, dashed wildly around the table, then galloped wriggling from the room followed by her distraught boyfriend. A man seated on the other side of the room with a date of his own beckoned to the waiter and said, "We'll have two of whatever *she* was drinking."

"I hate to go golfing with any of the executives from my own agency," complained the senior ad exec, while relaxing with his fourth Scotch and soda at the clubhouse bar. "Every time I yell 'Fore' they chime in with—he's a jolly good fellow!"

A millionaire we know has filled his swimming pool with Martinis. He claims it's impossible to drown, since the deeper you sink, the higher you get.

A friend of ours has come up with a cocktail he calls the David and Goliath—a small one and you're stoned.

The large, burly man approached the bartender and said, "I see by the sign in your window that you're looking for a bouncer. Has the job been filled yet?"

"Not yet," said the bartender. "Have you had any experience?"

"No," the man admitted, "but watch this!" He walked over to a loudmouthed drunk at the back of the room, lifted him off his feet, and threw him the length of the bar and sprawling out into the street. Then, returning to the bartender, he said, "How's that?"

"Great!" admitted the bartender. "But you'll have to ask the boss about the job. I only work here."

"Fine," said the burly man. "Where is he?"

"Just coming back in the front door."

A modern motto explaining the gentle art of conquest: Ply now, play later.

An irate *carabiniere* was in the process of arresting an inebriated young Roman who decided to take a nap in the middle of the Via Veneto. "It's my duty to warn you," he said sternly, "that anything you say will be held against you."

"Sophia Loren," whispered the drunk, and passed out.

Passing a cemetery in the wee hours, a drunk noticed a sign that read, RING THE BELL FOR THE CARETAKER. He did just that, and a sleepy-eyed man staggered to the gate. "What do you want at this hour?" the man demanded.

The drunk looked the caretaker over for a minute and then retorted, "I want to know why you can't ring the damn bell yourself!"

The classics professor walked into the bar and asked the bartender for a dry Martinus.

"Sorry, sir," the bartender replied. "You mean a Martini?"

"Now see here, my good man," exclaimed the prof. "If I wanted more than one, I'd ask for them."

"Happy New Year, everybody!" the drunk shouted as he staggered into a small neighborhood bar.

"Hey, man," said the somewhat amused bartender, "today is the first of April."

"April!" exclaimed the bewildered bibber. "Man, my wife's gonna kill me for being out on a bender this long."

One of our favorite new drinks is a French eggnog—two egg yolks, two teaspoons of sugar, and four jiggers of cognac mixed gently in a tall, warm lass.

Some people are discreet up to a point, and some are discreet up to a pint.

Two drunks wandered into a zoo, and as they staggered past a lion's cage, the king of beasts let out a terrific roar.

"C'mon, let's get out of here," said the first drunk.

"You go ahead if you want to," replied his more inebriated cohort. "I'm gonna stay for the movie!"

It was almost midnight and the attractive Mrs. Robinson had been standing at the bus stop for over half an hour, several Cosmos past her limit, when up drove a gent who offered to take her home. Sliding into the seat beside him, she managed to mumble her address, then slumped drowsily against the fellow's shoulder. Responding to the opportunity, the driver wrapped his free arm around his pretty passenger and pressed her closer to him, proceeding with as personal an appraisal of the terrain as possible without taking his eyes off the road, or his other hand off the wheel.

At first she seemed oblivious to what was going on, but then she suddenly came to life, exclaiming, "Man, you're passionate!"

Quite naturally flattered by this positive reaction to his romantic overtures, he attempted to take further liberties and was promptly greeted with a stinging slap across the face. Stopping the car abruptly, he turned to her angrily and said, "What the hell's going on here? On the one hand you tell me how passionate I am and with the other you smack me. Why don't you make up your mind?"

"I don't know what you're talkin' about, mishter," came the slurred reply, "but that's my house—and you're about to pash it again!"

A pair of intoxicated pals were seated in their favorite bar imbibing their favorite libation.

"I think I'll have a bite to eat," said the first inebriated fellow. Whereupon, he plucked the olive from his Martini and ate it.

"Ah," said his sozzled companion, "that calls for an after-dinner drink!"

The young man stepped up to the bar and ordered a Manhattan. The bartender returned shortly with the drink, in which floated a piece of parsley.

"What's that?" he asked, pointing to the glass.

"A Manhattan," replied the bartender. "Isn't that what you ordered?"

"Well, yes," said the young man. "But what's *that?*" He pointed to the parsley.

"Oh, *that,*" exclaimed the bartender. "That's Central Park."

A new housekeeper, accused by the man of the house of helping herself to the contents of the liquor cabinet when her employer was absent, waxed indignant. "I'll have you know, sir," she declared hotly, "that I come from honest English parents."

"I'm not concerned with your English parents," countered the man. "What's worrying me is your Scotch extraction."

A fat man was seated on his front steps drinking a can of beer when a busybody spinster from down the street began to berate him for his appearance.

"What a disgusting sight," she said. "If that belly was on a woman, I'd swear she was pregnant."

To which the man smiled and replied, "Madam, it *was* and she *is.*"

The elegantly dressed gentleman sauntered into the upscale cocktail lounge. After surveying the many patrons gathered there, he motioned for silence and called, "Bartender, I'd like the opportunity of buying a drink for everyone in the place."

After a brief pause, he added, "And please have one yourself." This generosity was hailed and toasted by one and all.

After downing his own drink and bidding everyone adieu, the fine fellow started for the door. His progress was interrupted by the slightly embarrassed bartender. "I hate to bother you, sir," he began, "but the tab comes to almost five hundred dollars...."

"So what are you bothering me for? I don't have as much as a penny," replied the gentleman.

Realizing that a cruel hoax had been perpetrated upon him, the enraged bartender seized the brash fellow by the collar, drove his fist into the guy's face, and threw the battered man into the street.

The following afternoon, the bartender was amazed to see the same man come into the lounge. The deadbeat stopped and motioned once again for silence. As a hush fell over the crowd, he snapped his fingers and shouted, "Bartender, drinks for everyone! Everyone, that is, except *you*—I've seen the way you act when you get a drink in you."

A well-dressed but obviously inebriated gentleman stumbled up to a policeman at a busy downtown intersection and voiced a thick-tongued complaint. "Somebody stole my car, officer," he announced groggily. "I had it right here on the tip of my ignition key."

"We'll go right to the station and report it," the beat cop replied, amused at the guy's condition. "But I think you should zip your fly up before we leave."

"Oh, my God," exclaimed the drunk, looking at his open barn door. "Somebody stole my girl, too!"

Storming into the frontier saloon, the fervid temperance evangelist boomed, "Repent, you vile sinners! Drinking that noxious fluid will send you all to hell. Join with me—all of you who want to go to heaven stand on this side."

All but one drunk staggered to his side. To the holdout, the evangelist shouted, "Don't you want to go to heaven?"

"No, I don't," replied the drunk.

"You mean to tell me that you don't want to go to heaven when you die?" asked the astonished evangelist.

"Oh," the drunk replied, crossing the room. "When I *die*. I thought you were making up a load right now."

The libidinous young woman listened patiently as her married sister extolled the benefits of the quiet life.

"That's not for me," she responded after hearing her sister out. "I once tried to give up drinking, smoking, and sex—and it was the longest twenty minutes I ever spent."

Never pour black coffee into an intoxicated person. If you do, you'll wind up with a wide-awake drunk on your hands.

A well-dressed gentleman seated at the bar was quietly guzzling Martinis. After finishing each one, he carefully ate the glass and arranged the stems in a neat row. The ninth time this occurred, the bartender could stand it no longer and commented to another customer, "There's a guy who's absolutely nuts."

"He sure is," agreed the other man. "The stems are the best part."

A new organization has been formed, called Athletics Anonymous. When you get the urge to shoot some hoops, play baseball, or participate in any other game involving physical activity, they send someone over to drink with you until the urge passes.

An acquaintance of ours has discovered a sure-fire way to avoid a hangover—keep drinking.

Several members of a temperance league approached a ninety-year-old teetotaler for a testimonial declaring that his longevity was due to a life of abstention from alcohol. The old gentleman said he would be pleased to sign such a statement and was in the process of making his mark when sounds of a riotous party came from an adjacent room. "My God, what's that?" gasped one of the visitors.

"Oh, that's my dad," the teetotaler said, shaking his head. "He's probably getting drunk again."

"Just look at me," declared the robust oldtimer. "I don't smoke, drink, or chase women and tomorrow I'll celebrate my eightieth birthday."

"How the hell are you going to do that?" asked a curious friend.

H*e did not drink, or smoke, or swear,*
His morals were not bad;
Nor did he live a century—
He only felt *he had.*

At the inquest the coroner gently asked the widow if she could remember her late husband's last words.

"Yes," she replied. "He said, 'I don't see how they make a profit out of this stuff at eight dollars a fifth.'"

It was Tracy's first crossing, and he was assigned to a table with a suave Frenchman. The first night out, the Frenchman rose, bowed slightly, and said, *"Bon appétit."*

Tracy got to his feet, bowed and said, "Tracy."

The following morning, at breakfast, then at lunch and again at dinner, the ceremony was repeated and Tracy found his politeness wearing a little thin. "It's beginning to annoy me," he told a companion in the lounge. "Same thing over and over: he tells me his name, *Bon appétit*, I tell him mine and we do it all over again at the next meal."

His companion laughed. "He's not introducing himself. *Bon appétit* is French for 'good appetite.' He's hoping that you enjoy your meal."

Tracy felt pretty silly. The next morning when he appeared at breakfast, the Frenchman was already seated. Tracy bowed and said, *"Bon appétit."* Whereupon the Frenchman jumped up, bowed, and answered, "Tracy."

A gourmet friend of ours advises that when preparing a dish for bedtime, champagne makes the best tenderizer.

Two cannibals were chatting over lunch. One said, "You know, I just can't stand my mother-in-law."

"Forget about her," the other replied. "Try the noodles!"

They made an attractive couple in the swank restaurant, he handsome, dressed in a hand-tailored suit, obviously well to do, and she ravishing, shapely, and obviously quite hungry. It was their first date.

"So, Margaret," he said. "What would you like?"

She scanned the menu with an experienced eye. "To begin," she said, "I'd like a champagne cocktail, then a dozen blue-point oysters on the half shell and a tureen of turtle soup. For the entrees I'll have the filet of Dover sole *aux chapignons* followed by the pheasant under glass. *Pommes de terre Lyonnaises*, plus an à la carte order of asparagus would be nice, too. And I'll have the tarragon oil dressing on
the salad. For dessert I'd like a great big plate of profiteroles, a few petits-fours, and a large cognac, X.O. That should do it."

Somewhat taken aback, the man smiled and asked, "Do you eat like this at home?"

Margaret favored him with a lazy grin. "No," she said. "But then, nobody at home wants to sleep with me."

Boys & Girls Together

LeRoy Neiman

A business friend was trying to convince us the other day that sex is so popular because it's centrally located.

The mother entered the darkened room unexpectedly and found daughter and boyfriend in passionate embrace on the sofa.

"Well—I never!" exclaimed mother.

"But, mother, you must have!" said daughter.

We've just received the results of a survey conducted to ascertain the various reasons men get out of bed in the middle of the night. According to the report, 2% are motivated by a desire to visit the bathroom and 3% have an urge to raid the refrigerator.

The other 95% get up to go home.

Everyone was surprised when fastidious, virginal Percy lispingly announced his intention to wed. "What, *you*, Percy?" was the amazed reaction. Some skeptics made bets that he wouldn't go through with it, but Percy fooled them. He even went on a honeymoon. Upon his return, one of the losers bitingly asked, "Well, is your wife pregnant?"

"I certainly hope so," said Percy with great sincerity. "I wouldn't want to go through *that* again!"

He held her close against him, a warm glow of satisfaction covering them both.

"Am I the first man you've ever made love to?" he asked.

She studied him reflectively. "You might be," she said. "Your face looks very familiar."

A socially prominent dowager from Boston was visiting friends in New York and a dinner party was held in her honor. She was seated next to another, younger woman, and began discussing the relative merits of Boston society.

"In Boston," she said, "we place all our emphasis on good breeding."

"In New York we think it's a lot of fun, too," agreed the other woman, "but we also try to pursue other interests."

The opera singer Giovanni Rotondo, star of the Metropolitan during its Golden Age, is credited with making the following common-sense statement: "It is not wise to make love in the morning—you never know whom you'll meet later in the day."

"Your Honor," said the husband suing for divorce, "my wife beats me."

"And just how often does she beat you?" queried the judge.

"She beats me every time, Your Honor."

Our tireless Research Department, after extensive house-to-house canvassing, has come up with the three best things in life: a Martini before and a nap after.

They moved apart as Frank lit their cigarettes; then she snuggled close to him again and pulled the bedsheets up around their chins. "Darling," she cooed, "how many others were there before me?" After a few minutes of silence, she said, "Well, I'm waiting...."

"Shh," he replied, puffing thoughtfully, "I'm still counting."

"**H**ow is it I find you sleeping with my daughter?" stormed the outraged father. "I ask you, you little bastard, how is it?!"

"Why, just great, sir," replied the calm young man, "just great!"

The moon shone silver on the waters of the lake, and the waves beating on the shore were hardly equal in intensity to the waves of passion nearby. One ardent couple pulled apart long enough for the young man to whisper, "Am I the first man to make love to you?"

Her tone, when she answered, was irritable. "Of course," she snapped. "I don't know why you men always ask the same ridiculous question."

"**M**y apartment serves as both my living quarters and laboratory combined," the brilliant young inventor explained to his friend as he showed him around the premises. With an uncharacteristic flourish, he drew back the velvet curtains enclosing a cozy alcove. There, stretched out on a divan, was a dazzling blonde, as nubile and as nude as any the visitor had ever seen. In her hand she held a glass, empty except for two ice cubes.

"This is my latest and greatest invention," the self-styled genius beamed proudly. "I call it instant sex. You just add Scotch."

To most modern writers, sex is a novel idea.

Mary had a little sheep,
And with the sheep she went to sleep.
The sheep turned out to be a ram—
Mary had a little lamb.

The 6:07 commuter train was quite late in leaving for its exurban destination, and Hank and Mack were enjoying their wait in the station bar. They had, in fact, been drinking long enough to have reached the stage of semimaudlin confession about their sex lives.

"You know," Hank said, "I never slept with my wife at all before we were married. Did you?"

Mack searched his thoughts with what was, under the circumstances, admirable reflection. "Gee," he finally said, "I dunno. What's her maiden name?"

Girls believe in love at first sight; men believe in it at first opportunity.

A wise man has observed that people who live in glass houses shouldn't.

"Wasn't it lovely out there on the lake?" the young man said to his date as they were returning from the canoe ride.

With a happy sigh she replied, "It's lovely anyplace."

A famed, but particularly succinct, psychiatrist had been invited to address an international conclave of his fellows on the subject of sex. When the day for his speech came, the amphitheater was packed and scores of reporters sat waiting at the press desk as the great, solemn man strode to the podium. A hush fell over the crowd as he adjusted his glasses and sipped a bit of water. He looked up and said in a firm, clear voice, "Gentlemen, it gives me great pleasure." And then he sat down.

We don't believe it, but we have a friend who insists that he recently met a girl who is so naïve that when he asked her if she knew the difference between a screw and a Caesar salad she said she had no idea.

"Did you explain it to her?" we asked.

"Hell no," said our friend. "But I have lunch with her every day."

Sam, one of the worst braggarts who ever bent a bar rail, was loudly lamenting to nobody in particular that his doctor had ordered him to give up half of his sex life.

"Which half are you going to give up?" asked a weary listener. "Talking about it or thinking about it?"

"Do you smoke after sex?" the man asked.

"I really don't know," the woman replied. "I've never checked."

Any girl who believes that the way to a man's heart is through his stomach is obviously setting her standards too high.

People who live in glass houses should screw in the basement.

Two young men seated in a restaurant were watching a customer busily disposing of a plate of oysters on the half shell. One of the young men remarked to his friend, "Did you ever hear that business about raw oysters being good for a man's virility?"

"Yes, why?" the friend replied.

"Well, take it from me, that's a lot of foolishness. I ate a dozen of them the other night and only nine worked."

When Ali, the sheik's most devoted eunuch, died unexpectedly in the middle of the night, the potentate's teenaged son asked his father how this unhappy event had come to pass.

"My son," said the sheik, "Ali's death teaches us a valuable lesson. Last night, upon retiring, I commanded him to hasten to my harem and select for my pleasure the one most beautiful among the hundred houris waiting there. He returned with surprising swiftness with a ravishing young woman, but this tasty morsel merely whetted my appetite, so I summoned Ali again and told him to fetch forth the most sensual female of the harem. This time he returned even more quickly—though the harem is a considerable distance from my quarters, as you know—with a female whose hair was as flame, with a passion to match.

"This erotic creature further increased my desire, and I instructed Ali to have the most innocent maiden he could find brought to my bedchamber; he reappeared soon after, short of breath and perspiring from his efforts in my behalf, with a raven-haired beauty who was the very image of innocence.

"So it went throughout most of the night—with a fourth, fifth, sixth, and seventh—faithful Ali scurrying back and forth between harem and bedchamber again, and again, and again, and again, until he dropped dead at my feet."

"And what is the valuable lesson to be learned from all this?" the perplexed son of the potentate wanted to know.

"There's no harm in sex," said the sheik. "It's running after it that can kill you."

LeRoy Neiman

The model climbed up the ladder,
As Titian, the painter, had bade her.
    Then her position
    Suggested coition,
So he climbed up the ladder and had her.

Shortly after his spaceship landed on the moon, the astronaut debarked and began exploring the strange new terrain. He had walked for only fifteen minutes when he came upon a lovely young moon girl, who was busily stirring the contents of a meteoroid pot.

"Hi," he said, introducing himself. "I'm an astronaut, here to discover everything I can about life on the moon."

The moon girl stopped stirring long enough to throw him a smile. "How interesting it is that you are formed just like our moon men," she observed, looking him up and down. Pointing to her own, quite naked body, she asked, "And am I structured as are earth women?"

"Yes, you are," answered the astronaut. "But tell me, why do you stir that pot?"

"I'm making a baby," she said. And sure enough, a few minutes later, a baby appeared in the pot.

"Would you like to see how we make babies on earth?" asked the astronaut, by now considerably aroused. The girl said she would, so the astronaut proceeded with a passionate demonstration.

"That was enjoyable," she said afterward, "but where is the baby?"

"Oh, that takes nine months," explained the astronaut.

"Nine months?" she asked. "Then why did you stop stirring?"

All girls are born good. Experience makes them better.

The strapping Australian farm boy on his first visit to Melbourne explained to a streetwalker he'd just met, "Ma run off when I was just a little critter, so there weren't no one to raise me 'ceptin' Pa. He taught me most of what I need to know, but he said I'd have to come to the city to learn about women, so I'd be obliged if you'd teach me that."

The sympathetic prostitute took the farm boy to her apartment. She told him to get undressed and then she went into an adjoining room and changed from her street clothes into a filmy black negligee. When she returned, she found all of her furniture stacked against the walls, the carpet rolled back, and the young man stripped and squatting in the middle of the bare floor.

"What's going on here?" she demanded.

The young man explained, "I don't know how it is with a woman, but I figure if it's anything like with kangaroos, we'll be needing plenty of room."

A philosophical friend of ours points out that at cocktail parties the men usually stand around getting stiff, and the women are usually tight, but when they get home they frequently find that neither is either.

The newly ordained young priest asked his monsignor a favor: Would the older and more experienced man audition the young man's handling of confessions, and give him a candid critique? The monsignor agreed, and at the end of the day called the priest to give his verdict.

"Quite good, on the whole," he said. "But I do have a suggestion. I'd have preferred to hear a few more 'Tsk! Tsk! Tsks!' and fewer 'Oh, wows!'"

As Sunday approached, the middle-aged minister grew slightly desperate, for he could think of no suitable subject for his sermon. When his wife suggested that he be original and preach on water-skiing, he decided he would do it.

Sunday came and the minister's wife—ill with a virus—remained at home. As the minister drove to church, his doubts about parables found in water-skiing increased. Finally, he decided to abandon the subject entirely, and instead, delivered a brilliant extemporaneous sermon on sex.

Later in the week, a matron of the church met the minister's wife in the supermarket and complimented her on her husband's magnificent talk.

"Where on earth did he ever get all that information?" she asked. "He seemed so positive and sure of himself."

"I'm sure I don't know," the minister's wife replied, thoughtfully. "He only tried it twice and fell off both times."

A friend tells us the only thing better than the sleep of the just is the sleep of the just-after.

Awakening the morning after the drunken orgy, the god of war was stretching sleepily when he noticed a lovely Valkyrie standing in the doorway.

"Good morning," he said. "I'm Thor."

"*You're* thor?" she replied. "I'm tho thor it hurth to thit down."

"Isn't the moon lovely?" she sighed.

"If you say so," answered her boyfriend. "I'm in no position to say."

"**N**ever make love on an empty stomach," admonishes a young woman we know. "Take him out to dinner first."

"**I**'m beat," confessed the popular sorority girl to her friend. "Last night I didn't fall asleep until after three."

"No wonder you're tired," her friend sympathized. "Twice is usually all I need."

A young man drove his date into the Hollywood hills in search of a suitable spot for a sexual interlude. They got out of the car, but the girl had reservations about making love in the open, so the boy suggested they crawl under the car, where no one could possibly see them. They were locked in passionate embrace when an authoritative voice demanded to know what the hell they thought they were doing.

Without opening his eyes, the young man answered, "Fixing the transmission."

"Oh, yeah," snapped the cop. "Well, you'd better fix your brakes, too. Your car is at the bottom of the hill."

"**I**t really *is* true," exclaimed the satisfied young woman to the man lying beside her. "Nice guys finish last!"

"**M**other," the young woman asked, "remember when you told me the way to a man's heart was through his stomach?"

"Sure," her mother answered.

"Well," the girl went on, "last night I think I may have found a new route."

The distinguished-looking elderly man asked at the department-store information kiosk where he might purchase some personal stationery. He was directed to the notions department on the third floor, but in the crowded elevator he became confused and got off on the fourth floor by mistake. Approaching the attractive floor manager standing near the elevator doors, he said, "Excuse me, Miss, but do you have notions?"

"Sure," she replied mischievously, "but during the work week I try to suppress them until after five o'clock."

"No, no, you don't understand," he stammered. "I mean to say, do you keep stationery?"

"No, I like to go with the flow right till the end," replied the floor manager, laughing. "And then I just start quivering all over."

A Chicago salesman on a business trip to Boston had a few hours to kill before catching a plane home. Remembering a friend's advice to try some some of Boston's famed broiled scrod, he hopped into a cab and asked the driver, "Excuse me, but do you know where I could get scrod around here?"

"Pal," replied the cabby, admiringly, "I've heard that question a thousand times, but this is the first time in the pluperfect subjunctive."

The learned judge looked down from the bench at the young woman who was suing her husband for divorce.

"Your Honor," the young woman said, "I just can't live with my husband anymore. He's a hobosexual."

"Just one moment," interrupted the judge, considerably confused. "Don't you mean *homo*sexual?"

"No, your Honor," insisted the woman. "I mean ho*bo*sexual. He's a bum lay!"

In an English-lit course on D.H. Lawrence, the irritated professor asked the young woman dozing in the back to explain the difference between fornication and adultery.

"Well," she said, rubbing the sleep from her eyes, "I've tried both, and they seem pretty similar."

An impious friend of ours explains that the difference between being "hard up" and "down and out" is about two minutes.

Upon taking a seat at the bar, the exec noticed that each stool had a number painted on it. Sitting next to him was a rather depressed-looking gentleman and an attractive young woman who was obviously enjoying herself. The newcomer turned toward the unhappy fellow and asked if he knew the purpose of the numbers.

"Sure," the guy said. "Every half hour, the bartender spins a wheel and whoever has the winning seat gets to go upstairs for the wild sex orgy they have up there."

"That's terrific!" exclaimed the surprised customer. "Have you won?"

"Not yet," the man said, miserably, "but my date has—four times in a row!"

"Is it a sin to have sexual relations before receiving Communion?" the young woman asked her pastor.

"Only if you block the aisle," he replied.

"I love you terribly," said the young man.

"You certainly do," agreed his girlfriend.

A recently deposed Eastern potentate was known for his prowess in the harem— often entertaining no fewer than a dozen wives per night. Shorn of his crown and possessions, he was seeking employment and was overjoyed when an American theatrical agent signed him up to perform these same feats at certain choice and private showings. The contract was signed, bookings were scheduled, and twelve willing young actresses hired for the premiere. The box-office sold out.

On opening night, the audience waited eagerly, having paid premium prices to see the fabulous potentate. A symphony orchestra struck up an overture, the lights dimmed, the curtains parted, and the women of the "harem" were revealed, reclining on couches. The potentate stepped briskly out from the wings, bowed to the audience, then proceeded. Naturally, after such a build-up, the audience was disappointed when the great man fell flat on his face after taking pleasure with only four of the beauties. They howled for their money back, and the theatrical agent regretfully had to comply. Later, he went backstage and wailed to the potentate, "I'm ruined! How could you do this to me? What happened?"

The potentate shook his head sadly. "I don't understand it," he said. "Everything went smoothly this afternoon at dress rehearsal."

An elderly gentleman visited his doctor with the complaint that he believed he was becoming impotent.

"When did you first become aware of this problem?" the doctor asked.

"Let's see," the old gentleman replied. "Yesterday afternoon, twice last night, and again this morning."

An elderly playboy we know has catalogued the three stages of a man's life: Tri-Weekly, Try Weekly, Try Weakly.

The aging playboy should find some satisfaction in the knowledge that though he's not as good as he once was, he's as good once as he once was.

Friend Bob Willoughby finally took his long-dreamed-of trip to *la belle* France. When he returned, after a two months' visit, we asked him about it.

"It was wonderful," he sighed, "especially Paris. My only regret is that I couldn't have made the trip twenty years ago."

"When Paris was really Paris, eh?" we said.

"No," he said, a little sadly. "When Willoughby was really Willoughby."

"I really don't know what you see in him, Susan," said the young trial lawyer to her lunch companion. "He's just an everyday sort of man."

"Well, jeez," Susan said, putting down her fork and giving her friend a look. "What more could a girl ask for?"

A very effective new potency pill developed for men has only one drawback—if it's swallowed too slowly, the user winds up with a stiff neck.

Everyone in the hip nightclub was amazed by the old gentleman, obviously pushing seventy, tossing off Manhattans and cavorting around the dance floor like a teenager. Finally, curiosity got the best of the bartender.

"I beg your pardon, sir," she said, "but I'm amazed to see a man of your age living it up like a club kid. Tell me, are all of your, uh, faculties unimpaired?"

The old fellow looked at the girl and shook his head. "Not all, I'm afraid," he said. "Just last evening I went nightclubbing with a girlfriend—we drank and danced all night and finally rolled into her place about two A.M. We went to bed immediately and I was asleep almost as soon as my head hit the pillow. I woke around three-thirty and nudged my friend. 'Why George,' she said in surprise, 'we did that just fifteen minutes ago!'

"So you see," the man said sadly, "my memory's beginning to go."

A pretty but curious young American tourist found herself in conversation with a ruggedly handsome, middle-aged Scot at a cocktail party. "Excuse my bluntness," she said, "but is anything worn under your kilt?"

"Nae, lass," he replied with a grin. "It's as fit as it ever was."

According to a sage old soothsayer we know, anyone who can still do at sixty what he did at twenty probably wasn't doing much at twenty.

Precisely nine months after the young couple were married, the wife was rushed to the hospital with an urgent call from the stork. Shortly after her arrival, the doctor came out of the delivery room and told the husband he was the father of a bouncing baby boy.

The new father consulted his watch, and said, "Well, nature certainly is precise. It's exactly seven o'clock."

Twenty minutes later, the doctor came out again, all smiles. "Congratulations again," he said. "You're also the father of a baby girl."

"Yessir, doc," came the father's reply, "right to the minute." Then, glancing at his watch, he added, "Well, I guess I'll just take a little nap. There shouldn't be another one until ten-thirty."

Imagine the dismay felt by the aging Don Juan who finds himself Don after Juan.

Having been married to each other for forty of their sixty years, the progressive couple decided to take separate vacations. After reveling for two months in the island paradise of Hawaii, the old gent called to their condo in Miami, where his wife had decided to vacation.

"I'm having a great time," he said. "I met the most fabulous thirty-year-old masseuse and we're really swinging."

His wife's voice crackled over the line. "Well, darling, I'm having a great time, too. I met a thirty-year-old man who has been squiring me all over town. In fact, I'm pretty sure I'm enjoying myself more than you are."

"How do you figure?" he responded.

"Simple mathematics, my dear sweet husband," she purred. "Thirty goes into sixty more times than sixty goes into thirty!"

In keeping with all self-respecting vehicles owned by traveling salesmen, Ed's car broke down in the middle of a blizzard, and he trudged to a nearby farmhouse. The farmer, being up in his lines, said, "We're short of beds, but you can sleep with my daughter." She proved to be eighteen, sloe-eyed, and a strapping figure of healthy young womanhood. So they went to bed. Not long after, Ed made a pass at the daughter.

"Stop that!" she said. "I'll call my father." He stopped. But half an hour later he made another attempt.

"C'mon, stop," she said. "I'll call my father." But she moved closer to him, so he made a third try. This time, no protest, no threat. Just as Ed, satisfied, was about to drowse off, she tapped his shoulder.

"Could we do that again?" she asked. Ed obliged, and this time fell asleep, only to be awakened by another tap.

"Again?" And again Ed obliged. But when his sleep was once more interrupted by gentle tapping, Ed rolled away from her and mumbled, "Stop that, or I'll call your father."

O'Mally hurried to church one morning to see his priest. "Father," he said excitedly, "I made love ten times last night!"

"O'Mally, I'm surprised at you," the priest replied sternly. "Is the woman married?"

"Oh yes, Father, she's my wife."

"But you don't have to come to confession if you make love to your wife."

"I know—but I just had to tell *somebody*."

"I won't say I'm getting old," the aging duffer told his golfing partner. "But lately my sex drive's turned into a putt."

By the middle of his senior year, the handsome history major had dated most of the girls on campus. One day, while seated in the student union, he looked up and saw the captain of the varsity football team coming toward him, an angry scowl on his face.

"I hear you went out with Susan Fremont," the huge fellow said menacingly. "Did you ever sleep with her?"

The young man thought for a moment and then answered, "Yes, once."

"Well, I'm her new boyfriend," the gridiron giant announced, "and I don't like it at all."

"You know," the senior mused, "I didn't like it much either."

Then there was the aging playwright who, no matter how hard he tried, could never get beyond the first act.

The haze and warmth of the summer evening added to the atmosphere of passion on the small lake, deserted except for a canoe drifting lazily on its surface. In it, clasped in close embrace, lay George and Marilyn, gazing into each other's eyes and murmuring lovingly to one another.

With a delicious silken rustle that set the canoe to gently rocking, she pressed herself still closer to him.

"Georgie," she sighed, "will you love me always?"

"Of course, my darling," he whispered tenderly. "Which way should we do it first?"

An attractive young med student was having coffee with her girlfriend and complaining about her fiancé's extraordinary sexual appetites. "I barely have the strength to come to work in the morning," she murmured. "And now that he's on his vacation, things will probably be even more intense when he gets back."

"How long is he off?" the assistant inquired.

"It varies," she replied. "But usually it's just long enough to smoke a cigarette."

An elderly French playboy entered the door of his favorite sporting house and asked the Madam if he might have an audience with Renée.

"Alas, monsieur," replied the Madam. "Renée is visiting her dear mother in Provence. Would you care to see Musette?"

The old gentleman smiled. "No, thank you, *chère madame*, I will return another day. When do you expect Renée to be back?"

"Saturday next," said the Madam. "Your devotion is to be admired. But can you not find diversion in the company of Clothilde? Or Gaby? Or the lively Yvette?"

To each suggestion, the old man shook his head. Curious, the Madam asked, "Renée is, of course, charming, but what does she possess that the other girls do not?"

"Patience, *chère madame*," he replied, "patience."

Trouble with being the best man at a wedding is that you rarely get a chance to prove it.

Then there was the determined young woman who finally got so fed up with her shy boyfriend's fumbling advances she decided to put him in her place.

"**H**ow did this accident occur?" asked the doctor.

"Well," explained the patient, "I was making love to my girlfriend on the living-room rug when, all of a sudden, the chandelier came crashing down on us."

"Fortunately, you've only sustained some minor lacerations on your buttocks," the doctor said. "You're a very lucky man."

"You said it, doc," exclaimed the man. "A minute sooner and it could have fractured my skull!"

"**I**'d like to buy some body make-up for my girlfriend," the young lawyer told the clerk at the cosmetics counter.

"Certainly, sir," the clerk remarked. "What color would you like?"

"I hadn't thought much about that," the attorney said. "What I really want to know is what flavors you have."

"**M**y mother is really such a prude," the high school girl sadly told her locker partner. "She said that my boyfriend could feel me up only if he didn't touch me below the waist."

"Bummer," her schoolmate commiserated.

"Yeah," the first girl said. "That's why I've decided to learn how to stand on my head."

The young patient nervously asked the doctor to perform an unusual operation—the removal of a large chunk of green wax from her navel. Looking up from the ticklish task, the physician asked, "How did this happen?"

"Well, doctor," the girl said, "my boyfriend likes to eat by candlelight."

Upon applying for admission to one of the most exclusive country clubs in New England, the reserved, unimpressive-looking young man was notified that he must play a round of golf with the club officers as a prerequisite to his acceptance.

On the appointed afternoon, he met them on the first tee equipped with a hockey stick, a croquet mallet, and a billiard cue. The officers looked him over incredulously, but nevertheless proceeded to tee off. To their dismay, the young man coolly drove three hundred and ten yards with the hockey stick, gracefully arced his second shot to the green with the croquet mallet, and sank a twenty-foot putt with the billiard cue.

After soundly drubbing the baffled officers with an under-par 68, the applicant retired with them to the club bar. There he ordered a Scotch and soda, and when it arrived, he mixed the drink himself by tossing the contents of the shot glass over his shoulder into the waiting soda behind him on the bar. This further display of the young man's incredible physical coordination was too much for the officers of the club.

"You're miraculous," they exclaimed. "What's the story behind these fantastic talents of yours?"

"All my life," the man explained, "physical activity of any sort has been child's play for me. To overcome the boredom of being naturally gifted at everything, I try to do almost everything in the most difficult way possible. Thus, I play tennis with a Ping-Pong paddle, Ping-Pong with a tennis racket, and so on."

"Wait a minute," interrupted one of the club officers. "If it's true, as you say, that you do everything physical in the most difficult manner possible, I have one question...."

"I know," said the talented young man, smiling. "Everyone asks me the same thing and I don't mind telling you. Standing on my head... in a hammock."

After trying to fix a flat tire during a raging blizzard, the young man jumped back into the car with his date and began rubbing his nearly frozen hands. "Let me warm them for you," she offered, placing his hands between her thighs.

When his fingers had thawed out, the chap rushed back to continue working on the tire, but he quickly returned again, complaining that his hands were numb with cold. As he reached under her skirt, she slid forward and whispered, "You know, your ears are pretty cold, too...."

We know a guy who complains that last winter was so cold it took him forty-five minutes to get his girlfriend started.

Then there was the basketball player who was so tall that his girlfriend had to go up on him.

The shapely sophomore was undressing for the night when she noticed a puzzled look on her roommate's face. "Do you know there's the impression of a large 'M' on your stomach?" the roommate asked.

"Oh, yeah, that," the young woman said, looking down. "My fiancé's in town this weekend, and he likes to make love with his letter sweater on."

"Which school does he go to, Michigan? Minnesota?" questioned her friend.

"Wisconsin, actually."

We know a cautious man who, upon discovering that his girlfriend had forgotten to take the pill one night, gave her a tongue-lashing.

We know a movie fan who's very excited by current trends in films—the hero still gets the girl in the end, but he's never sure which end it will be.

Animals

LeRoy Neiman

The circus was finishing its final performance in the small town when one of its zebras had a stroke. The local veterinarian prescribed a few weeks' rest for the beast, so the circus owner made arrangements to board it at a nearby farm.

The zebra took to the new life immediately and spent the first day meeting all the animals of the barnyard.

He came across a chicken and said, "I'm a zebra, who are you?"

"I'm a chicken," said the chicken.

"What do you do?" asked the zebra.

"I scratch around and lay eggs," said the chicken.

Moving on, the zebra found a cow. He introduced himself, saying, "I'm a zebra. Who are you?"

"I'm a cow," said the cow.

"What do you do?" asked the zebra.

"I graze in the field and give milk," said the cow.

The zebra met a bull next. "I'm a zebra," he said. "Who are you?"

"I'm a bull," said the bull.

"And what do you do?" asked the zebra.

"What do I do!" snorted the bull, pawing at the turf with a forefoot. "Why you silly looking ass—take off your pajamas and I'll show you!"

The old bull's active days were over, but the kindly farmer permitted him to stay on in the pasture with the cows. Of course, the farmer also turned a young bull loose in the field and the newcomer went to work immediately. Seeing this, the old bull began snorting and pawing the ground with his hoof.

"You're wasting your time," said the farmer. "You're too old for that sort of thing now."

"I know," said the bull, "but I can show him I'm not a cow, can't I?"

The old maid bought herself a parrot to brighten her lonely hours. The parrot's name was Bobby, and he was a charming bird, with but one small fault. Whenever the mild-mannered lady had company in, Bobby would cut loose with a number of obscene expressions he'd picked up from his previous owner, a retired madam.

The lady discussed this problem with her pastor, and after witnessing a particularly purple display, the good man suggested, "This parrot needs company. Get him interested in another of his species, and he'll soon forget his sinful past.

"I, myself, have a parrot. Her name is Sarah and she is an unusually devout bird. She *prays* constantly. Let me bring her with me the next time I call. We'll keep them together a few days—I'm certain her religious background will have a marked influence on this fellow's character."

Thus, the next time the pastor called, he brought his parrot, and the two birds were placed in a single cage. They spent the first couple of minutes hopping about and sizing one another up, then Bobby spoke. "I go for you, sweetie," he whistled. "How about you and me shacking up?!"

"You betcha, you big stud," said Sarah. "My prayers have finally been answered!"

A performing octopus could play the piano, the zither, and the piccolo, and his trainer wanted him to add the bagpipe to his accomplishments. With this in mind, a bagpipe was placed in the octopus' room and the trainer awaited results.

Hours passed, but no bagpipe music was heard. Since the talented octopus usually learned quickly, the trainer was disturbed. Opening the door the next morning, he asked the octopus, "Have you learned to play that thing yet?"

"*Play it?*" retorted the octopus. "I've been trying to lay it all night!"

Two small mice were crouched under a table in the chorus girls' dressing room at Radio City Music Hall.

"Wow," exclaimed the first mouse, "have you ever seen so many gorgeous legs in your life?"

"Doesn't really do anything for me," said the second. "I'm a titmouse."

Perhaps you've heard of the impecunious snake who was so poor he didn't have a pit to hiss in.

Of course, you've heard the definition of an emasculated dinosaur: A colossal fossil with a docile missile.

The young woman and her son strolled through the zoo, and finally stopped in front of the monkey island. Mystified as to the whereabouts of the animals, she queried the keeper, "Where are all the monkeys today?"

"They're back in the cave, Miss—it's mating season."

"Will they come out if I throw them some peanuts?"

The keeper scratched his head. "I don't think so. Would you?"

Screams of delight piercing the air attested to the fact that Harry's tomcat was indeed the cat's meow. But, after numerous complaints from the neighbors, Harry sadly agreed to allow a veterinarian to render the cat fit to guard a sultan's harem.

"I'll bet," ventured one of Harry's neighbors weeks later, "that that ex-tom of yours just lies on the hearth now and gets fat."

"Actually," said Harry, "he still goes out. But now he goes along as a consultant."

The little old lady rushed into the taxidermist and unwrapped a package containing two recently deceased monkeys. Her instructions to the proprietor were delivered in a welter of tears.

"Favorite pets...*(blubber, sob)*...caught cold...*(moan)*...don't see how I'll live without them...*(weep, sob)*...want to have them stuffed... *(blubber, blubber)*...."

"Of course, Madam," said the proprietor in an understanding voice, "and would you care to have them mounted?"

"Oh, no," she sobbed, "just shaking hands. They were just close friends."

A pink elephant, a green kangaroo, and two yellow snakes strolled up to the bar.

"You're a little early, boys," said the bartender. "He ain't here yet."

A kangaroo hopped into one of the better midtown Manhattan bars and requested a gin Martini, not too dry and very cold, with a twist. The bartender had never seen a kangaroo outside the zoo, but he complied with the request.

"How much?" asked the kangaroo.

"Sixteen dollars," said the bartender.

As the marsupial downed the drink, the bartender remarked, "I've never seen a kangaroo in here before."

"No," said the kangaroo, "and at these prices, you're not likely to again."

Our zoologist friend tells us that long reasearch has shown definitively why mice have small balls: Apparently, not many of them know how to dance.

When we asked our zoologist friend how porcupines have sex, we were told, "Carefully, very carefully."

Marvin, a devoted amateur naturalist, spied a grasshopper perched on a blade of grass. He got down on his knees and said, "Hello, friend grasshopper. Did you know they've named a drink after you?"

"Really?" replied the grasshopper, obviously pleased. "They've named a drink Fred?"

Attend now to a fable that proves that lasting fame is not always built upon success: Once upon a time, two boll weevils from the Deep South traveled to New York, there to seek their fortune. Upon arriving, the first boll weevil got a job as a ringmaster in a small flea circus. As time went by, he moved to bigger and better flea circuses until he became internationally renowned as a flea-circus impresario. The other boll weevil, however, was unable to find any employment and, as time passed, he faded into total obscurity.

That was fifty years ago. But today, do you suppose anyone remembers that boll weevil who was once impresario of the world's greatest flea circuses? No! But we do remember the other one— the failure—for, even today, we refer to "the lesser of two weevils."

When a newly purchased rooster died after only three weeks on the job, the farmer was determined that the replacement would last longer. So, before putting the rooster into the hen coop, he dosed it heavily with vitamins and pep pills. The instant the bird was released, it charged into the coop and serviced every one of the hens therein. Then, before the farmer could stop it, it flew into the adjoining coop and proceeded to do the same for the geese. At this point, the farmer gave up and went back to the house, shaking his head and muttering, "He'll never last out the day."

Sure enough, around sunset the farmer was crossing the yard, and there lay the rooster, legs aloft, flat on its back, with two hungry buzzards slowly circling above his supine body. "Damn it!" groaned the farmer. "Now I've got to buy me another new rooster!" At which point the rooster opened one eye, winked, and, pointing at the nearing buzzards, said, "Shh!"

The new rooster caused a great stir in the barnyard. From resplendent comb to defiant spurs, he was the picture of young bantamhood. Almost immediately upon his arrival, he was greeted by an elderly rooster who took him behind the barn and whispered in his ear, "Young fellow, I'm long past my prime. All I want now is to live out my remaining days in peace and solitude. So you take over right now as ruler of the roost with my blessings."

The newcomer did just that. He went about his squirely duties as only a young rooster could. After several days, however, the elder rooster again took the young champion behind the barn.

"Kid," he whispered, "the hens have been after me for giving up my position so easily. So why don't we have a race—say, ten laps around the farmhouse? The winner becomes undisputed keeper of the henhouse, and then the hens will stop nagging me."

The young rooster, with only contempt for his elder's athletic ability, quickly agreed. Surprisingly, the older one jumped off to an early lead. His younger counterpart, weakened by the activities of the previous week, was never quite able to overtake him. As they rounded the barn for the fourth time, the elder rooster still maintained a formidable lead.

Suddenly, a shotgun blast rang out. The young rooster fell in the dust, his plumage riddled with buckshot.

"Dammit, Emmy," said the farmer. "That's the last rooster we buy from Ferguson. Four of 'em this month, and every one's been queer."

The little white-haired spinster was rocking on her front porch with her tomcat at her feet when a good fairy suddenly appeared and offered her three wishes.

"Aw, go on," the little old lady said. "If you can grant wishes, let's see you turn this rocking chair into a pile of gold."

A wave of the good fairy's wand and the spinster found herself atop a pile of pure gold. Her face lighting up, she asked, "I get two more wishes?"

"Yes," the good fairy assured her. "Anything your heart desires."

"Then make me into a beautiful, voluptuous young woman again," she ordered. Another wave of the wand and her wish was granted.

"Now," she said, "make my faithful old cat into a tall, dark, and handsome young man."

The good fairy waved her wand and disappeared as the third wish came true and a muscular swain stood where the tomcat had just been sleeping.

The young man approached the beautiful young woman, took her in his arms, and murmured gently, "Now aren't you sorry you sent me to the vet?"

A newlywed couple established a household routine that included having sexual relations each evening at 5:15. After several weeks, the bride contracted the flu and received an injection that killed all but three germs. The trio of survivors frantically discussed how they might escape. "I'm moving to the tip of her ear," said the first. "They'll never get me there."

Thinking for a moment, the second bug chirped, "I'm going to the tip of her toe!"

"You guys do what you want," retorted the third, "but when the old five-fifteen pulls out tonight, I plan to be on it."

"If you're looking for a really unusual pet," said the shop owner, "this cage contains a giant Crunch Bird. Its powerful beak and claws are capable of completely demolishing almost anything."

"How horrible," said the female customer.

"Not at all," the pet-shop owner replied, "for the bird is remarkably well behaved and completely obedient. It is only when he is given a direct command, such as 'Crunch Bird, the chair,' or 'Crunch Bird, the table,' that he attacks and destroys the thing that was named."

"Could he destroy a television set?" the woman asked, with new interest.

"Plasma, rear-projection, LCD—you name it. If the Crunch Bird was given the command he could turn any set into a pile of scrap in a few seconds."

"I want him!" the woman exclaimed. "I don't care what he costs, I want him!"

When the woman returned home, she found her husband in his usual spot—directly in front of their enormous television set. No amount of coaxing could draw him away. Her once-loving spouse had lost all interest in sex, in conversation, in everything except TV. But things will be different from now on, she thought, opening the Crunch Bird's cage.

"What sort of pet did you buy?" her husband asked, without looking up from the set. "A poodle, a parakeet?"

"I bought a Crunch Bird," she replied, preparing to give the command that would smash her electronic rival into a million pieces.

"Crunch Bird, my ass," said her husband.

The boor tapped on the sleeping parakeet's cage and said, "Hey, birdie, can you talk?"

"Sure, nimrod," said the bird. "Can you fly?"

"**N**o!" cried the girl centipede, crossing her legs. "A thousand times, no!"

A Broadway bookie was given a parrot in lieu of cash payment. The bird's vocabulary included choice phrases in English, French, Spanish, and German. Sensing a winner, the bookie hauled the bird off to his favorite bar.

"This bird is a genius," he said to the bartender, who snorted in disbelief. "Wanna bet this bird can speak four languages?" the bookie challenged.

Annoyed, the bartender finally agreed to a fifty-dollar wager. The bookie turned to the parrot and said, "*Parlez-vous français?*" There was no response.

Nor was there any reply to the question in English, Spanish, or German. The bartender picked up the bookie's wager from the bar and went about his business.

On the street, the bookie glared at the bird. "You asshole!" he exclaimed. "I've got fifty bucks riding on you and you clam up on me. I oughta strangle you!"

"Don't be a dick," the parrot replied. "Just think of the odds we'll get tomorrow!"

Complaining of the distance between campus buildings, the veterinarian's daughter wrote home for money to buy a bicycle. But by the time the money arrived, she'd changed her mind and bought a monkey instead. After a few weeks, the animal began losing its hair. Hoping her father might know a cure, she sent an e-mail: "All the hair is falling off my monkey—what should I do?"

Later that day came the terse advice: "Sell the bicycle."

During camouflage training in Louisiana, a private disguised as a tree trunk made a sudden move that was spotted by a visiting general.

"You moron!" the officer barked. "Don't you know that by jumping and yelling the way you did, you could have endangered the lives of the entire company?"

"Yes, sir," the soldier answered apologetically. "But, if I may say so, I did stand still when a flock of pigeons used me for target practice. And I never moved a muscle when a large dog pissed on my lower branches. But when two squirrels ran up my pants leg and I heard the bigger say, 'Let's eat one now and save the other until winter'—that did it."

Anna accidentally sat on a hill of fire ants while vacationing with her sister in Africa, with most unfortunate results. Her sister sent a telegram to their mother from the nearest village to let her know what had happened. The sister, having only enough money (after the hospital expenses) for a six-word wire, sent the following message: "ANACIN HOSPITAL ADAMANT BITTER ASININE PLACES."

WESTERN UNION
TELEGRAM

Payment
233 E Ohio St
Chicago Ill.

HAPPY BIRTHDAY
FROM PLAYBOY

WESTERN UNION
TELEGRAM

LeRoy Neiman

"**G**rrr," said the wolf, leaping at Little Red Riding Hood. "I'm going to eat you up!"

"For God's sake," Red replied. "Doesn't anybody screw anymore?"

Desperate for work, the young actor took a job at the zoo masquerading as a gorilla, replacing a prize animal who had died. The fellow launched into his act with gusto, screaming at the top of his lungs and pounding his chest as he swaggered around the cage. The crowd applauded wildly. Inspired, he scrambled up and over his cage into an adjoining pen occupied by four fierce lions and started goading them. As the animals approached him, the faux gorilla suddenly came to his senses and started screaming, "Help, they're going to kill me!"

"Shut up, you asshole," whispered one of the lions, "or we'll all lose our jobs!"

The chicken and the egg were lying in bed, the sheets and pillows surrounding them in post-coital disarray. A satisfied look on its face, the chicken reached over to the side table for a cigarette.

The egg grabbed the sheet, rolled over to face the wall, and said in a disgusted tone of voice, "I guess we answered *that* question once and for all."

Figures & Figleaves

Engineers are continually surprised to find that girls with the most streamlined shapes offer the most resistance.

An attractive young woman was having difficulty keeping her skirt down about her shapely legs while waiting for the bus on a windy street corner. She was aware of a man watching her struggles with considerable interest and she addressed him in an irritated voice, "It is obvious, sir, that you are no gentleman."

To which the man replied, "It's obvious that you're not, either."

For every girl with curves, there are a dozen men working the angles.

"I was a 97-pound weakling," the man said to his drinking companion, "and whenever I went to the beach with my girl, this 197-pound bully came over and kicked sand in my face. So I took this weight-lifting course I read about, and in a little while I weighed 197 pounds."

"So what happened?" his friend wanted to know.

"I went to the beach with my girl and a 257-pound bully kicked sand in my face."

Mike had just moved into his apartment and decided he should get acquainted with his across-the-hall neighbor. When the door was opened he was pleasantly surprised to be confronted by a very attractive girl. A trifle flustered by this smiling apparition, Mike came up with the following remark: "Hi, I'm your new sugar across the hall—can I borrow a cup of neighbor?"

Nothing keeps a girl on the straight and narrow more than being built that way.

A girl with an hourglass figure can often make grown men feel like playing in the sand.

A stunner walked into a dress shop and asked the manager, "I wonder if I might try on that blue dress in the window?"
    "By all means," he said. "It will only help business."

With due respect to old Charlie Darwin, although man has learned through evolution to walk in an upright posture, his eyes still swing from limb to limb.

It's usually a woman's geography that determines her history.

A middle-aged executive was becoming increasingly irritated by the constant ribbing he received at the hands of junior employees who couldn't resist making fun of his bald head. One morning, a particularly brash trainee had the gall to run his hand across the older man's skull and exclaim, "Feels just like my wife's ass!"
    With a genuinely thoughtful look on his face, the aging exec also felt his gleaming pate. "So it does," he said, "so it does."

A leading musicologist asserts that J.S. Bach had twenty children because there were no stops on his organ.

An American on a business trip to Glasgow entered a restaurant and asked the waitress what the specialty was. "Roast and rice," the lass replied in a heavy brogue.

"You certainly do roll your *R*s," the visitor observed.

"Only when I wear high heels," she replied, blushing.

Reminiscing with her girlfriend about their childhood, the young woman asked, "Did you ever play with jacks?"

"Oh, yes," her friend replied. "And with Tommy's and Freddy's, too."

When a girl says she's got a boyish figure, it's usually straight from the shoulder.

As Sam the fruit man reminded us the other day, the apple of the average playboy's eye is usually the prettiest peach with the roundest pear.

Charlie entered the airline ticket office in a rush, but did a double-take almost immediately when he saw the devastating woman behind the counter. What's more, she was sporting a silk blouse with a plunging neckline. For a couple of minutes, she was unaware of his presence, and he shamelessly took advantage of the fact. Finally, she looked up and saw him.

"Oh! How can I help you?" she asked.

Charlie heard his breath hissing in his ears like steam, but he smiled broadly and soldiered on. He did, after all, need two tickets to Pittsburgh.

"Uh—" he began, distractedly, "give me two pickets to—"

At the risk of differing with Dorothy Parker, a friend of ours insists that men often make passes at girls who wear glasses. It really depends on their frames.

Being troubled with coughing spells, a teenage girl was taken by her mother to see a doctor. He explained that the girl's chest must be examined for a proper diagnosis. Placing his stethoscope above her heart, he said, "Big breaths."

"Yeth," she replied. "And I'm only thixteen!"

Shapely limbs help many a girl to branch out.

A nurse was telling a gorgeous co-worker about the Canadian sailor who was a patient in Ward Ten. "He's tattooed," she confided in a low voice, "in a very intimate place!"

"You mean—" gasped the beautiful nurse.

"Yes! Isn't that odd? There's actually a word tattooed there: 'Swan.'"

"This I've got to see," exclaimed the voluptuous one, and she hurried off to Ward Ten. Half an hour later, she returned. "You were right," she said, "he is tattooed there. But the word is 'Saskatchewan'!"

The *maître d'hotel* at the Ritz was interviewing waiters for an important society banquet to be held in the hotel that night. There were very few applicants for the jobs and time was running short. One applicant named Angelo, when asked where he had previously worked as a waiter, gave Harry's Hash House as a reference. The maître d' reluctantly engaged Angelo, with a word of warning to mind his manners, "for this is the Ritz."

During the banquet, after serving the turtle soup, Angelo noticed that the left breast of an attractive but tipsy young debutante had fallen out of her low-cut gown into her plate of soup. Quick as a flash, Angelo jumped forward, seized the young lady's breast, dried it with a table napkin, and slipped it back into her gown.

As he was returning to the kitchen to serve the next course, the maître d' seized him by the arm and furiously denounced him as a clumsy oaf.

"But what was I to do?" Angelo cried. "I couldn't very well just leave it out there lying in the soup."

"Well of course not!" the maître d' said, stiffening noticeably. "But when an incident such as that occurs at the Ritz, one uses a warmed serving spoon!"

Peters was the university's star fullback. A few days before the big game, he injured his leg during a practice scrimmage and was told he would be unable to play in the most important game of the year. The college paper planned to announce the sad news with the headline, "Team Will Play Without Peters."

However, the Dean caught this bit of college humor before the paper went to press and ordered the editor to change it or be kicked off the paper. The editor complied, and Saturday morning the paper hit the campus with the headline, "Team Will Play With Peters Out."

As far as we're concerned, the perfect gift for the girl who has everything is a topless bathing suit.

"What part of the human body," asked the anatomy professor, "is harder than steel?" Nobody in the class volunteered the information, so he looked in the direction of a female student and asked, "Can you tell me, Miss Riley?"

She blushed a deep scarlet and lowered her eyes, stammering, "I— I can't answer that, professor!"

Crisply, he said, "The answer is the tissue of the nails. And you, Miss Riley," he added with a smile, "are an optimist."

Three female members of an exclusive country club walked into the women's shower room and were shocked to see the lower part of a man's anatomy behind the door of one of the shower stalls. "Well!" said one of the ladies, "that certainly isn't my husband!" The second one added, "He isn't mine, either."

And the third, the youngest of the three, said, "Hell, he isn't even a member of this club!"

The psychiatrist was holding a group consultation with three young mothers and their small children. "You all have obsessions," he told them. To the first one, he said, "Your obsession is eating. Why, you've even named your little girl Candy." The second, he said, was obsessed by money. "Again, it manifests itself in your child's name, Penny."

At this point, the third mother arose and, taking her little boy by the hand, whispered, "Let's go, Peter."

There was a young fellow named Lancelot
Whom the neighbors all looked on askance a lot.
For whenever he'd pass
A presentable lass,
The front of his pants would advance a lot.

A beachcomber of twenty-five had been shipwrecked on a desert island since the age of six. One day, while in search of food, he stumbled across a beautiful woman lying on the beach almost entirely naked; she'd been washed ashore from another shipwreck just that morning. After they got over their initial surprise at seeing each other, the girl wanted to know how long he had been alone on this barren bit of land.

"Almost twenty years," he said.

"Twenty years!" she exclaimed. "But how ever did you survive?"

"Oh, I fish, dig for clams, and gather berries and coconuts," he replied.

"And what do you do for sex?" she asked.

"What's that?" He looked puzzled.

Whereupon she pulled the innocent beachcomber down onto the sand beside her and proceeded to demonstrate. After they had finished, she asked how he had enjoyed it.

"That was amazing!" was the reply. "But look what it did to my clam digger!"

"Why do you have to buy such expensive brassieres?" the irate husband snapped nastily as he looked over the latest credit card statement. "You don't have much to put in them."

"By those standards," she replied, "you haven't needed a new pair of underwear in years!"

The busy Park Avenue veterinarian impatiently assured the well-dressed woman with the schnauzer that there was nothing wrong with the animal's hearing. "There's just too much hair around the dog's ears," he said. "Get some hair remover and he'll be all right."

She purchased a bottle of depilatory at a nearby pharmacy, and the clerk instructed her to use it at full strength for leg hair and to dilute it by half for underarms. "Thanks," said the woman with a puzzled frown, "but I want to use this on my schnauzer."

"Oh," said the clerk, somewhat taken aback. "Well, in that case you'd best use it at one-third strength…and…uh, I wouldn't advise bike riding for a while!"

Taking a shortcut through a graveyard on their way home, the fellow and the girl began to feel the eerie mood of the place.

"Scary, ain't it!" said the youth, putting his arm protectively around the girl.

"Yes, isn't it!" said the girl.

"Weird, ain't it!" said the fellow, holding her closer.

"Yes, isn't it!"

"Gruesome, ain't it!"

"Yes, hasn't it!"

While swimming in the nude at a deserted California beach, the young man sustained a painful sunburn over his entire body. Later that night, while in bed with his date, he found the agony almost unbearable. Stepping into the kitchen, he poured a tall glass of cold milk and submerged the object of his greatest discomfort.

"A-ha!" the girl exclaimed, watching him from the doorway. "I've always wondered how guys load that thing!"

"**W**hat floors, please?" asked the hotel elevator operator, and a young man at the back of the car called out, "Ballroom, please."

At which the man in front of him turned and said, "Oh, I'm sorry, I didn't realize I was crowding you."

After meeting at a discothèque, the young couple repaired to a local lovers' lane, where they proceeded to cement their new relationship. Having freed her of blouse and bra, he was helping remove the rest of her clothing when a police car drove by.

"Fuzz," he whispered excitedly, ducking his head.

"What did you expect," she replied, "a ponytail?"

"**F**or several weeks," the distraught factory worker confided to his psychiatrist, "I was obsessed with the idea of putting my dick in the pickle slicer. The thought kept me awake nights. When I finally fell asleep, I would dream about it. I couldn't work effectively. All I could do was stare at the pickle slicer and daydream. Finally, I couldn't control my passion. During lunch hour yesterday, I stayed in the factory and acted on my obsession."

"My God!" gasped the psychiatrist. "What happened?"

"The foreman came back from lunch early," said the worker, "saw what was going on, and fired me on the spot."

"What happened to the pickle slicer?"

"She was fired, too," the man replied.

Two career girls were discussing plans for their forthcoming vacations. "I'm going to Monaco for the Grand Prix," bubbled one enthusiastically.

"I'm afraid you're in for an awful letdown," remarked her friend. "For one thing, that's not even how it's pronounced."

Strolling through London's Soho district, the young Cockney noticed an attractive girl furiously struggling to hold down her micro-mini in the brisk wind. Tipping his hat, he said, "Airy, ain't it?"

"What the 'ell did you expect?" she replied. "Feathers?"

In the darkness of the all-but-empty theater balcony, the couple embraced so passionately that the man's toupee slid from his head. Groping to find it in the darkness, he reached under his date's skirt.

"That's it, that's it," she gasped.

"It can't be," the fellow whispered back. "I part mine on the side."

"Do you really think I can be a star?" cooed the young actress, snuggling closer to the famous producer.

"I certainly do," replied the showman. "You're already starting to make it big."

"I have a friend who thinks he may have a venereal disease," said the embarrassed young man to his doctor.

"Well," replied the physician, "take him out and let's have a look at him."

It's possible to lie with a straight face, but it's much nicer to lie with a curved body.

"Do you enjoy cocktails?" the young man asked the woman sitting to his left at the dinner party.

"I certainly do," she said. "Heard any good ones?"

Impressed by the impeccable cleanliness of the restaurant, the customer summoned his waiter over to the table to compliment him.

"We take pride in our sanitary precautions," the waiter explained. "For example, the manager makes us carry a large spoon, so we don't have to touch any of the food we serve with our hands, and we even have a string attached to our pants fly, so that we don't touch the zipper after we take a leak."

"But how do you get it back into your trousers?" the customer asked.

"I don't know about the others," the waiter confided, "but I use my spoon."

A man returned from a convention and proudly showed his wife a gallon of bourbon he'd won for having the largest sex organ of all present.

"What!" she exclaimed. "Do you mean to tell me you exhibited yourself in front of all those people?"

"Only enough to win, darling," he replied. "Only enough to win."

Shortly after arriving at the Bible-themed amusement park for their honeymoon, the nervous groom became worried about the state of his bride's innocence. Deciding on a direct confrontation, he quickly undressed, pointed at his exposed manhood, and asked his mate, "Do you know what this is?"

Without hesitating, she blushingly answered, "That's a wee-wee."

Relieved to be so successfully instructing his wife in the ways of love, the husband whispered, "From now on, dearest, this will be called a prick."

"Oh, come on now," the girl chided. "I've seen lots of pricks, and I can assure you, that's a wee-wee."

Stopping to pay a call on some of his suburban constituents, the Congressman found that they were having a party and volunteered to return at a more convenient time.

"Don't go," the host begged. "We're playing a game that you might enjoy. We blindfold the women and then they try to guess the identity of the men by feeling their genitals."

"How can you even suggest such a thing to a public servant such as myself?" the politician said.

"Oh, c'mon, you might as well play," the host urged. "Your name's already come up three times."

Two American tourists in France stopped a gendarme on the street and complained about the behavior of the pharmacist down the block. "We went there to buy some condoms," one admitted, "but the pharmacist didn't speak English and we couldn't make him understand what we wanted."

"Please continue," the officer urged.

"I tried to communicate by example," the tourist explained. "I exposed myself to him, put some money on the counter and pointed to my organ. He still didn't get the point, so my friend did the same."

"Did he understand then?" the gendarme asked.

"He smiled as if he did," the American grumbled. "But then he just opened his fly, took out the largest penis I've ever seen and scooped up the money."

Then there was the amorous actor who tried out for a part in the latest nude play only to find that the position he wanted had already been taken.

The beautiful woman had just stepped out of the bathtub in her hotel suite and was about to reach for a towel when she caught sight of a window washer taking in all of her charms. Too stunned to move, she stood staring at the man.

"Whatcha lookin' at, lady?" he finally asked. "Ain'tcha never seen a window washer before?"

"Love of my life," said the enraptured husband, "your beauty is such that it should be captured in the nude by the finest sculptor in the world."

Two gentlemen passing by the hotel room happened to overhear the conversation, paused for a moment, then rapped on the door.

"Who's there?" asked the husband.

"Two world-class sculptors from New York," came the answer.

A fashionable woman knows that bare skin never clashes with anything she's wearing.

"I know a place," said the college student to her sorority sister, "where men don't wear anything, except maybe a watch once in a while."

"Where is that?" the sister asked eagerly.

"Around the wrist, silly."

Don't ask us where we've been, but we just heard about the two nudists who decided to stop dating because they felt they were seeing too much of each other.

We know a girl who was chased out of a nudist colony because she had something on her mind.

Vacation time was suntan time as far as Janine was concerned, and she spent almost all of her day on the roof of her hotel sopping up the warm sun's rays. She wore a bathing suit the first day, but on the second, she decided that no one could see her way up there and she slipped out of it for an overall tan. She'd hardly begun when she heard someone running up the stairs; she was lying on her stomach, so pulling a towel over her derrière, she continued to recline as before.

"Excuse me, miss," said the flustered assistant manager of the hotel, out of breath from running up the stairs. "The Hotel Plaza doesn't mind your sunning on the roof, but we would very much appreciate your wearing your bathing suit as you did yesterday."

"What difference does it make?" Joan asked rather coolly. "No one can see me up here and besides, I'm covered with a towel."

"Not exactly," said the man. "You're lying on the dining room skylight."

It's easy to admire a good loser at strip poker.

Strip poker is one game in which the more you lose, the more you have to show for it.

You're playing strip poker for high stakes when you play pantyante.

An artist's model is nearly always unsuited for her work.

Then there was the little old lady with varicose veins who won first prize at a costume ball. She went nude, as a road map.

She had just finished her shower when the doorbell rang. Tiptoeing to the front door, shivering in plump, pink nudity, she called, "Who is it?"

"The blind man," came a mournful voice, so she shrugged and opened the door with one hand while reaching for her purse with the other. When she turned to face the man, he was grinning from ear to ear, and she saw that he was holding a large package in his arms.

"You can see!" she exclaimed.

"Sure," he nodded happily. "Now, where do you want I should put these blinds?"

A couple was strolling hand in hand across the nudist camp when the young male suddenly lowered his head and confessed, "Don't look now, Sally, but I think I'm falling in love with you."

Did you hear about the fellow who took a girl to a nudist camp and discovered that nothing looked good on her?

"How did you like your first stay at the nudist camp?" asked one bachelor of another.

"Well," responded his friend, "the first three days were the hardest."

We've always been partial to absent-minded professor jokes. Like the one about the guy who walked into the men's room, unbuttoned his vest, and pulled out his necktie.

A fashion expert of our acquaintance predicts that if stretch pants get any tighter, they'll be replaced by spray paint.

"That was the dullest party I've ever been to," complained the glamorous young style editor to her roommate. "God, was I bored."

"But you stayed quite a while, didn't you?" asked her roommate.

"Yes—but only because I couldn't find my clothes."

A friend of ours, just back from a nudist wedding, reports that he came within an inch of being best man.

Then there was the neophyte nudist who, despite his efforts to appear inconspicuous, stuck out like a sore thumb.

A heartening note in women's fashion is that they're now running truer to form.

A sophisticated friend claims that nothing can replace the modern swimsuit—and practically has.

Girls' dresses have gotten so short we wonder what the designers will be up to next.

Sign at the entrance of a nudists' colony: "Please bare with us."

An old roué of our acquaintance recently pointed out that about the only thing you can look down on and approve of at the same time is a plunging neckline.

It has recently been brought to our attention that a definite parallel exists between a Martini and a woman's breasts. One is not enough, and three are too many.

There's nothing like a girl with a plunging neckline to keep a man on his toes.

A New York fashion designer warns that if hemlines get any shorter, women won't dare sit down and men won't dare stand up.

And then there was the retired brassiere manufacturer who still liked to keep his hand in the business.

Women

"**D**o you know what virgins eat for breakfast?" he asked his date.

"No, what?" she replied coyly.

"Hmmm," he said, "just as I suspected."

"**I** never slept with a man until I married your father," declared the stern mother to her wild young daughter. "Will you be able to say the same thing to your daughter?"

"Yes," replied the girl, "but not with such a straight face."

A beautiful girl appeared at the gates of Paradise and asked to be admitted. Saint Peter asked her the routine question, "Are you a virgin?"

"Of course," she replied.

To be sure, Saint Peter instructed an angel doctor to examine her. When he was finished, the doctor reported, "I think we can let her in, but I must report that there were seven slight dents in her maidenhead."

Saint Peter decided that he couldn't deny her admittance for such a trifle, so he sent her along to the registration clerk. "Your name?" asked the clerk.

"Snow White," she answered.

The guy who first said, "You can't take it with you," had probably never known an old maid.

All it really takes to separate the men from the boys is girls.

A word to the weight-conscious: If you want to get a youthful figure, ask a woman her age.

The very proper spinster didn't go out very often, but she'd had some important shopping to do that morning and so decided to have her lunch in a what appeared to be a nice and quite nearby restaurant. With the noontime crowd, many customers shared their tables with strangers; the spinster selected a seat next to an attractive young woman. The girl finished her sandwich and coffee, then settled back and lit up a cigarette. The older woman controlled herself for a few moments and then snapped, "I'd commit adultery sooner than smoke at the table!"

"So would I," said the girl, "but I only have half an hour for lunch."

We've just heard about the old maid who sued a Miami Beach hotel for cruelty. Seems they gave her a room between two honeymooning couples.

The reason today's girls will do things their mothers wouldn't think of doing is that their mothers didn't think of doing them.

Some women, like prizefighters, won't go into action until they see a ring.

Women are the kind of problem most men like to wrestle with.

Women are to blame for most of the lying men do. They insist on asking questions.

Then there was the nymphomaniac who just hated to be stood up.

We heard of a club for nymphomaniacs whose meetings consist entirely of screening prospective members.

Some men don't give women a second thought. The first one covers everything.

The best years of a woman's life are usually counted in man-hours.

Many women could add years to their life if they'd just tell the truth about their age.

Since one woman we know was warned by her mother not to talk to strange men, she only speaks to those who act familiar.

A stunning blonde boarded a bus and, finding no vacant seats, asked a gentleman for his, explaining that she was pregnant. The man stood up at once and gamely gave her his seat, but couldn't help commenting that she didn't look pregnant.

"Well," she replied with a smile, "it's only been about half an hour."

"Blessed are the pure," a waggish friend of ours misquotes, "for they shall inhibit the earth."

Heard tell about a widow who wears black garters in remembrance of those who have passed beyond.

When a girl can read the handwriting on the wall, she's usually in the wrong restroom.

Girls who think they will hate themselves in the morning should learn to sleep till at least noon.

A girl's conscience doesn't really keep her from doing anything wrong—it merely keeps her from enjoying it.

The attractive young hostess was entertaining guests at a cocktail party with an account of the time she had miraculously escaped injury in an elevator whose cable had snapped.

"After you realized you were falling," interrupted one intrigued listener, "did the sins of your entire life pass before your eyes?"

"Hardly," she responded. "I only fell eleven floors!"

The crowded elevator had just begun to rise when one of the young women on board screamed and said, "I've been geesed!"

"You mean you've been goosed?" asked the elderly gentleman in front of her her.

"Listen, buddy, I know how to count," came her reply.

The young woman had just purchased some lingerie and asked if she might have the sentence "If you can read this, you are too damn close" custom embroidered on her panties.

"Yes, madam," said the clerk. "I'm quite certain that can be done. Would you prefer block or script letters?"

"Braille," said she.

If a man expects to marry a beautiful woman he has to exhibit a generous nature—or else how generous nature has been to him.

A fashion expert we know tells us that miniskirts are really quite functional, because they enable girls to run faster—which is a good thing because when they wear them, they have to.

You can't judge the modern girl by her clothes. There just isn't enough evidence.

What some young women refer to as a diary might be more aptly described as a whodunit.

Over morning coffee, the three up-and-coming public defenders were considering what kind of man they'd prefer being shipwrecked with on a desert island.

"I'd want a guy who was a wonderful conversationalist," said the first.

"That would be nice," agreed the second, "but I'd rather have a guy who knew how to hunt and could cook the things he caught."

The third said, "I'd settle for a good obstetrician."

Wits &
Halfwits

leroy neiman

The passionate divorcee was having a very difficult time getting across what she wanted from her handsome, but rather dense, date. In a final attempt at seduction, she asked, "Would you like to see where I was operated on for my appendicitis?"

"God, no!" he replied. "I hate hospitals."

The naïve young woman was seated in her doctor's office.

"Our tests indicate that you are pregnant," said the physician, "and there is every indication that you are going to have twins."

"But how can that be, doctor?" the girl protested. "I've never been out on a double-date in my life!"

Alfred had been married to lovely Arlene for less than a year and already he was beginning to suspect she was untrue to him.

Forced to leave town for the weekend on a business trip, Alfred explained the problem to his close friend, Wendell, and asked him to keep an eye on his wife while he was away.

Upon his return, Alfred demanded a complete account of Arlene's activities.

"Well," Wendell said, "the night you left a good-looking guy came over to the house. Arlene got all dressed up and they went out to a nightclub. I followed them and saw them drinking together and dancing very closely. Finally, around three in the morning, they got into a cab and I could see them hugging and kissing in the back seat. I followed them back to your house and watched through the living-room window while they mixed more drinks and hugged and kissed each other some more. Then they went into the bedroom and they switched out the lights, so I couldn't see anymore."

"That's the trouble," exclaimed Alfred. "Always that element of doubt!"

The husband emailed home that he had been able to wind up his business trip a day early and would be home on Thursday. When he walked into his apartment, however, he found his wife in bed with another man. Furious, he picked up his bag and stormed out; he met his mother-in-law on the street, told her what had happened, and announced that he was filing for divorce in the morning.

"Give my daughter a chance to explain before you take any action," the older woman pleaded. Reluctantly, he agreed.

An hour later, his mother-in-law phoned the husband at his club.

"I knew my daughter would have an explanation," she said, a note of triumph in her voice. "Her email was down!"

A *do-it-yourselfer named Alice*
Used a dynamite stick for a phallus.
   They found her vagina
   In South Carolina
And part of her anus in Dallas.

An attractive, but hard-of-hearing, young woman of our acquaintance nearly ruined herself before discovering that what the doctor ordered was not, as she misunderstood, "three hearty males a day."

Sign in a pharmacy window: FOR THE MAN WHO HAS EVERYTHING—PENICILLIN.

The distraught father hurried down the beach to the spot where his lovely daughter lay. A bronzed lifeguard stood over her.

"I've just resuscitated her, sir," he said.

"Then, by God," exclaimed the father, "you'll marry the girl!"

Some guys go out every Saturday night and sow their wild oats, then go to church on Sunday and pray for crop failure.

The two office workers were complaining about the short lunch hours.

"The boss takes an hour-and-a-half every day and expects us to get by on thirty minutes," said Tom.

"If I had an extra fifteen, I could go home for lunch," agreed Bill.

"The boss is never around at noon. Why don't we just take the extra fifteen minutes," Tom suggested.

Bill agreed and that very day he went home for lunch. Naturally his wife wasn't expecting him and when he didn't find her in the front part of the house, Bill looked in the bedroom. When he opened the door, he discovered his wife in bed with his boss. Bill backed out of the room quietly, slipped out of the house without being noticed, and hurried back to the office.

The following morning Tom asked him if he was going to take the extra fifteen minutes again that day.

"Hell, no," said Bill. "I almost got caught yesterday!"

We've just received this tidbit from a usually reliable source concerning a certain Senator who, it seems, had to visit Chicago recently for a Committee Hearing and wanted to take a female acquaintance along.

"I have senatorial immunity," he assured her, "so you needn't be afraid of the Mann Act."

"Afraid of it?" she said. "Why, Senator, I just adore it!"

An engaging but somewhat vacant young man we met recently thought "vice versa" referred to limericks.

The high-priced lawyer was sitting in his office when his secretary announced the arrival of a new client, who turned out to be a very sexy young mother.

"I want to divorce my husband," said the woman.

"On what grounds?" the lawyer asked.

"Infidelity," came the reply. "I don't think my husband has been faithful to me."

"What makes you think that?"

"Well," she said, "I don't think he's the father of my child."

Janice, the cute au pair in the Johnson household, came to her mistress with a sad story to tell. Janice, it seemed, was going to have a baby—out of wedlock—and she would have to quit. Mrs. Johnson, though stunned, came back with a game offer, for good childcare is hard to find, and Janice was good.

"You'll do no such thing, my dear," she said. "You'll have your child here and we'll adopt it and raise it as our own." And so it was arranged, and everybody was happy.

But the following year, it was the same story. Once again, Mrs. Johnson insisted that the family adopt the child and Janice stay on. The third year was a repeat performance.

When Janice came to her for the fourth time, Mrs. Johnson shook her head from side to side. "Janice, Janice," she said, "whatever are we to do with you?"

"There's nothing to be done, madam," said Janice. "This time I'm truly leaving. I refuse to take care of so many children."

A bookseller of our acquaintance admits to having been momentarily flustered when a dim young customer asked for a volume he referred to as How to Make Friends and Influential People.

I believe you have the wrong number," said the man into the phone. "You'll have to call the weather bureau for that information."

"Who was that?" his young wife asked.

"Some guy wanting to know if the coast was clear."

The young woman stood at the teller's window in the bank, an attractive figure marred only slightly by the fact that the light in her baby-blue eyes was more than somewhat vacant. The teller examined the woman and the check she wished to cash with equal concentration. Then he asked her to identify herself.

For a moment, her lovely brow was corrugated by puzzlement; then, her expression brightening, she pulled a small mirror from her handbag, glanced in it, and, with relief, said, "Yes. It's me all right."

Strolling into the admitting office of a large hospital, a ravishing young woman told the nurse on duty that she wanted to see an upturn.

"You mean an intern, don't you, dear?" asked the kindly nurse.

"Well, whatever you call it, I want a contamination," replied the girl.

"You mean examination," corrected the nurse.

"Maybe so," allowed the girl. "I want to go to the fraternity ward."

"Maternity ward," said the nurse, with a slight smile.

"Look," insisted the girl, "I don't know much about big words but I do know that I haven't demonstrated for two months and I think I'm stagnant."

Her name was Clarissa and she was curved, Harry decided, in a manner that could only be called awesome. She was also, alas, virtually brainless, but luckily this lack was not a hindrance to the type of entertainment Harry had in mind for the evening. He was, therefore, delighted when she agreed to accompany him to his apartment.

As he mixed the drinks with fingers nervously nimble with anticipation, Clarissa wandered aimlessly around his apartment, pausing here and there to cast a perplexed eye over a book title or painting that eluded her. Finally, she stopped stock-still before his fireplace.

"What in the world is that thing?" she asked, pointing to a carved wooden object resting on the mantel.

"Oh, that's African," he responded. "It was used in fertility rites. Actually, it's a phallic symbol."

"Well," Clarissa said, demurely patting her hair into place, "I hate to tell you what it looks like."

Flustered and flushed, Carol sat in the witness chair. The beautiful young woman had gotten herself named corespondent in a divorce case, and was being questioned in court.

"So, Miss Jones," the lawyer intoned, "you admit that you went to a hotel with this man?"

"Yes, I do, but I couldn't help it."

"Couldn't help it? Why not?"

"He deceived me."

"And how did he do that?"

"Well," Carol said earnestly, "he told the clerk at the reception desk that I was his wife."

An acquaintance of ours thinks the Playboy Foundation is some kind of cosmetic.

Grace and Martha were recent graduates of a very strict Christian academy, and they were spending their summer together in New York, doing outreach. On this particular afternoon, they had accepted an invitation to the opening of his new show from a young painter whom they had met out in Brooklyn a few weeks before. As they approached an extremely provocative nude, Grace couldn't help noticing that the canvas bore a striking resemblance to her girlfriend.

"Martha," she gasped, "that painting looks exactly like you. Don't tell me you've been posing in the nude!"

"Certainly not!" Martha stammered, blushing furiously. "H-he must have painted it from memory."

A number of showgirls were entertaining the troops at a remote Army camp. They had been performing all afternoon and were not only tired but very hungry. Finally, at the close of the show, the major asked, "Would you girls like to mess with the enlisted men or the officers this evening?"

"Either way," spoke up one of their number. "But we've just got to have something to eat first."

The young reporter was interviewing a woman who had just reached her hundredth birthday.

"To what do you attribute your remarkable good health?" he asked.

"Well," she said, thoughtfully, "I've always eaten moderately, worked hard, I don't smoke or drink, and I keep good hours."

"Have you ever been bedridden?" the reporter asked.

"Well, sure," said the elderly lady, "but don't put that in your paper."

Simple George was no great catch, so when he met a remarkably beautiful girl who seemed to be wildly in love with him, he immediately proposed marriage.

"Poor dear boy," she said, "don't you realize that I'm a nymphomaniac?"

"Darling," replied ardent George, "I don't care if you steal, as long as you're faithful to me."

A young simpleton we know who is mad for the horses thought he had a sure winner the other day at the track. The tote board listed his horse as starting at 25 to 1, and he knew the race didn't begin until 1:00 P.M.

The new bride complained to her doctor about the birth-control pills he had given her.

"What seems to be the problem?" he asked.

"They must not be the right size, doctor," she said. "They keep falling out."

Coming home early from work one afternoon, the exec found his wife lying naked in bed, breathing heavily and clearly distracted.

"Alice, what's the matter?" he asked.

"I think I'm having a heart attack," she gasped.

Quickly, he rushed downstairs to the phone and was dialing a doctor when his son hurried in and exclaimed, "Dad! There's a naked man in the front closet."

Going over to the closet, the exec opened the door and found his best friend cowering there. "For God's sake, Frank," blustered the husband, "my wife is upstairs having a heart attack and here you are sneaking around scaring the children!"

The perky bride returned home with an ultra-Mod, clear-plastic minidress and held it up for her stodgy husband's approval.

"Why, you can see right through it," the astonished husband gasped.

"No you can't, silly," she answered. "Not when I'm in it."

A wiseguy had made a lot of money in "carting" and was beginning to move into the higher levels of society, and he was afraid his favorite mistress would embarrass him with her unpolished language. He decided to send her away for a very expensive crash course in grammar. She returned three months later, burst into his office and exclaimed, "Were you blue while I was gone?"

"All that money," the mobster moaned, "and she still has her tenses wrong."

"I hope you're not planning to be alone in that bachelor's apartment tonight," the worried mother cautioned her daughter.

"Don't be silly," the young woman answered. "He'll be there with me."

The cute and efficient young maid seemed to enjoy her work in the Governor's mansion until one day, without warning, she gave notice.

"Why do you wish to leave?" the First Lady, a fervent evangelical just like her husband, asked her. "Is there anything wrong?"

"I just can't stand the suspense in this house a minute more," the maid replied.

"Suspense?" said the confused mistress. "What do you mean?"

"It's the sign over my bed," the girl explained. "You know, the one that says: WATCH YE, FOR YE KNOW NOT WHEN THE MASTER COMETH."

On the last night of his first buying trip to Paris, a young furniture importer from the United States met an attractive French girl in the hotel elevator. She spoke no English, however, and neither could understand a word the other was saying until the resourceful merchant devised a means of communication for the occasion. Taking out a pencil and notebook, he drew a sketch of a taxi. She nodded approvingly, and off they went for a ride in the Bois de Boulogne. A little later, he drew a picture of a table laden with food and wine bottles, and when she nodded her assent, they headed for a sumptuous repast at Taillevent. After dinner, she was delighted with a sketch he made of a dancing couple, so they danced the evening away at a popular Left Bank *boîte*. Finally the girl picked up the pencil and, with a knowing glance at her clever escort, she proceeded to make a crude drawing of what was clearly intended to be a four-poster bed. He stared at his charming companion in amazement; and when he took her home, while he was kissing her good night on her doorstep, during the long ride back to his hotel, and even on his flight back home the following afternoon, he still couldn't figure out how she had known he was in the furniture business.

An experienced steward on a plush cruise ship was giving a young apprentice advice on how to handle unexpected situations. "If you enter a cabin at an embarrassing moment, pretend not to notice and try to say something to put the passenger at ease. For instance, yesterday I entered a cabin just as a lovely young woman was about to step into the shower. Without a moment's hesitation, I turned away, saying, 'Excuse me, sir,' and went out."

That afternoon, while serving tea to the passengers, the young steward walked in on a couple in the middle of having energetic sex. Remembering what he had been told, he promptly turned away and, fumbling with the cups, politely inquired, "Either of you gentlemen take sugar?"

A movie-studio president who was not exactly noted for his knowledge of the English language received a well-written story titled "The Optimist." After reading the manuscript, he called a meeting of the company's most creative minds and announced, "Gentlemen, we got us a great story here, but I want all of you to think of something simpler for a title. There ain't many people will know the technical term for eye doctor."

When the announcer on the Armed Forces radio network finished the newscast, he closed with the correct time. "For you Navy men," he said, "it's now eight bells. For you men in the Army, it's now 0800. And for all you officers," he concluded, "the little hand's on eight and the big hand's on twelve."

A colonel was chatting with a young second lieutenant in the officer's club when a major approached, coughed discreetly, and said he'd like to speak to the colonel about a matter of some importance. "Go ahead," said the colonel.

"I'd rather not in front of the lieutenant, sir," murmured the major.

"Well," observed the colonel, "spell it, then."

Plays on Words

Our Research Department tells us that in the days of Queen Elizabeth I, some ladies-in-waiting liked to curl up with a good book, while others were satisfied with one of the pages.

Imagine the girl's surprise when she walked into the playboy's apartment and discovered he had no chairs, no tables, no bed, no furniture at all. She was floored!

We just overheard a couple of our new interns discussing one of the more dashing members of our staff. "He dresses so well," said one.

"And so quickly," replied her girlfriend.

From London comes the story of the three professors of literature who, while returning from lunch, encountered several ladies of pleasure who were patrolling the street en masse. "What might one call such a congregation?" mused the first professor, a Shakespearean specialist. "A flourish of strumpets?"

The second professor, being an authority on the novels of Anthony Trollope, chuckled and said, "A chapter of trollops?"

But the best description, we think, came from the youngest among them, a generalist by training: "An anthology of pro's."

Canned and frozen juices are becoming more and more popular, but most men still prefer to squeeze their own tomatoes.

We just heard about the street cleaner who got fired because he couldn't keep his mind in the gutter.

"To me," said one, "he's a pain in the neck."

"Strange," said the other, "I had a much lower opinion of him."

The movie producer traveled all the way to Europe, but returned to Hollywood disappointed. He had contacted the beautiful Italian actress he'd been seeking, all right, but, unfortunately, she refused to come across.

"Darling," he breathed, "after making love I doubt if I'll ever be able to get over you—so would you mind answering the phone?"

The snooty woman was approached on the dance floor by a man slightly her junior.

"I'm sorry," she said in a superior tone, "but I couldn't dance with a child."

"Oh, sorry," he said. "I didn't know your condition."

A world-traveling friend who has just returned from Tibet, informs us that in those parts a "coolie" is a quickie in the snow.

In a recent discussion on world affairs, a friend observed the difference between war and peace is there has never been a good war.

"My mother," said the young woman to her date, "says there are some things a girl should not do before twenty."

"Your mother is right," said her boyfriend. "I don't like a large audience either."

Verily, a man never knows whether he likes bathing beauties until he has bathed one.

Girls who look good in the best places usually get taken there.

"Hey, wise guy," complained the mistress to her lover, "what's the big idea? You promised you'd take me to Florida!"

"I said nothing of the sort," insisted her gentleman friend. "I merely commented that I was going to tamper with you."

The new accounts director was dictating a note to her personal assistant. She paused, uncertain about the proper phrasing in the next sentence.

"Do you 'retire a loan'?" she asked the young man.

"Not when I can help it," he replied with a smile.

Word is in from the Middle East about the sultan who left a call for seven in the morning.

The sexy freshman returned to the sorority house after spending the night with her boyfriend. Asked what she had for breakfast, she replied with satisfaction, "Him and eggs."

"May I be of help, sir?" asked the impeccably attired salesman in the foreign-car showroom.

"Yep," said the casually dressed and obviously self-made man of means. "My girlfriend isn't feeling well. Whatcha got in the way of a get-well car?"

"Don't you think he dresses nattily?" asked one colleague of another regarding the young executive walking past the water cooler.

"Natalie who?" her co-worker demanded.

An ornithologist of our acquaintance is troubled by the fact that the stork is too often held responsible for circumstances that might better be attributed to a lark.

A woman with a past attracts men who hope history will repeat itself.

Passionate picnickers should bear in mind that some girls are like flowers—they grow wild in the woods.

Cynthia's fine figure had been poured into a beautiful form-fitting gown and she made a point of calling her date's attention to it over and over again throughout the evening. Finally over a nightcap in his apartment he said, "You've been talking about that dress all evening long. You called my attention to it first when we met for cocktails, mentioned it again at dinner, and yet again at the theater. Now that we're here alone in my penthouse, what do you say we drop the subject?"

Next to a beautiful girl, sleep is the most wonderful thing in the world.

Almost as pitiable as the fellow who was tried and found wanting is the guy who wanted and was found trying.

History credits Adam and Eve with being the first bookkeepers, because they invented the loose-leaf system.

You never know how a girl will turn out until her folks turn in.

Latest word we have from Hollywood concerns a young producer moving into lavish new offices who had his interior decorator on the carpet because she'd forgotten to include a studio couch.

Pierre, a passionate masseur, was recently fired when he rubbed a female customer the wrong way.

Sometimes a woman attracts a man with her mind, but more often she attracts him with what she doesn't mind.

After a pleasant picnic in the woods, Alice described her boyfriend as the down-to-earth type.

Women who don't repulse men's advances advance men's pulses.

Whether or not a girl in a rented bathing suit attracts a lot of attention depends primarily on where the rent is.

The man who can read a woman like a book usually likes to read in bed.

Some men make friends quickly. With strangers it takes a little longer.

Gently massaging the trick knee of his attractive young patient, the doctor inquired, "What's a joint like this doing in a nice girl like you?"

Americans are people who insist on living in the present, tense.

"But Robert," she gasped, "why did you park here when there are so many nicer spots farther down the road?"

He stopped what he was doing just long enough to mutter, "Because I believe in love at first site."

The John Birch Society is reportedly organizing a youth auxiliary— the Sons of Birches.

Many a man has been slapped because his hand was quicker than the "aye."

We know a girl who thinks she's a robot just because she was made by a scientist.

"Laura," said the disapproving girlfriend, "that young man who's been walking you through the park strikes me as being exceedingly unpolished."

"Well," Laura answered, "he is a little rough around the hedges."

"What are you reading?" asked the prison librarian.

"Nothing much," replied the prisoner. "Just the usual escapist trash."

We've just heard that the Italian government is installing a clock in the Leaning Tower of Pisa. After all, what good is it if you have the inclination, but not the time?

A young woman of our acquaintance who always sleeps in the buff awoke one morning to find herself completely dressed.

"My God," she cried, "I've been draped!"

Then there was the coffee bean who, though she could be made instantly, still preferred the old grind.

Then there was Christian-college girl who was expelled from school for having a record player in her room—the local disc jockey.

Then there were the two Burmese girls looking for a Mandalay.

Why a man would want a wife is a big mystery to some people. Why a man would want two wives is a bigamystery.

The next phase in the exploration of space is sure to make headlines: Scientists are planning to put three hundred head of cattle into orbit. It'll be the herd shot round the world.

When the sultan entered his harem unexpectedly, his wives let out a terrified sheik.

The man who likes to lie in bed can usually find a girl willing to listen to him.

The manufacturer of a well-known tonic for people with "tired" blood received this inadvertently racy testimonial from a little old lady who lived on a farm in Tennessee:

"Before taking your tonic," the woman wrote, "I was too tired to hoe the fields or pick the cotton. But after only two bottles of your delicious mixture, I've become the best cotton-picking hoer in the county!"

When her gardener suddenly took ill, the wealthy matron decided to visit him in the hospital. Approaching the visitors' desk, she announced, "I've come to see Mr. Johnston in room six-thirteen."

"Are you his wife?" asked the nurse on duty.

"Certainly not!" retorted the haughty dowager. "I'm his mistress."

Overheard at our local nightclub: "She's the kind of girl you could fall madly in bed with."

The British anthropologist was doing some research in an isolated African village, and the local tribal leader asked if he would like to attend a trial his people were conducting that afternoon. "I think you'll be surprised," said the chief, "at how well we've copied your country's legal procedures. You see, we have read the accounts of many English trials in your newspapers."

When the scientist arrived at the crudely constructed court-house, he was indeed amazed at how closely the African court officials resembled those of his native land. Both counsels were suitably attired in long black robes and the traditional white powdered wigs worn by all British jurists, each arguing his case with eloquence and proper judicial propriety. But he couldn't help being puzzled by the occasional appearance of a bare-breasted tribal girl who ran through the crowd waving her arms frantically. After the trial, the anthropologist congratulated his host on what he had seen and then asked, "What was the purpose of having a seminude woman run through the courtroom during the trial?"

"We were careful to copy every detail," replied the tribal chieftain, "and all the accounts we read in your papers about British trials invariably mention something about 'an excited titter' running through the gallery."

During his examination of a newly arrived Viennese immigrant, the gynecologist inquired, "Have you had a checkup within the past year?"

"I don't believe so, darlink," she said. "Just an occasional Hungarian or two."

We were not particularly surprised to learn recently that Democrats generally have more children than Republicans. After all, who ever heard of anyone enjoying a good piece of elephant?

The battle of the sexes will never be won by either side, because there's too much fraternizing with the enemy.

A friend reports that during a recent trip to Ireland he was a lunch guest at a monastery and was served such delicious fish and chips that he asked the good brothers if he might be allowed to meet the cook, in order to thank him personally for the delicious meal. There were several men working in the kitchen and our friend asked which of them had prepared the fish and chips.

"Well, I'm the fish friar," one man replied, "and that's the chip monk over there."

A wedding ring may not be as tight as a tourniquet, but it does an equally good job of stopping circulation.

A friend of ours says that an ounce of suggestion is sometimes worth a pound of lure.

The prof was telling his early morning class, "I've found that the best way to start the day is to exercise for five minutes, take a deep breath of air, and then finish with a cold shower. Then I feel rosy all over."

A sleepy voice from the back of the room said, "Tell us more about Rosy."

A young man walked into a drugstore that was being tended by the owner's shrewish wife. "May I have six condoms, miss?" he asked.

"Don't you 'Miss' me," the elderly woman snippily replied.

"OK," the man said, "better make it seven."

We've heard about a girl who wanted a divorce because her husband was getting indifferent.

A knowledgeable friend of ours informs us that when a girl tells her boyfriend she's a perfect thirty-eight, she expects him to grasp what she's talking about.

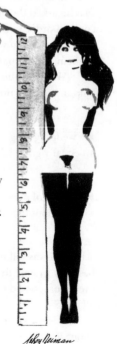

Some college kids have a faculty for making love, while others just have a student body.

The slightly overweight sophomore visited the kindly campus psychiatrist to report despondently that she thought she was losing her boyfriend.

"Why don't you diet?" asked the good doctor.

"That's a good idea," she said. "What color do you think he'd like?"

During a visit to the zoo, the inquisitive child asked, "Mommy, how do lions make babies?"

"I don't know, dear," replied the mother. "Most of your father's friends are Rotarians."

"**M**y wife's an angel," observed the man to the guy sitting next to him at the bar.

"You're lucky," answered the other unhappily. "Mine's still alive."

According to one pundit we know, the trouble with political jokes is that they sometimes get elected.

Then there was the sweet young nymph who hated to be laughed at but didn't mind being satyrized.

Then there was the bachelor who continually felt the need to insert his masculinity.

A muscle-bound beach rat was showing off by lifting two bikinied women high in the air, one on each arm.

"Wow," said a nearby girlwatcher to his buddy, "look at the girls on that boob!"

A handsome advertising executive attended a party given by a female colleague and left with an extremely attractive guest. In the office the next morning, he thanked the hostess and explained that he really liked her friend.

"Oh, she's not really a friend of mine," the girl responded. "Just an acquaintance."

"Well, in that case," the man chuckled, "I'm happy to have made your acquaintance."

Then there was the lusty swan who left his pond during the mating season, stopped the first human he saw, and demanded, "Take me to your Leda."

The shapely topless dancer went to Mass dressed in her working clothes, but was stopped at the door by the priest. "Miss," he said, "you can't go in like that."

"But, Father," protested the churchgoer, "I have a divine right."

"Aye, and your left isn't bad, either," the man of the cloth responded, "but you still can't enter the church without proper attire."

One nice thing about the battle of the sexes—it will never be a cold war.

Convicted of murder and sentenced to death, the shapely young woman asked, as a last request, that she be hanged in the nude. Although the warden thought this unusual, he felt a last request was not something to be denied. When the condemned prisoner arrived at the gallows, the hangman gasped, "My God, you have the most beautiful body I've ever seen."

Came the whispered reply, "It's all yours if you keep your trap shut."

Definitions

Acute Alcoholic   An attractive drunk.

Adolescence   The age between puberty and adultery.

Adultery   When a husband is too good to be true.

Adult Western   One in which the hero still loves his horse, only now he's worried about it.

Alcoholic   A guy you don't like who drinks as much as you do.

Alcoholic Actor   Ham on rye.

Alimony   Bounty on the mutiny; A system by which, when two people make a mistake, one of them has to pay for it; The billing without the cooing; Having an ex-husband you can bank on; Disinterest, compounded annually; A splitting headache; The high cost of leaving.

Anatomy   Something that everybody has, but it looks better on a girl.

Appetizers	Little things you eat until you lose your appetite.
Artificial Insemination	Copulation without representation; Inoculate conception.
Artist's Model	Attireless worker.
Asphyxiation	A fanny fetish.
Assault	What everyone likes to be taken with a grain of.
Autoeroticism	Doing your own thing.
Automated	A couple making love in a car.
Avalanche	A mountain getting its rocks off.
Bachelor	A man who believes in life, liberty, and the happiness of pursuit; A man who has no children to speak of; A fellow who is crazy to get married—and knows it; A man who never makes the same mistake once; One who's footloose and fiancée free; A fellow who can take women or leave them and prefers to do both; A man who thinks seriously about marriage; A rolling stone who gathers no boss; A man who never has a bride idea; A man who believes in wine, women, and s'long; A guy with a strong will looking for a girl with a weak won't; A fellow who prefers to ball without the chain.
Bachelor Apartment	A wildlife sanctuary.
Bad Trip	Acid indigestion.
Bar Belle	Something to be picked up.

Bar Stool	What Daniel Boone stepped in.
Bathing Beauty	A girl worth wading for.
Beatnik	Santa Claus the day after Christmas; A man who's dropped the job but kept the coffee break.
Beatnik Cannibal	One who eats three squares a day.
Bedbug	A nymphomaniac.
Beer Baron	Malty millionaire.
Belly-Dancer's Agent	Abdominal showman.
Bigamist	A man who has loved not wisely but two well.
Bikini	A bare trap.
Bisexual	A man who likes girls as well as the next fellow.
Bore	A guy with a cocktail glass in one hand and your lapel in the other.
Braggart	A man who enters all conversation feat first.
Bragging	The patter of little feats.
British Atheist	One who doesn't believe in John Lennon.
Brothel	Home Is Where the Tart Is.
Brothel Sprouts	The children of a madam.
Buccaneer	You have one on each side of your buccan head.
Buddhist	One who practices yoga bare.
Buffalo	A greeting between two nudists.

Bulldozer	Someone who sleeps through office meetings.
Burlesque	A broad takeoff.
Burlesque Theater	A place where belles peel.
Cad	A man who refuses to help his date with the breakfast dishes.
Castration	A eunuch experience.
Cat-O'-Nine-Tails	A hipster with a busy social life.
Censor	A person who sticks his No's into other people's business.
Centaur	The world's cheapest hooker.
Chafing Dish	A girl who has been stood up on a date; A girl in a tight leotard.
Chaperone	One who could never make the team but is still in the field intercepting passes; An older woman who accompanies young women to see that they do not indulge in any of the things she would have indulged in if she hadn't been chaperoned when she was a young woman.
Chastity Belt	An antithrust suit.
Cherry Cobbler	A virgin shoemaker.
Cherry Tart	A contradiction in terms.
Chestnut	A man who is crazy about breasts.
Chest Protector	A bouncer at a topless restaurant.
Chimpanzee	A gay monkey.

Chinese Voyeur	Peking Tom.
Chiseler	A man who goes stag to a wife-swapping party.
Chivalry	A man's inclination to help a woman from everyone but himself.
Clear Conscience	Poor memory.
Clothes Line	"How would you like a new Dior gown and a Prada bag?"
Cobra	The kind worn by Siamese twins.
Cocktail Party	A gathering at which you meet people who drink so much you can't even remember their names.
Cocktails	Sips that passion the night.
College	A fountain of knowledge where all go to drink.
Comic Strip	A burlesque queen who tells jokes while she peels.
Compulsive Gambler	A guy who'd rather lay a bet than anything else.
Condom	A labor-saving device; An article to be worn on every conceivable occasion.
Condominium	A prophylactic for midgets.
Confirmed Bachelor	A man who goes through life without a hitch.
Connoisseur	A man who collects old masters and young mistresses.
Continence	Mind over what matters.

Conversation Piece	A girl men like to talk about; A girl who likes to talk in bed.
Cookie	A virgin doughnut.
Cooperation	An exchange between a man and woman in which she coos while he operates.
Cooperative Girl	A woman who reclines to answer a question.
Counterfeit Money	Homemade bread.
Courtship	An entertaining introduction to a dull book.
Death	Nature's way of telling us to slow down.
Debate	What lures de fish.
Difficult Age	When she's too old to be a Brownie and too young to be a Bunny.
Divorce Court	A hall of blame.
Double Joint	Tea for two.
Drip-Dry	An ignorant teetotaler.
Drive-In	Place where a guy parks his car to try out his clutch.
Drive-In Movie	Wall-to-wall car-petting.
Dry Dock	A nondrinking member of the medical profession.
Ecstasy	Something that happens between the Scotch and soda and the bacon and eggs.
Efficient Nurse	One who can make a patient without disturbing the bed.

Egotist	A guy who suffers from I strain.
Eloquence	The ability to describe Halle Berry without using one's hands.
Entrance Exam	A premarital checkup.
Erogenous Zone	"The skin you love to touch."
Eunuch	A man cut off from temptation.
Eunuch King	An impotentate.
Executive Suite	A sugar daddy.
Exhibitionist	A person who discards three aces in a strip-poker game.
Exotic Dancer	A girl who brings home the bacon a strip at a time.
Experience	The wonderful knowledge that enables you to recognize a mistake when you make it again.
False Pregnancy	Laboring under a misconception.
Falsies	Hidden persuaders; Padded attractions; Absentease.
Falsie Salesman	A fuller bust man.
Feast of the Vestal Virgins	Cherries' jubilee.
Flag-Waving Speech	Star-spangled banter.
Football Game	A contest where a spectator takes four quarters to finish a fifth.
Fornication	Adultery without benefit of clergy.

Frustration	A transvestite in a nudist colony; Nixed emotions; The first time you discover you can't do it the second time. *See also* **Panic**.
Fun-Loving	The only kind there is.
G-String	A gownless evening strap.
Gay Blade	The Fire Island fencing champion.
Genius	A nudist with a memory for faces.
Gigolo	A fee-male.
Girls' School	An institution of higher yearning.
Gold-Digger	A girl who breaks dates by going out with them; A human gimme pig; A guy who's got what it takes to take what a girl's got; A girl who believes in sinner take all; A fund-loving guy.
Good Clean Fun	Taking a bath together.
Gossip	Someone who puts one and one together— even if they're not.
Gourmet	A man who is invited for an evening of wine, women, and song—and asks what kind of wine.
Grimace	A fighter pilot with one wing shot away.
Hangover	Wrath of grapes.
Happiness	Finding the owner of a lost bikini.
Harlot	A place that sells used hars.
Harp	A nude Steinway.

Henpecked Husband	One who needs to tell his pregnant wife that he is sterile.
Hermaphrodite	Bisexual built for two.
High-Fidelity	A drunk who goes home regularly to his wife.
High Noon	A four-Martini lunch.
Hollywood	A city where they put beautiful frames in pictures; A place where you can lie on the sand and look at the stars—or vice-versa.
Home Cooking	The place a cuckold thinks his wife is.
Homogeneous	A wise old queer.
Homosexual	A man's man.
Hula	A shake in the grass.
Hungarian	A well-endowed man from Gary, Indiana.
Husband	A man who began by handing out a line and ended by walking it.
Hymen	A greeting to male companions.
Hypochondriac	One who can't leave being well enough alone.
Illegitimate Child	A bungle of joy.
Immaturity	Knowing where it's at—but not what it's for.
Impotence	Emission impossible.
Incest	Sibling revelry; A sport the whole family can enjoy; Rolling your own; Sibling ribaldry.
Individualist	A man who lives in the city and commutes to the suburbs.

Inhibitions	Being tied up in nots.
Intoxication	A physical state in which one feels sophisticated without being able to pronounce it.
Jamaica	What's usually asked of a man by his friends when he comes back from a date.
Jury	A group of twelve people selected to decide who has the better lawyer.
Kiss	An application for a better position.
Las Vegas	A great place to get tanned and faded at the same time.
Latent Homosexuality	Swishful thinking.
To Lay	The object of a proposition.
Lesbian Cocktail Lounge	A her-she bar.
Lesbians	Bosom buddies.
Libertine	A swinging adolescent.
Liquor Store	A stupor market.
Locomotive	A crazy reason for doing it.
Logarithm	A Catholic birth-control record.
Love Letter	Something that often turns out to be a noose paper.
Lover's Leap	The distance between twin beds.
Low-Class Brothel	Humpty-dumpty.

Luck	What a man experiences when he meets a girl who's at the age when her voice is changing from "No" to "Yes."
Madam	Someone for whom the belles toil; One who offers vice to the lovelorn.
Mad-Money	Psychiatrist's fee.
Maiden Aunt	A girl who never had sense enough to say "uncle."
Maidenhead	A virgin who smokes a lot of pot.
Manic Depressive	A person whose philosophy is easy glum, easy glow.
Marijuana	The only kind of grass capable of mowing down the gardener.
Masochism	The agony of the ecstasy.
Masochist	One who would rather be switched than fight; A person who gets his kicks getting kicks.
Masseurs	People who knead people.
Maternity Dressmaker	A mother frocker.
Mate Swapping	Intermarital extracourse.
Mermaid	A bottomless girl in a topless suit.
Meteor	What most girls are than Kate Moss.
Meteorologist	A man who can look into a girl's eyes and predict whether.
Minimum	A tiny British mother.

Minute-Man	A fellow who double-parks in front of a house of ill repute.
Mistress	A cutie on the Q.T.; Halfway between a mister and a mattress.
Monastery	A home for unwed fathers.
Money	The poor man's credit card.
Monotony	Marriage to one woman at a time.
Morality	That instinctive sense of right and wrong that tells some people how everyone else should behave.
Motel	A love-inn.
Mother's Day	Nine months after father's day.
Neurotic	A person who worries about things that didn't happen in the past, instead of worrying about something that won't happen in the future, like normal people; Anyone who likes a psychiatrist's couch better than a double bed.
Nice Girl	One who whispers sweet nothing-doings in your ear.
Nightclub	A place where the tables are reserved but the patrons aren't.
Noel Coward	A guy who's afraid to go home to his wife after the office Christmas party.
Nudism	A different way of looking at things; Exposure with composure.

Nudist One who suffers from clothestrophobia; A buff buff.

Nudist Camp A place where the peeling is mutual; A place where nothing goes on.

Nudist Colony A place where men and women air their differences.

Nudists People who go in for altogetherness.

Nymphomania "Aye" trouble; A disease in which the patient enjoys being bedridden.

Nymphomaniac A go-go-go-go girl; A girl who belives that it's every man for herself.

Old Age A time when a man sees a pretty girl and it arouses his memory instead of anything else.

Old-Fashioned Girl The one who gets kissed good-night instead of good morning.

Old Maid A confirmed hope addict.

Optimist A husband who goes down to the marriage bureau to see if his license has expired; A man who sits in the last row of a theater and winks at the showgirls; A pregnant woman who rubs vanishing cream on her stomach; A man who makes a motel reservation before a blind date; A man who, after coming home unexpectedly and finding cigar butts in the ashtrays, decides his wife must have given up cigarettes.

Oral Contraceptive The word "no."

Orgasm	The gland finale.
Orgy	Group therapy; A screw ball.
Pajamas	Item of clothing usually placed next to the bed in case of fire.
Panic	The second time you discover you can't do it the first time. *See also* **Frustration**.
Paranoid	A couple interrupted by a cop in lovers' lane.
Parlay	One that is just average.
Peeping Tom	A window fan.
Peer Group	A voyeurs' club.
Perambulator	Last year's fun on wheels.
Pessimist	One who has no faith in future degenerations.
Petting Party	An affair that lasts until someone gives in, gives up, or gives out.
Peyote	A trance plant.
Philanderer	A man with a perfect sense of two-timing.
Piéce de résistance	A French virgin.
Pillage	About sixteen, for most girls.
Pimp	A snatch purser; A fornicaterer
Platonic Friendship	What develops when two people grow tired of making love to each other.
Platonic Relationship	Mind over mattress.
Playboy	A man with an eye for an "aye."

Poise	Raising only your eyebrows on your first trip to a nudist camp.
Political Moderate	A guy who makes enemies left and right.
Polyunsaturated	A dry parrot.
Popular Girl	One who has been weighed in the balance and found wanton.
Population Explosion	The result of too many overbearing women; When people take leave of their census.
Potholder	What you don't want to be when the police arrive.
Pot Roast	Cookout for 'heads.
Powder	What a cad takes if his girlfriend forgets her pill.
Practical Nurse	One who falls in love with a wealthy old patient.
Pregnancy	Taking seriously something that was poked in fun.
Primate	A sultan's favorite wife.
Prostitution	Fee love; The only business in which profits go up when the assets go down.
Protein	A prostitute too young to vote.
Prudery	Meddle-class morality.
Psychiatrist	Someone who doesn't have to worry as long as other people do.

Psychologist	A man who watches everybody else when a beautiful girl enters the room.
Puberty	That time in every girl's life when she's fit to be tried.
Puritan	A man who No's what he likes.
Pushover	A girl who is dedicated to the proposition.
Pylon	What a nymphomaniac might say at a nude beach party.
Queer	One who likes his vice-versa.
Racehorse	An animal that can take several thousand people for a ride at the same time.
Race Riot	A din of inequity.
Race Track	A place where windows clean people.
Ramification	What made Mary have a little lamb.
Relay	The second time around.
Remarriage	The triumph of hope over experience.
Repeal	A stripteaser's encore.
Sadist	One who is kind to masochists; That little old whine-maker; A man who gives a paralytic friend a self-winding wristwatch.
Safety Belt	The one you don't drink before driving home.
Saint Valentine's Day Massacre	A gang-bang.

Salesman	A guy who can make his girlfriend feel sorry for the chick who lost her bra in his car.
Scabbard	A non-union poet.
Score Pad	A bachelor apartment.
Scratch Pad	A hipster bank.
Seduction	The art of genital persuasion.
Sex	The most fun you can have without laughing.
Sex Drive	A trip to a motel; Trying to find a motel that has a vacancy.
Sex Lecture	A sermon on the mount.
Sex Survey	A pubic-opinion poll.
Sexual Revolution	Copulation explosion.
Shebang	A girl who can't say no.
Short Affair	Leer today, yawn tomorrow.
Shotgun Wedding	A case of wife or death.
Shrunken Head	A pot-smoking midget.
Singing Stripteaser	A skin diva.
Sleep	That which if you don't get enough of, you wake up half a.
Slipcover	A maternity dress.
Snake Dancer	A woman who can writhe to the occasion.
Snow Job	Something a man uses to defrost a woman.
Spice	The plural of spouse.

Spinster	A girl aged in the wouldn't; An unlusted number.
Sport of Kings	Queens.
Stagnation	A country of fun-loving males.
Stalemate	Last season's girlfriend; A moldy spouse.
Stick Shift	One of Callista Flockhart's dresses.
Stoic	De boid what brings de babies.
Strapless Evening Gown	A bust-truster.
Strip Poker	A card game that begins according to Hoyle and ends according to Kinsey.
Suburb	A community in which a man will lend you his wife but not his golf clubs.
Suburban Husband	A gardener with sex privileges.
Success	Making enough money to pay the taxes you wouldn't be paying if you hadn't made so much money in the first place.
Sugar Daddy	A man who can afford to raise Cain.
Suicide	The ultimate form of self-criticism.
Summertime	The season when there's nothing much on radio, TV, or the people at the beach.
Sun Bathing	A fry in the ointment.
Sycophant	A mentally disturbed pachyderm.
Sympathy	That which one woman offers another in exchange for the details.

Synonym	A word you use when you can't spell the other one.
Tax Office	A den of inequity.
Taxpayers	People who don't have to pass a civil-service exam in order to work for the government.
Tease	A girl who is always thinking of a man's happiness—and how to prevent it.
Titillate	A tardy meal for a breast-fed baby.
Toll-House Cookie	A cute prostitute.
Trade Relations	What incestuous couples do at a wife-swapping party.
Transistor	A girl who used to be your brother.
Transvestite	A fellow who likes to eat, drink and be Mary; A drag addict.
Triplets	What you might get from small doses of LSD.
Twist Expert	The torque of the town.
Urination	What Israel was told in 1948.
Van Dyke	A truck-driving Lesbian.
Virgin	A chick who No's everybody; A girl who hasn't met her maker.
Virgin Bride	A right-ring extremist.
Voluptuous Woman	One who has curves in places where some girls don't even have places.
Voyeurism	Looking at the world through roué's-colored glasses.

Wedding Ring	A one-man band.
Whipped Cream	Masochistic milk.
Whippersnapper	The photographer at an S&M party.
Wife	The woman who stands by her husband through all the trouble he wouldn't have had if he'd stayed single.
Wife-Swapping	A type of sexual fourplay.
Will	A dead giveaway.
Window Dresser	A girl who doesn't pull down the shades.
Wolf	A man who has a retirement plan for girls; A man with a little black book of canceled chicks; A man who treats all women as sequels.
Yes Man	One who stoops to concur.
Zebra	The largest size a woman can buy.